Jimmy Log...

The Life and Career of a Notts County legend

David Fells

Published in Great Britain by David Fells, 57 Countrymans Way, Shepshed, Loughborough, Leicestershire, LE12 9RA.

Email: davidfells66@gmail.com

First published 2019

(c) David Fells, 2019

ISBN 978-0-9546143-3-1

DEDICATION

This book is dedicated to my late mother-in-law, Doreen Vernon, a keen Notts County fan who passed away during March 2019.

ACKNOWLEDGEMENTS

Reaching the point of publication of this book has taken a lot of research and work over a number of years but it would not have come to fruition without the help of the following people:

Sue Fells — My wife, for her excellent proofreading and her positive attitude and unflinching support whenever I weakened in my task.

Ayr's Carnegie Library — A host of questions, all answered with the utmost care and thoroughness by the very helpful staff.

David McVay — An ex Notts County footballer turned journalist and author of numerous Nottinghamshire football books. He was therefore my perfect proofreader and an incredible help who pointed me in the right direction on numerous occasions.

Contents

INTRODUCTION

By David McVay

THIS is the story of Jimmy Logan, a Scottish teenager who was determined to become a professional footballer at a time when only amateurs were allowed to play the game north of the border (in theory at least).

That passionate desire to achieve his ambition cost him dearly. His father, a relatively wealthy man of the sea, never forgave him. Doubly heartbreaking as Jimmy left his wife and family behind to pursue his dreams while they lived under his father's roof.

His torturous journey to the top and back embraces several strands of the game at the time. The power struggle between rival governing bodies and the role of disreputable agents trying to poach players by any means foul or fair. Sounds familiar? If there are parallels to the modern malaise afflicting football, remember this is the state of play at the turn of the 19th century when Scottish shamateurism was also rife.

Players forced to don disguises to escape the unwanted and violent attention of rowdy fans is more in keeping with the Victorian era as well as the fact that Scotland were the dominant force in the Home internationals!

Football pitches then were brutal environments, a predominantly working-class sport executed with maximum energy by some of the toughest of men, no place for the faint-hearted with hostile crowds crammed close to the field of play awaiting to pounce. In vivid contrast to the Premiership as we know it today, contact with the opposition was virtually compulsory and actively encouraged.

Still it is a tale of raw courage and talent if ultimately one of heartache, a young man seemingly with the world at his feet but also destined, by self-will, bad luck or faltering health, to take a premature, final bow in a classic tragedy.

And yet before the final curtain, there had been the glittering prizes and the acclaim for the centre-forward that were almost overwhelming. A goal on his Scotland debut against Wales, courted and signed by the leading clubs in England and a dazzling hat-trick that secured the FA Cup for Notts County against Bolton Wanderers in the 1894 final at Goodison Park.

If that was the peak, as ever a trough soon followed for the Ayrshire lad. The zenith of adoration by the Nottingham public swiftly descended to the nadir of familiar rejection and acrimonious departure from a city and club that had so recently bestowed legendary status on his fragile shoulders.

So did art mimic life or was it a case of vice versa for the Scotsman? Like the famous striped shirt of the Notts County Magpies that he sported with such glory, it was always black and white for Jimmy Logan. Nothing grey. Famine or feast.

In the end, he died pitifully young, undernourished and unloved, at least by his paternal family back home. Perhaps also misunderstood, but nevertheless laid to rest in a pauper's grave.

Above all, perhaps that was the real tragedy of Jimmy Logan.

CHAPTER ONE

1870-1890

Early Scottish Football

JIMMY Logan began his football career in the early 1880s with organised football in Scotland still very much in its infancy. The game in Scotland had followed the game in England in its early formation. The Football Association had been formed in London in 1863 with the Scottish Football Association following on ten years later in 1873. The FA Cup was instituted in the 1871/72 season while the Scottish version made its first appearance two years later in the 1873/74 season.

Association football quickly became the most popular sport in Scotland, with the Scottish FA Cup being dominated by Queen's Park and Vale of Leven. Between them, the pair won the first nine competitions (in fact Queen's Park had won it NINE times themselves by 1890).

Queen's Park FC – winners of the first Scottish Cup in 1874
Back row L to R: A. McKinnon, J. Dickson, T. Lawrie, C. Campbell, R. Neill
Front row: R. Leckie, J. Taylor, H. McNeil, J. Thomson, J. Weir, W. McKinnon

Vale of Leven FC – Scottish Cup winners from 1877 to 1879

Dumbarton appeared in four finals (winning only one) in the 1880s and Renton must also be mentioned as they reached four early finals (winning two). Before both the Football and Scottish Leagues existed, winning the national cup in either country was extremely prestigious at a time when England and Scotland were the two leading football nations in the world. A meeting of the English Cup winners, West Bromwich Albion, and their Scottish counterparts, Renton, at Cathkin Park in Glasgow in May 1888 resulted in a 4-1 win for the Scots. Renton then laid claim to being Champions of the World!

Renton FC 1887/88 – 'Champions of the World'
Back row: Club officials.
Middle row: Kelso, Hannah, Lindsay, McCall, McKechnie.
Front row: McCallum, H. Campbell, Kelly, J. Campbell, McCall, McNee

Football in Scotland in the 1880s was still an amateur sport (in theory at least) but in England they had succumbed to the mounting pressure from northern clubs and those from the Midlands, officially opening the floodgates in 1885, formalising what had been happening 'under the counter' for a number of years by legalising professionalism.

England and Scotland had been meeting in annual international games since 1872 but in the 14 years from 1874 to 1887 England managed only one victory, 5-4 at the Oval in London in 1879. Thus Scottish players, particularly at international level, were held in high regard and they had a big influence on English football, favouring a passing game as opposed to England's early preference to dribble.

This meant that English clubs in need of new players would regularly send representatives, or employ agents acting on their behalf to find quality Scottish players for their clubs, offering wages above what the average working man would be earning.

These representatives or agents who prowled Scotland looking for possible recruits were very much disliked by supporters who were not keen to lose their best players. Ooccasionally this resulted in the agents being roughly treated and left in no doubt that they were not welcome in that vicinity.

Other major factors helped the organisation of the game in Scotland. Firstly, in the early part of the 19th century the working man's hours were reduced, from six-days-a-week to having Saturday afternoons off when they could play or watch their favoured sport. The second important change was the arrival of the railways.

By the middle of the 19th century Scotland's major cities were linked to each other and the rail network south of the border. The second half of the century saw a rapid expansion and before 1900 virtually every major town on the Scottish mainland had a railway station. At the same time trains became more comfortable, faster and more frequent whilst the cost of travel declined relative to wages, very useful when having to transport a football team from Ayr to Glasgow. This was also very important in the formation of the leagues where teams found it necessary to travel greater distances.

There was no Scottish League until the 1890/91 season so before then all Scottish football clubs had fixture lists comprising of national, county and local cup competitions and friendly games which were usually arranged on a 'home and away' basis. Officially, there were no professional footballers in Scotland at that time, so to earn a living from the game players had to 'take the English shilling' and move south to play.

Here are just a few basic facts about football in the early 1880s in Scotland:

i) Players' shirts carried neither numbers nor names for identification. This often led to misidentification in newspaper match reports.

ii) Goalkeepers often wore exactly the same strip as the outfield players in their team. Although they were allowed to handle the ball, kicking was the usual way to deal with attacks. Handling was more of a last resort.

iii) Crossbars had just replaced the tape that joined the top of the two goalposts.

iv) Nets affixed to the goal posts and crossbar didn't come into regular use until about 1890 so the first ten years or so of Jimmy Logan's career would have been mainly without the advantages of nets.

v) A belt was usually required to hold up the shorts.

vi) Shin pads were worn outside the socks.

The usual formation, based on attack, was as follows:

(Forwards)   Outside-Left Inside-Left Centre-Forward Inside-Right Outside-Right

(Half Backs)   Left-Half Centre-Half Right-Half

(Backs)   Left-Back   Right-Back

                                 Goalkeeper

CHAPTER TWO

1840-1887

The Early Years

JIMMY'S father, James Logan, was a seaman. He was born in 1840 in Newton-on-Ayr, a small parish on the Ayrshire coast about ten miles south of Troon. It sits north of the River Ayr which separates it from the town of Ayr. From about 1770 it was a mainly coal mining town but by 1830 the coal seams had been exhausted so other types of work had to be found. The sea was in James' blood (with his father John being a shipwright[1]) and the sea held a great attraction to him, so much so that in 1854, aged only 14, he signed up to become a merchant seaman, based at Ayr harbour, learning his trade as he served on a number of sailing ships including *Niagara, Wallachie, Bondicar, Volumnia, Express, Reaper, Chancellor and Eleanor.*

One of the first photographs of Ayr harbour, probably taken in the 1850s, showing the sailing ships on which James learned his trade as a seaman

On February 24 1863, aged 23, James married Elizabeth Connell of Troon at the United Presbyterian Church and the couple decided to live nearby in Portland Street, Dundonald, Troon. Over the next seven years James and Elizabeth had four children – John, Thomas, Janet and Jimmy.

---

[1] *A person who builds and launches wooden vessels or carries out the carpentry work in connection with the building and launching of steel or iron vessels.*

The United Presbyterian Church built in 1843 as it looks today (now the Seagate Evangelical Church) on West Portland Street in Troon where James and Elizabeth were married

An old postcard showing Portland Street in Troon

With four young children at home, James temporarily stopped travelling the world and arranged, for several years (1865-1869), while the children were very young, to be responsible for the pilot boat in Troon Harbour. The basic role of the pilot was to ensure the ships took the correct channel entering and leaving the port. All ports vary so it requires someone with local knowledge of the waterways to act as a guide.

James wasn't satisfied with being an 'ordinary seaman' forever and clearly worked hard to improve his lot in life. In 1869 he passed the necessary examinations to make himself a Second Mate.

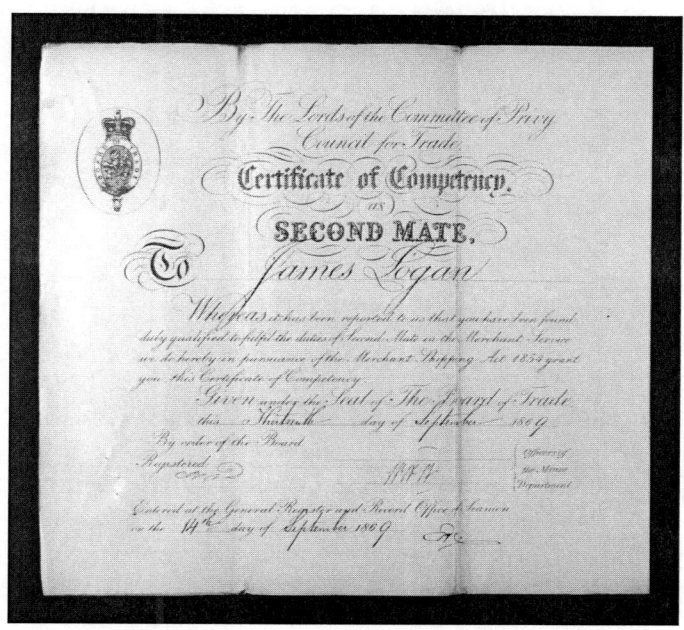

James Logan's certificate as he qualified to be a Second Mate in September 1869

Two years later, after more hard work, he had more exam success as he qualified to become a First Mate.

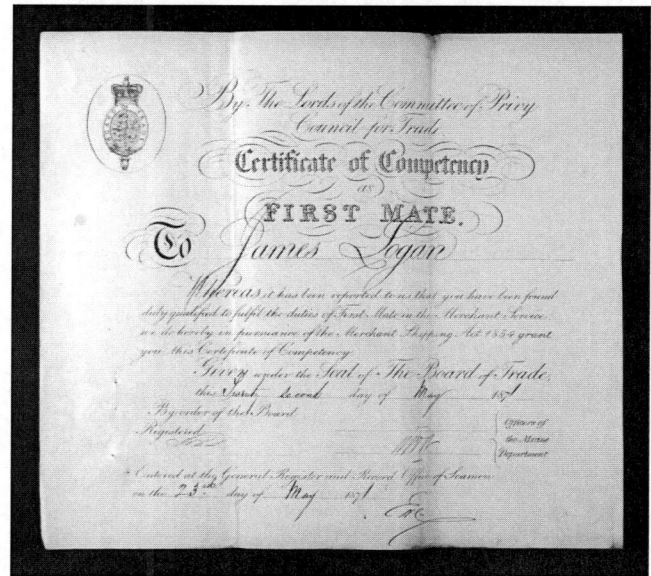

James Logan's certificate as he qualified to be a First Mate in May 1871

Ultimately, in 1874, James passed his final examinations to qualify as a Master Mariner which meant he could now captain ships on the 'high seas' anywhere in the world.

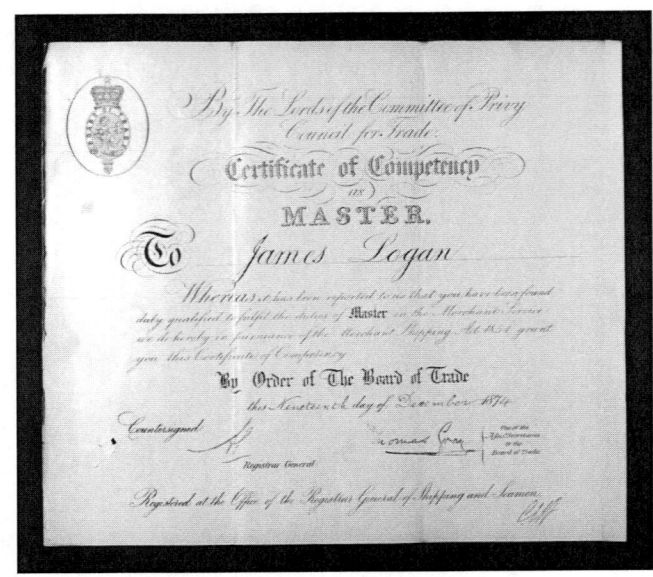

James Logan's certificate as he qualified to be a Master Mariner in December 1874

In early 1875 the Logan family move just around the corner from their home to live in Ayr Street, Troon.

Ayr Street, Troon

In June of the same year the couple's fifth child was born and named after her mother, Elizabeth. Tragically the following year Elizabeth died, just 16-months-old after being ill for a month with acute hydrocephalus.[2]

Their new home on Ayr Street certainly didn't bring the family much joy as Thomas, their second child, also died in December of the same year of tuberculosis. He was ten years old.

---

2 *A build up of fluid inside the skull*

James Logan purchased a family lair or plot in Troon cemetery.

The stone on the Logan plot is now broken (front, centre of photo) but it would have stood tall and proud like the others around it when it was first erected

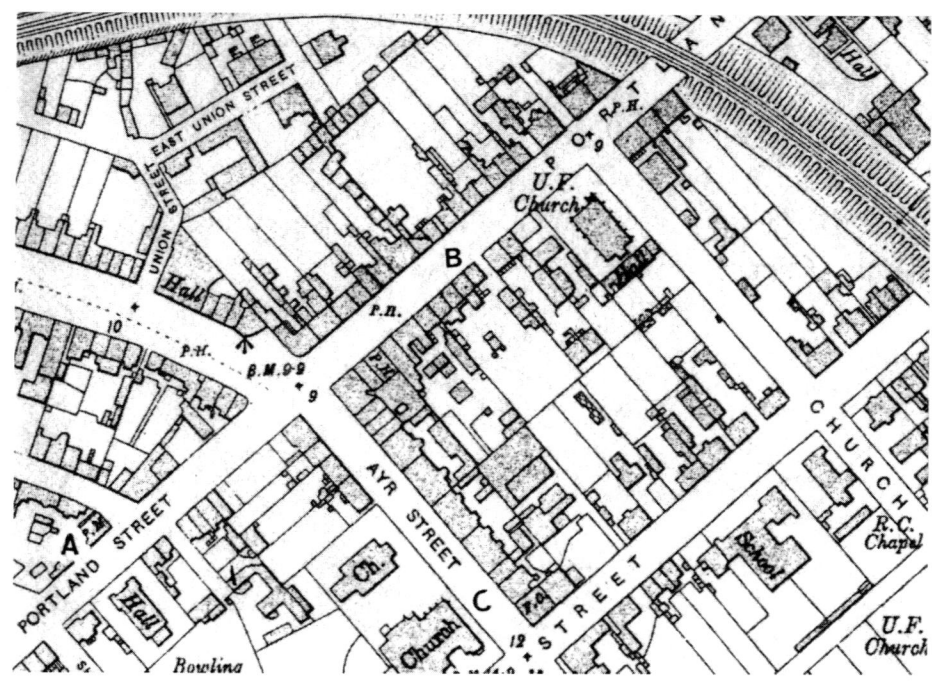

The streets of Troon from a 1909 map
A - The site of Seagate Church where James and Elizabeth married
B - Portland Street – James and Elizabeth's first home after their marriage
C - Ayr Street – where the family moved to in 1874

Whether the death of two of their children was the reason or whether James' career would be better served working from the busier harbour in Ayr rather than the one in Troon is not clear but in 1875 the family moved ten miles down the Ayrshire coast to live in Newton-on-Ayr, where James had been born and raised. Later that same year another daughter was born whom they also named Elizabeth.

Ayr, or the 'Old Taun' as it is referred to locally, is famous for the poet and lyricist Robert (or Rabbie) Burns who was born there in 1759, though his actual birthplace was in Alloway just a couple of miles from the town centre. To most people, he is best known for his poem *Auld Lang Syne* written in 1788. It was set to the tune of a traditional folk song and it is now regularly sung to bid farewell to the old year on the stroke of midnight on New Year's Eve.

Initially, the family didn't appear to settle, moving house regularly, living in York Street Lane, Taylor Street, Waggon Road and Allison Street for short periods but finally stayed for longer on Viewfield Road which was convenient, being as it was the road where the three children attended the Newtonhead School.

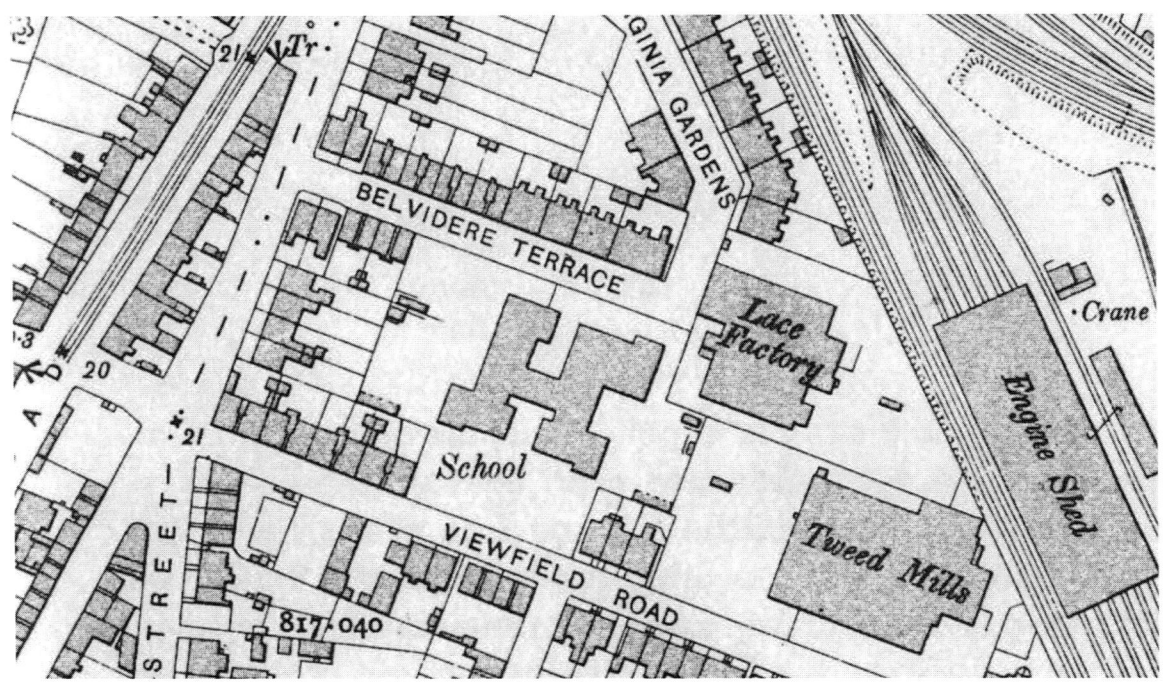

The Newtonhead School on Viewfield Road taken from a 1908 map.
The road on the left, at the end of Viewfield Road, is Allison Street where the family also lived at one point

The eldest child John, on leaving school, followed in his father's footsteps by becoming a seaman but after a spell on the *Griffin* and *Lord Palmerston* from early 1880 through to March 1881 he decided it wasn't for him and instead decided to train as a confectionery manufacturer working for a company called J. Richmond. They were manufacturers and wholesalers of confectionery products in the Ayr area and run by Andrew Richmond at 54 Allison Street, Newton-on-Ayr – the next street to where the Logan family were living in Viewfield Road.

An aerial photo of Newton-on-Ayr in 1982 showing the Newtonhead School, that the Logan children attended, on Viewfield Road. Shortly after, it was demolished

J. RICHMOND

WHOLESALE CONFECTIONER,

AYR CONFECTIONERY WORKS,

ALLISON STREET, NEWTON, AYR.

POMFRET CAKE AND ROLL MANUFACTURER

Maker of Richmond's Celebrated Butter Scotch.

HOUSE—54 ALLISON STREET, NEWTON.

An advertisement for the Confectionery Works where John worked as a confectioner
Taken from the Post Office Trade Directory of the mid 1880s

Meanwhile, John's younger brother Jimmy, still at school, had discovered football and didn't miss an opportunity to join in with the local lads whenever there was a game to be had. He soon began to stand out amongst his school mates and so for season 1885/86, aged just 15 he joined his first organised football team – Arden Villa FC. They were a junior team and, as leagues were a thing of the future, they played friendly games against other local sides that hardly warranted coverage from the local press except for the occasional result. Jimmy played for Arden Villa for two full seasons, turning out in almost every position in the team during his time there. Arden Villa played their games on what is now affectionately known as the 'Old Racecourse' the new racecourse having opened in 1907.

The former racecourse is still used today as playing fields as well as being part of Seafield golf course. The Old Racecourse hosts junior football teams in the town with its six football pitches for 7-a-side games and three full size pitches for 11-a-side games.

The Old Racecourse in Ayr where Jimmy Logan had his first taste of organised football with Arden Villa FC

Since there were no leagues in Scotland as Jimmy began his football journey in the mid-1880s, each club's fixture list comprised 'friendly' games, usually arranged on a 'home and away' basis.

After two seasons with junior club Arden Villa he decided it was time try his luck on the next step up the football ladder, joining the senior team in the town – Ayr FC for the 1887/88 season.

Around the same time, in the summer of 1887, the Ayr Burns Club set the ball rolling with a fund-raising scheme to erect a statue of Robert Burns in a public place in the town centre. Soon after the announcement, concerts, lectures and football matches were organised to help reach the £1,000 total needed to complete the project – an awful lot of money then.

Two lines from a Robert Burns poem entitled *Tam O'Shanter* shows where the nickname of Ayr FC (and later Ayr United FC) The Honest Men derived:

"Auld Ayr, wham ne'er a town surpasses,
For honest men and bonnie lasses."

CHAPTER THREE

July 1887 - June 1888

Beresford Swifts – the Ayr third team

**Ayr FC in 1885 – two years before Jimmy Logan joined the club.
The trophy on the left is the Ayr Charity Cup and on the right is the Kilmarnock
Charity Cup**

AYR Football Club was formed in 1879 by a merger of Ayr Thistle and Ayr Academicals. Their initial home had been Springvale Park but by the time Jimmy joined them in 1887 they had moved to play at Beresford Park which was south of the river Ayr. All of Jimmy's parents' various homes were all north of the river in an area called Newton-on-Ayr, making Jimmy's walk to the ground about a mile-and-a-half.

Ayr FC ran three teams, with the third team being the Beresford Swifts while the reserves were the wonderfully named Ayr Strollers. As a newcomer to the club and aged only 17, Jimmy began life with Ayr in the Swifts' line up, probably hoping that with some fine performances he could one day progress through the ranks and eventually reach the dizzy heights of the first team.

Beresford Park – with sheep grazing to keep the grass at a reasonable level

In addition to the arranged friendly games, each district had its own cup competitions, in Ayr's case these would be the national Scottish Cup, the Ayrshire Cup and the local fundraiser, the Ayr Charity Cup.

A disadvantage for Jimmy's Swifts team was that in the Ayrshire Junior and 2nd XI cup competition, as the title suggests, they were lumped together with all the other 2nd XI sides meaning that progress in the competition was very unlikely – and so it proved. In the first round they were drawn against Irvine's Reserve team, Irvine Rangers and although no specific match report could be found a later match report for Irvine Rangers described their passage through the first round as being carried out *'very successfully'*.

That season, Ayr FC appointed a new trainer, William Munro. William was a tobacco pipe-maker by trade and in the late 1870s he, his wife Helen and their family had moved from Glasgow to live in Ayr. By 1881 they and their five children were living in Elba Street, which, like Jimmy's home was north of the river.

But then October 31, 1887 proved a harrowing time for the Logan family when news reached them that James Logan's ship the *Bellona*, containing 10 tons of sugar, had capsized and sunk in Mauritius harbour. Thankfully, everyone on board was unharmed and after a few days of negotiations with the insurers, the ship was re-floated. An astonishing feat which must have been an interesting operation to watch. Within a few days it was returned to normal usage.

In the **Scottish Cup**, Ayr had a comfortable passage through the first round as they put six goals past the Monkcastle keeper without conceding. The second round saw them travelling to Maybole progressing with an even more comfortable scoreline. A thumping 13-0 victory for the visitors. Goals from Millar, Jack and Tannock (2) ensured another convincing win for Ayr this time over Port Glasgow Athletic by four goals to nil.

After three rounds Ayr had scored 23 goals and were yet to concede a goal so confidence must have been high – at least until the draw was made for the next round.

The fourth round saw Ayr draw the mighty Vale of Leven, who had a tremendous reputation in the game. In the early days of Scottish football, Vale of Leven from the town of Alexandria, in the Vale of Leven an area of West Dunbartonshire, were a real powerhouse in the land. Vale won the Scottish Cup three times in succession (1877, 1878 and 1879) and in 1878 they travelled down to England and beat the FA Cup winners, The Wanderers, 3-1

14

at Kennington Oval. Even the Ayr fans were therefore talking of their team having 'the wind taken out of their sails' by being paired with 'The Vale'. But the game surprised everyone. It was played at Beresford Park in good conditions in front of *the largest turn out of spectators ever seen in a football field in the town'*. Both teams were met with 'hearty cheers' as they made their way onto the playing area. The Vale immediately went onto the attack forcing two corners in quick succession but nothing came of them.

After 14 minutes The Vale took the lead from a goalmouth scrimmage and although they continued to dominate the game, half-time arrived with just the single goal separating the two teams. In the second half Ayr were much more in the game and after an hour's play scored the equaliser with much excitement in the ground. Ayr continued to press and two more goals were scored by Ayr to give them a 3-1 advantage. A late reply by the visitors could not spoil the day and the ground erupted in scenes of celebration as the final whistle sounded with the score stood at Ayr FC 3, Vale of Leven 2.

Ayr FC were now the only Ayrshire club remaining in the Scottish Cup and confidence was sky high. On November 26, they travelled to Cambuslang for the fifth round tie. Interest in the town was running high but when the Ayr party arrived at the ground conditions were found to be deplorable. The match was played in incessant rain on a field which was already ankle-deep in mud.

While Ayr really struggled in the mud just to stay upright, their opponents actually revelled in it with the final score being 10-0 to Cambuslang. How can the same team perform so contrastingly as Ayr did in these last two rounds of the Scottish Cup – one sublime, the other substandard, as poor as it gets!

Their run in the **Ayrshire Cup** was much less successful. After an initial first-round win 13-1 away at Ensign Androssan, the next stage saw Ayr drawn at home against East Ayrshire team Mauchline – about ten miles away. A good many of their fans made the trip by railway, which offered return tickets for one shilling.

Ayr were expected to win comfortably but struggled just to achieve a 2-2 draw. The replay at Mauchline was a repeat performance a fortnight later on Saturday, November 12, with this time a 1-1 scoreline. On December 3, the second replay was moved to a neutral venue at Rugby Park, Kilmarnock. Once again a special train, leaving at one o'clock on the Saturday, was laid on for the Mauchline supporters and 112 responded to the invitation arriving at 'Killie' at 1.30 for the 2pm kick-off.

There had been a storm the previous night and the high winds continued on the day of the game. Mauchline won the toss and decided to play against the high winds in the first half showing little intent to try and score. The Ayr forwards attacked for the full 45 minutes but were thwarted by opponents who had achieved their ambition by turning round at half-time with a clean sheet at 0-0. Then a solitary goal in the second half was enough for Mauchline to progress into the next round of the competition at the expense of a hugely disappointed Ayr.

A large crowd greeted the Mauchline team as they arrived back home at the station and on the following Monday evening the players and committee were treated to a celebratory meal at the Loudoun Hotel by an old, but still very enthusiastic, ex-player who promised the meal if his team could knock Ayr out of the cup – the promise was fulfilled.

The **Ayr Charity Cup** was started in 1884/85 when eight clubs usually competed. There was always a 'keen competition' whenever the two local teams of Kilmarnock and Ayr were drawn together. Ayr had a very good record having won all three previous competitions in 1884/85, 1885/86 and 1886/87. More importantly, over those same three seasons, the local Ayr County Hospital had benefited by £200. In 1887/88, all games were played at Beresford Park and as only four teams entered it went straight to the semi-final stage.

Ayr were given chance for revenge when they were drawn to play Mauchline, the team that had put Ayr out of the Ayrshire Cup and this time there were no mistakes. Ayr went through to the final with a comfortable 4-0 scoreline. Meanwhile in the other semi-final Kilmarnock had beaten Hurlford 4-0.

For the final, between 3,000 and 4,000 fans were in attendance, the weather was fine and the field was in 'capital condition'. Both teams arrived in good time and were met with tremendous cheers as they entered the field with the excitement outside the ropes intense. There was just one problem. The referee had missed the train so kick-off was delayed by 45 minutes awaiting his eventual arrival. It was not Ayr's day. In a hard fought contest Ayr missed a number of good chances while Kilmarnock took most of theirs running out comfortable winners 5-1 thus ending Ayr's sequence of success in the finals.

Although Ayr's first team had a reasonable 1887/88 season with a decent run in the Scottish Cup, reached the final of the Ayr Charity Cup and had victories in friendly games over major English clubs Sunderland and Aston Villa - the Ayr Strollers were clearly the team to watch that season.

The Ayr second team were a good side, a good balance of promising youngsters and experienced players on the fringes of the first team – and they were also a big physical side. This point was driven home after news was received that Aston Villa were unable to play Ayr FC at Beresford Park on the agreed date of December 31, due to an FA Cup tie with Preston North End (the game was eventually re-arranged to take place at the end of the season on May 7, a historic fixture for the home team as it transpired).

Ayr tried to set up replacement opposition but were unsuccessful so arranged a game against their reserves and as it turned out, the Strollers were convincing 4-0 winners. No excuses, either, because only a few weeks later the first team beat Sunderland 4-1 with an equally confident performance.

In the **Ayrshire 2nd XI Cup** the Strollers got off to a flying start with an 11-1 victory over Kilmarnock Winton in the first round followed by an 8-2 win in the semi-final over Kilmarnock Thistle at Holm Quarry. In the final the Strollers met yet another Kilmarnock team – Kilmarnock's second team, the Rangers. An even game ended 2-2.

The replay was designated to take place at Meadow Park, Irvine and this time the Strollers prevailed in style, contolling the game throughout, resulting in a 4-0 victory for the Strollers who were delighted to have a trophy already in the bag.

The Ayr Strollers were also advancing well in the national **Scottish 2nd XI Cup** having beaten Kilmarnock 3-2 in the first round, followed by another 3-2 win, this time over Hurlford. The third round saw the Strollers visit Larkhall where they despatched Royal Albert easily enough by four goals to one. On the same day that the Strollers were beating Royal Albert (October 22) their first team were short of players for a friendly against Renfrew at Beresford Park so a few of the third team, the Beresford Swifts, were promoted for the day, including a 17 year old Jimmy Logan, who was making his senior debut. He was selected out on the left wing. The goal scorers were not recorded but Jimmy played his part in a comprehensive 6-1 victory.

The quarter-final saw the Strollers drawn at home to the Clyde second string. The crowd at Somerset Park was a small one due to a large contingent of Ayr fans leaving the town on a special train for Mauchline to watch the first team in the Ayrshire Cup. Clyde began well having the better of the play in the early stages but the longer the game went on, the more the Strollers took a firm grip and progressed to the semi-finals of the national 2nd XI Cup on the back of an 8-1 scoreline.

A meeting of the Scottish Football Association saw the draw for the semi-final as follows:

Abercorn	v	Heart of Midlothian
Cambuslang	v	Ayr Strollers.

A tough draw because the Cambuslang first team had beaten Ayr FC 10-0 earlier in the season in the 5th round of the Scottish Cup.

The Strollers faced Cambuslang reserves at Beresford Park in the 2nd XI Cup semi-final. Inclement December weather and a 'sixpenny' gate did not deter many fans from attending. Five minutes from the end Strollers edged 2-1 ahead and Cambuslang could offer no comeback. A fortnight later, in the other semi-final, Paisley club Abercorn, the holders, unexpectedly sustained a 4-3 home defeat from Hearts.

Early in the New Year, William Munro, the club's trainer talked about a youngster in the Ayr third team saying that he was eagerly looking forward to the day when a certain *'chestnut colt'* began to make an impression at the club – could this have been Jimmy?

The player was not named but by a strange coincidence the very next game for the Strollers was a friendly game against Kirkintulloch Central on Monday, January 2, and Jimmy was selected as centre-forward for his Strollers' debut.

The score was a resounding 9-1 victory for the Strollers and although the scorers were not detailed it is hard to imagine a side scoring nine without the centre-forward contributing his fair share. After that debut one of the sporting newspapers carried the following:

"Another addition to the Ayr Strollers on Monday, a fine dashing centre-forward of great promise." Jimmy retained his place for the next Strollers' game, another friendly, this time away at Maybole – against the Maybole first team. Part of the match report read as follows: *"The Ayr Strollers visited Gardenrose to tackle the Maybole first XI. The excitement in the capital of Carrick over this game was unprecedented and the gate was the largest that has been seen in Maybole for years. The game, we are assured, was the roughest that the Ayr Strollers ever took part in. The match was devoid of the finer points of the game and ended, according to the referee's decision, in a draw of five goals each. The last two goals 'scored' by the home team were strongly disputed, one being deliberately fisted through and the other going slowly about two feet over the bar."*

Having now played for the Strollers in two friendly games after the team had won their semi-final against Cambuslang, Jimmy must have been secretly hoping to play in the final against Hearts – but it wasn't to be.

There was a good reason for his omission from the Scottish 2nd XI Cup final. He had not been selected to play in the earlier rounds of the competition so why would the selectors change a successful side.

What followed, though, must have eased his feeling of disappointment a little, because on the same day that the Strollers were playing their cup final on January 28, Jimmy was selected to play his second game for the Ayr first team in a friendly against Morton at Beresford Park. Ayr triumphed 4-2. The local press, perhaps unsurprisingly, described Jimmy's performance as *'nervous'*.

When the venue for the Scottish 2nd XI final was made known, no-one could quite believe it. Hearts had been given the gift of playing the final in their home city of Edinburgh at Easter Road. The task for the Strollers to win the national competition had just been made so much more difficult.

The date was fixed for January 28 and the team selected to represent Ayr were: George Glendinning (goal); John Ferguson and John Tannock (backs); John Dickie; Daniel Christie and Adam Dunnachie (half-backs); Samuel Feggans; Robert McMurtrie, Anthony McWhirter, John Murray and Robert McBurnie (forwards).

Although the majority of the 2,000 crowd were behind Hearts, Ayr Strollers nonetheless received vocal encouragement on taking the field. At the interval Strollers were 2-0 in front and the cup was in sight. The first team, as mentioned, were playing Morton at Beresford Park and when a telegram arrived with the half time score from Easter Road, great excitement ensued, all attention being taken off the match in progress.

When Strollers scored again it was all over 'bar the shouting' but Hearts were successful in pulling one back. The immense physique of the Ayr team had won the day and home came the Scottish 2nd XI Cup. Not for many a year was the victors' reception forgotten.

"Seldom has Ayr witnessed such a sight in the dead of night as that at Ayr Station on that Saturday. The cheering as the train dashed into the station was something tremendous, and the players, as they left the compartment, were borne in triumph to the stirring strains of the Ayr Burgh Band. So dense was the crowd that many in the crowd never managed to see the victorious team at all!

Ayr Strollers 1887/88
Back row: Daniel Christie, John Fergusson, George Glendinning, D. White (12th man), Adam Dunnachie
Middle Row: Samuel Feggans, John Dickie, Anthony McWhirter, John Tannock, John Murray.
Front row: Robert McMurtrie and Robert McBurnie

The Strollers' record in a remarkable season in the cup competitions was as follows:

Pl	W	D	L	F	A
10	9	1	0	48	13

Twenty-five years later, in 1913, the players were assembled together in a celebration of this national cup success. Sadly, two members of the team had passed away by then – John Fergusson and Robert McMurtrie – and one player, Adam Dunnachie had moved to live in America. The eight players who did make the celebration are pictured below:

Ayr Strollers 1913
Back row: John Dickie, John Tannock, George Glendinning, A. Thomson, Joseph Glendinning (match secretary)
Front Row: Daniel Christie, Samuel Feggans, Anthony McWhirter, Robert McBurnie, John Murray

Jimmy spent the first half of the season with the third team, the Beresford Swifts, but he was improving swiftly and progressing. After that second appearance for the first team Jimmy played most of his football for the Ayr Strollers rather than the third team, usually at centre-forward but occasionally at wing-half.

Towards the end of the 1887/88 season the club found itself caught up in a major difficulty. Every year Beresford Park was taken over along with the adjoining fields in order that the Annual Cattle Show could be staged on this site.

In 1888, however, the field was unexpectedly requisitioned earlier than usual. It was April and there were fixtures still to be played. Aston Villa had agreed to visit Ayr on May 7 but Beresford Park would not be free for a month. A front page advertisement was published in the *Ayr Observer* headed *Ayr Football Club. A Special General Meeting will be held in Carrick Street Hall, on Wednesday first, at 8pm. A*s the advertisement (below) shows, there was only one item on the agenda – the ground.

Ayr, 13th April, 1888.

AYR FOOTBALL CLUB.

A SPECIAL GENERAL MEETING will be held in CARRICK STREET HALL, on WEDNESDAY FIRST, at 8 P.M. Business—Ground.

By Order of Committee.
JOS. GLENDINNING, Hon. Sec.

A short distance away was a field which was to the liking of some of the committee members. It was situated to the south of Walker's Chemical Works, just at the junction of the Glasgow and Mauchline railways. The grass was in poor condition due to a 'lack of grazing' but this site being adjacent to Somerset Road was convenient to the thickly populated districts of Newton-on-Ayr and Wallacetown. Rapid negotiations were entered into with the owners of the chemical works and a satisfactory rent was agreed. Prophecies of doom and gloom were fired at Ayr FC, the general line going: "The club will go to the dogs. The gates will never be as big as they were at Beresford." Fears of bankruptcy and letters of resignation from committee members did not deter the club and they 'christened' their new field Somerset Park.

The pitch was on a north-south alignment running almost parallel to the railway. It ran parallel to Somerset Road with the stand backing onto the railway. The entrance was near the top of Tryfield Road (now Tryfield Place). With the ground being developed in this location, a further expanse of field lay between Somerset Park and Somerset Road. This spare land would become crucial to future improvements, while local opponents Ayr Parkhouse moved into the now vacant Beresford Park.

Ayr FC had moved across the water and in the lands of Hawkhill the old clubhouse and stand from Beresford Park were dismantled and re-erected at Somerset Park in time for the inauguration of the new field on Monday, May 7, 1888 against Aston Villa. It was pure coincidence that the ground was opened by such prestigious opponents.

The match had been initially arranged for December 1887 when Aston Villa found it necessary to call off a match at Beresford Park, at only a few days' notice because of an FA Cup tie against Preston.

Both teams found the surface difficult but Ayr FC set about mastering the difficulties and two goals by Campbell gave a comfortable half-time lead. The second half had barely started when Feggans completed the rout - Ayr FC 3 Aston Villa 0 in Somerset Park's first game!

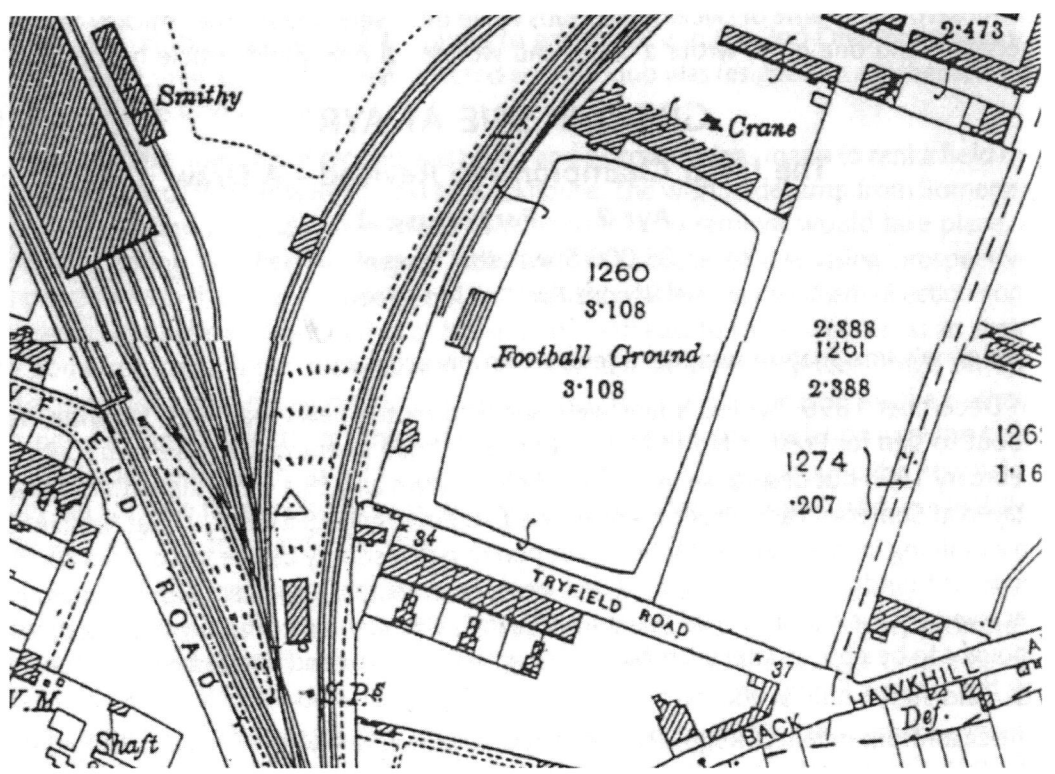

Somerset Park taken from an 1896 map

20

Somerset Park (with Walker's Chemical Works in the background)
Ayr FC kick off against Ayr Parkhouse on April 9, 1910, shortly before the two clubs
merged to form Ayr United

One person who would have been pleased with the ground move was Jimmy Logan because, instead of the mile and a half walk to Beresford Park from his parents' home, Somerset Park was now less than a quarter of a mile away.

CHAPTER FOUR

July 1888 – June 1889

Jimmy has a finger amputated!

AYR FC's AGM was held in the summer at the Wallace Tower Hall on Ayr High Street.

The original Wallace Tower was built in honour of William Wallace. In 1832 the original tower was declared unsafe and replaced by the current one – a sculpture of William Wallace stands in the side of the tower

The costs involved in moving to the new field at Somerset Park had placed the club in a poor financial situation but, now settled, it was hoped the coming season would see the finances improve. The following officials were appointed for the coming season: Match Secretary – Mr J Glendinning, Captain – Mr James P Campbell, Vice Captain – Mr R Cunningham, Captain of the second team (Strollers) – Mr John Ferguson, Vice Captain for the second team – John Dickie. Captain of the third team (Somerset XI – changed from the Beresford XI after the move to Somerset Park) – James Howie.

The campaign began strangely with Jimmy taking no part in football whatsoever for the first three or four months of the season but there were no reports of illness or of an injury.

Jimmy's father, James, had shown himself to be a hard working seaman, who, by sheer determination and graft went from joining the Merchant Navy as a 14 year old 'ordinary seaman' to working his way up various levels until at the age of 34 be became a Master Mariner or ship's captain.

John, the eldest of the Logan children, also proved to be a chip off the old block and like his father, was a dedicated grafter. Although he didn't take to being a seaman he concentrated on training as a confectioner. Jimmy, on the other hand, was an 18-year-old who was completely consumed by the love of playing football and clearly that was this teenager's priority.

In contrast, football was of little interest to his father, a man who had spent most of his life at sea. It is more than likely that Jimmy's obsession with the game was causing rifts and disagreements at home, where it seems Jimmy was fast becoming the black sheep of the family.

I think that is most probably the reason for his four-month absence from football. As far as Jimmy's father was concerned, football was never going to earn his son a decent living. Footballers in Scotland were amateurs. From his father's point of view, the only way Jimmy could ever earn enough from football was to be offered a contract with an English club. Since that seemed a remote possibility his father stood firm and probably told Jimmy to set about 'getting a proper job'.

Ayr FC had strengthened their squad with the signing of full-back John Somerville, an outstanding local teenager who had spent the previous season with local rivals Ayr Parkhouse.

At the beginning of August 1888, just one year after its launch, the Ayr Burns Statue Fund stood at £500 – half the amount required – a tremendous effort by the local residents, football teams etc.

September 1888 saw the start of the first season of the new Football League in England. The 12 member clubs were all from the midlands and the north: Accrington, Aston Villa, Blackburn Rovers, Bolton Wanderers, Burnley, Derby County, Everton, Notts County, Preston North End, Stoke, West Bromwich Albion and Wolverhampton Wanderers. Each club played the others twice, once at home and once away, with two points awarded for a win and one for a draw. The introduction of the League would only increase the pressure on teams to be successful and find more outstanding players.

It was always going to be difficult to live up to the previous season's success and so it proved as the Strollers exited both the Scottish 2nd XI Cup and the Ayrshire 2nd XI Cup before the end of November. Conversely, the first team were more impressive reaching the final of both the **Ayr Charity Cup** and the **Ayrshire Cup** but they fell just short losing both finals to Kilbirnie and Hurlford respectively.

The season had got off to a flyer with a 13-0 hammering of Beith in a friendly. Things got much tougher the following Saturday, September 1, when the club somehow managed to 'double book' themselves with a game at Aston Villa in Birmingham as well as a **Scottish Cup** tie at Hurlford.

Hurlford were asked to put the game back a week but they could not oblige as they were due to play Glasgow Thistle, so half the first team travelled to England, along with half the Strollers team and a similarly organised team went to Hurlford. Aston Villa won 10-0 and Hurlford won 7-0 – 'a very bad day at the office' in the current vernacular.

On Thursday, September 13, 1888, Ayr FC faced the touring Canadian national team at Somerset Park. Rangers had failed to beat the Canadian side but Ayr FC enjoyed a convincing 4-0 victory.

In the **Ayr Charity Cup** there was a local derby between Ayr FC and Ayr Athletic in the semi-final at neutral Beresford Park. It had all the trappings of a big occasion. Ayr F.C. changed at the Star Hotel in Fort Street and from there travelled in some style to the ground in a horse-drawn brake, followed by many of their supporters. Athletic were beaten 8-2 and it was a record "threepenny gate" for the town amounting to over £24.

An advert from the local press for the Star Hotel in Ayr in 1886

In the final, versus Kilbirnie at Somerset Park, the roof quite literally fell in on Ayr FC as the grandstand collapsed! Fortunately, nobody was seriously injured. It got worse as Kilbirnie won 3-1. Apparently the main reason for the collapse was a weakening of the structure when it was dismantled at Beresford Park and transported across town and reassembled.

Ayr reached the final of the **Ayrshire Cup** under unusual circumstances. After victories over Damconner, Kilbirnie and Lanemark, Ayr were drawn in the semi-final away against Lugar Boswell.

Owing to the death of a Lugar player's relative the club notified Ayr FC the day before the game that they would not be able to fulfil the fixture 24 hours later. However, Ayr had already committed to travel arrangements and so continued on their journey to Lugar on the day of the game. It was not in Ayr's power to postpone the game as the Ayrshire FA had chosen that date for the match to be played.

Therefore they journeyed to Lugar to meet their opponents, who failed to turn out to meet them. On arrival Ayr changed into their strip and went through the farcical show of taking a run down the pitch, scoring a 'goal' and then claimed the tie. Lugar protested to the ruling body but the case was immediately dismissed and Ayr had a walkover into the final.

Since its inception the **Ayrshire Cup** had proven elusive to the county town of Ayr. To change that trend, they would need to overcome an in-form Hurlford at Rugby Park. The fans were hopeful and two trains at Ayr Station took 795 aboard, with 215 mounting at Newton to swell the 'army' to 1010. On arrival, confusion reigned as admission to the game was by a ticket obtained at a wooden hut in a neighbouring field, which created a chaotic scene with people milling everywhere. Sadly, all the enthusiasm was in vain as Hurlford won 2-0.

I am sure Jimmy Logan had tried very hard to comply with his fathers' wishes to put his work before football but at the end of November the lure of football proved too much and he returned to the Ayr team.

His first match back in action came on the left wing against Glasgow University in a 3-2 defeat, followed by a 4-2 defeat against Ayr Parkhouse. A single appearance at centre-forward for the Strollers in a 7-2 victory with Jimmy once again amongst the goals and just maybe the 'rustiness' from his lay-off was beginning to disappear.

So, after his early season exile he was now making gradual progress in regaining his sharpness and best form, but in late January his season was brought to a second shuddering halt when an accident at work derailed a career that was just getting back on track.

It was unclear what Jimmy's line of work was at that time but the *Scottish Sport* carried the following paragraph:

"James Logan, one of the most promising forwards in the town of Ayr, met with a serious accident while at his work last week. His hand became entangled in some machinery and was badly bruised, necessitating the amputation of one of his fingers.[3] Logan, as a centre forward during the last month or two, has come rapidly to the front. He has a fine command of the ball and is a most deadly shot at goal. It will be some weeks before he is able to resume his place in the Ayr Strollers."

Ayr County Hospital opened in 1883 where Jimmy would have been taken after his accident at work. The surgeon at the hospital who could have performed the operation was Dr William John Naismith – who was also the president of Ayr FC

It was the beginning of April before Jimmy was able to turn out again, just in time to compete in the second round of the **Kilmarnock Charity Cup,** in which Ayr were making a rare appearance, against Kilmarnock Athletic – and Jimmy was back with a bang as he scored two fine headed goals in a 4-2 win.

In the next round, the semi-final, Ayr were drawn against Hurlford, who had beaten Ayr 2-0 in the Ayrshire Cup final – but there was no mistake this time with Ayr progressing into the final with a 4-2 win – but a shock decision awaited them. Ayr were victorious, but both teams were ejected from the competition for staging the game on a date not specified by the organising committee – so the other two semi-finalists Kilbirnie and Kilmarnock both received a bye into the final!

---

[3] *Looking at the small number of photographs available of Jimmy, it was probably one of the fingers on his left hand that was amputated as whenever he was photographed he always folded his arms in such a way as to hide his left hand.*

On February 2 1889 the *Greenock Telegraph and Clyde Shipping Gazette* carried the following paragraph which explained how Jimmy's father James, would be taking receipt of a brand new ship – the *Enterkin*:

LAUNCHES TODAY

Messrs Robert Duncan & Co, will launch this afternoon a steel sailing ship of 1,700 tons for Mr Thomas C. Guthrie's Village Line of sailing ships. The dimensions are 245 feet by 39 feet by 24 feet moulded and the vessel has been built to class 100 A1 at Lloyd's and carry 9,750 tons dead weight on Lloyd's freeboard. She is supplied with John Hastie & Co.'s patent halyard winches for fore and main masts; Clark, Chapman & Co.'s patent windlass, arranged so that it can be driven from a powerful steam winch at main hatch made by George Russell & Co., of Motherwell; Mills patent main and bilge pumps; McConachy's patent ventilators for holds, cabins and deckhouses and McConachy's patent life-saving gangway and accommodation ladder combined. She will be named the Enterkin by Miss Edmiston, Ibrox House, Glasgow and commanded by Captain James Logan, formerly of the Bellona. This is the fifth sailing ship Messrs Duncan & Co. have built for the Village line and they have another in course of construction, which will be launched in a few months.

The *Enterkin*

CHAPTER FIVE

July 1889 – June 1890

The English agents move ever closer

IN AUGUST 1889, the *Ayrshire Post* carried the following paragraph on the efforts of the agents from English professional football clubs:

"Almost every one of the Ayr FC team have had offers from across the border, but we are glad to say that not one of them would listen to the tempter, one of them running the agent into the street with little ceremony. Some of these prowlers will receive a rough handling one of these nights if they don't take care."

The AGM of Ayr FC took place in the summer where the financial situation of the club had greatly improved over the last year, nearly all of the club's debt had been cleared off. A committee was formed to improve the current ground including the laying of a cinder track around the playing area. The office-bearers were then appointed for the coming season as follows: President – Dr Naismith, Vice President – Mr A H Chambers, Hon. Treasurer – Mr W Piper, Secretary – Mr J Glendinning, Representative to the Scottish Football Association – Mr C H Robertson, Representative to the Ayrshire Association – Mr J Glendinning, Match Secretary – Mr J Glendinning, Captain – Mr R Cunningham, Vice Captain – Mr J Sommerville, Captain of Strollers – Mr J Watson.

Having beaten Beith 13-0 at the start of the previous season, Ayr FC were drawn to meet Beith again, this time in the first round of **The Scottish Cup** – Ayr managed even more goals this time in a 16-0 win!

Round two brought a trip to Rosebank Field in the familiar territory of Lugar Boswell with Ayr winning 2-0. The *Sport* reported *"The Lugar men took their defeat very badly and the Ayr umpire was severely assaulted by one of the players on entering the pavilion. The matter has been handed into the police and the Association will also be asked to rule in the matter."* The Scottish FA suspended the assailant from October 1889 until April 1890, almost the entire season.

An Ayrshire XI including four Ayr FC players (Sommerville, Christie, Campbell and Ross) beat a Glasgow XI 5-0 at Third Lanark's Cathkin Park with the gate money being donated to the Burns Statue Fund. By the autumn of 1889 the fund had reached £800 – £200 short of the target.

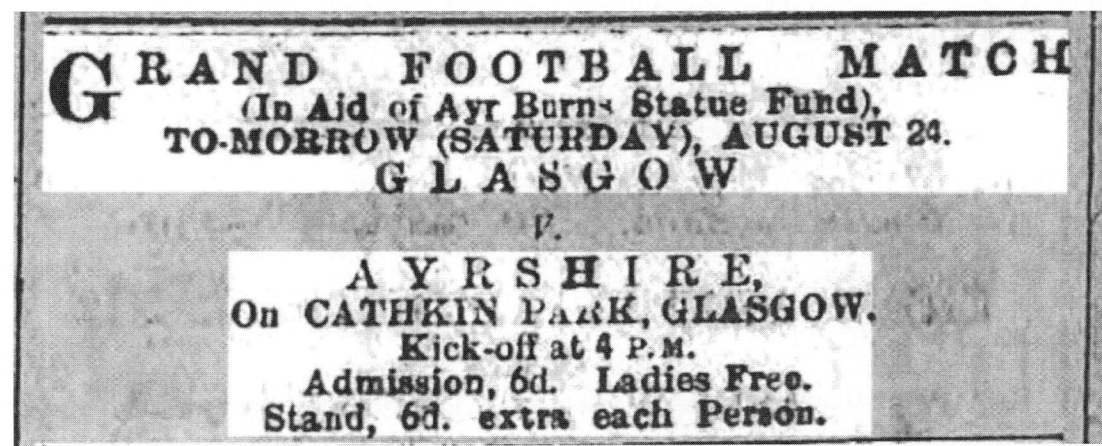

Ayrshire v Glasgow – typical of the games used to raise money for the Ayr Burns Statue Fund

A 4-1 victor over Morton, at Greenock, in the third round gave Ayr FC 22 cup goals for the loss of only one. Ayr FC were drawn against Leith Athletic in the 4th round of the Scottish Cup at home where four goals were shared and Leith winning the replay 4-1.

In the **Ayrshire Cup,** Ayr FC fared even worse. After Ayr FC's opponents Maybole had scratched from the competition in the first round, they lost in the second round to Newmilns by a shock score of 5-2 - and that at Somerset Park!   In the final Annbank beat Hurlford 3-2 at Rugby Park, Kilmarnock. The crowd of almost 7,000 was, at the time, a record for an Ayrshire Cup Final.

In the first round of the **Ayr Charity Cup** Ayr Athletic faced Kilbirnie at Somerset Park. With ten minutes remaining and Kilbirnie leading 2-0, Athletic claimed that they had the ball a clear yard through their opponents' goal but the referee was unimpressed. The unsatisfactory result was the abandonment of the game after the crowd surged through the ropes and attacked the referee.

In a similar manner, voices were raised at the half-yearly meeting of Ayr FC. It was almost Christmas but the festive spirit was nowhere to be seen. The cause of the raging controversy was the question as to whether players should be paid for lost time or not. It was argued that *"The players of five seasons ago did not get paid for lost time, they did not even have a trainer, but they had what was of more importance, enthusiasm and a determination to do their best."* Obviously someone was getting on his 'high horse' but this old-fashioned, strictly amateur mode of thinking was defeated.

The 1880s finished with Ayr FC overpowering Parkhouse by five goals to one.

During the summer of 1890, the Scottish Football League was formed but it was to be a further seven years before the town of Ayr was represented under League auspices.

1889/90 was a good season for Ayrshire side Annbank whose team, without exception, were miners. As well as winning the Ayr Charity Cup they also won the Ayrshire Cup, and only lost 3-2 to Hurlford in the final of the Kilmarnock Charity Cup, with 20 year old George Kerr the season's outstanding player.

Meanwhile, Jimmy Logan now aged 19 was still honing his football skills in the Ayr second team, the Strollers, where publicity, particularly of individual players was thin on the ground.

This season's Strollers were a young team and not as strong as a couple of seasons earlier when they won the Scottish National 2nd XI cup. Some of the players had moved on while others, like Daniel Christie, Samuel Feggans and John Murray were now first team regulars. The lack of strength of the Strollers team was exposed for all to see when they crashed out of the **2nd XI Scottish Cup** in the first round to Kilmarnock 7-1.

The Strollers fared slightly better in the **Ayrshire 2nd XI Cup**. In the 1st Round away at Dalry, the ground was waterlogged and declared unfit for football – so instead the two teams played a friendly game! When the game was finally played at a later date the Strollers took it 4-2 and their second round draw saw them at Somerset Park against Mauchline.

A sound performance saw the Strollers in control and an emphatic 4-0 win reaped the reward of a third round bye. The quarter-final saw the Strollers travel to Largs in North Ayrshire where an evenly contested game ended 3-3. In the replay, the Strollers could not repeat the feat and went out of the competition at Somerset Park losing 3-1.

Despite exiting all the cup competitions there was still plenty of football to be played with the highlights for the Strollers being the wins against Irvine (3-0), Ailsa (10-0), Annbank (6-2), Tarbolton (7-4), and Irvine (8-4) with Jimmy usually collecting his share of the goals.

In March 1890 Ayr were dealt a blow when their fine young full-back and captain, John Somerville, who only joined Ayr from Ayr Parkhouse in the summer of 1888, accepted an offer to turn professional with Bolton Wanderers and left for Lancashire.

This is the first 'desertion' that Ayr FC had experienced. James Ross had also been approached by Preston North End but had so far rebuffed their advances.

John Somerville[4]

---

[4] *John Somerville turned out to be an excellent signing for Bolton, playing almost 300 times for them. In 1898 he became Bolton's first player/secretary and was then made manager from 1908-1910 – serving Bolton for 20 years.*

CHAPTER SIX

July 1890 – June 1891

From Stroller to Scottish International

A number of things had happened around this time in Jimmy's family life. During 1890 elder brother John had completed his apprenticeship and had become a Master Confectioner. Coincidentally, the Richmond family (Andrew, wife Janet and children John and Jean) with whom John Logan had worked his apprenticeship as a confectioner, had moved out of 54 Allison Street to a brand new building in North Park Terrace just off the Prestwick Road. Jimmy's father James did not hesitate and moved his family into the vacant 54 Allison Street complete with a confectionery workshop. Soon after this, Jimmy finished his job as a timekeeper and joined brother John in the confectionery business.

By moving his family to the house in Allison Street I am certain James hoped it would achieve two things. Firstly, it would set his son John up in a situation where he could run his own business but he also knew John couldn't do it alone so James looked for a major commitment from son Jimmy who he hoped would work hard to assist John to make the venture a success.

On August 8, 1890, Jimmy's sister Janet married Henry Harkins, a time keeper and cashier, at the Council Rooms in Newton-on-Ayr. At the time of the marriage Janet was living in the family home at 54 Allison Street.

HARKINS — LOGAN — At Newton Council Rooms, Ayr, on the 8th August, by the Rev. William Rainie, Henry Harkins, Denny, to Janet A. Logan, eldest daughter of Captain James Logan, 54 Allison Street, Ayr.

Janet Logan's marriage announcement in the local press

By now Jimmy had a girlfriend – Mary Munro, the daughter of the Ayr FC trainer, William. The 1890/91 season would change the 20-year-old's life completely.

1890/91 was the first season of the Scottish Football League. The teams that comprised the initial League were: Dumbarton, Rangers, Celtic, Cambuslang, Third Lanark, Heart of Midlothian, Abercorn, St Mirren, Vale of Leven and Cowlairs. The season ended with Dumbarton and Rangers as joint champions after a play-off finished 2-2, St Mirren and Vale of Leven were re-elected, while Cowlairs were not re-elected. Renton began the season as part of the initial League but were found to be professional, so were removed from the League and their record was expunged.

Jimmy began the season playing for the Ayr Strollers, who seemed in fine fettle as a 5-0 win over Stevenson Thistle and an 8-1 victory against Dalry indicated. There were also positive comments about Jimmy Logan's early season form.

In early September Ayr progressed through the first round of the **Scottish Cup** without too much effort when their opponents Kilbarchan scratched from the competition. In the second round, in late September, they had a comfortable 3-1 victory over Rutherglen away at Phoenix Park.

In the third round, in October, Ayr FC had to travel again, this time to Barrowfield Park on the north bank of the River Clyde in Glasgow to meet Clyde FC.

Clyde had moved to Barrowfield in 1877. There was a cycle track around the pitch, an uncovered seated stand on the eastern side and a pavilion in the south-eastern corner of the ground, whilst embankments were developed at the north and south ends. Depending on which newspaper is believed to be nearest the mark there were between 3,000 and 5,000 spectators to see this important clash between two of the more senior non-league Scottish clubs.

With Stewart unavailable Jimmy Logan was selected at half-back. The Ayr team were first on to the field closely followed by Clyde. Both teams went straight onto the attack. Clyde scored first after 20 minutes but Ayr responded and equalised ten minutes later only for Clyde to re-take the lead five minutes later. Determined not to be outdone, Ayr once again equalised and a fast and furious first half ended with two goals apiece.

Clyde versus St Mirren in a Scottish Football League game at Barrowfield Park in 1894 – still without goal nets despite their use having been sanctioned three years earlier

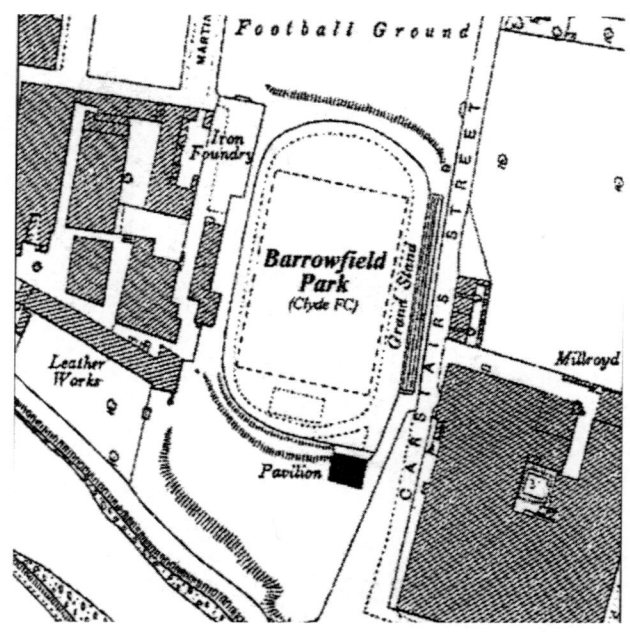

Clyde's Barrowfield Park from an 1896 map

Early in the second half a shot from Clyde went across the face of Steel's goal as the Ayr netminder stood by his post and watched it sail just wide. Without nets in place, it was not always clear which side of the post the ball travelled and to the wonderment of everyone in the ground the referee awarded a goal and signalled a re-start to the game.

The Ayr players were *'disgusted beyond measure'* and had serious thoughts of not continuing with the game. Eventually, after a short delay where the players lodged a protest with the referee, they took up their places to re-start the game. On the hour, Ayr's pressure won a corner and from it, for the third time in the game, Ayr were level at 3-3.

With only a few minutes remaining the visitors, through Cunningham, scored the winner for a full time final scoreline of 4-3 to Ayr. In a contest of seven goals, the newspapers were consistent in their praise for the two goalkeepers, Steel and Fortune for Clyde, being the outstanding performers in the game. The *Scottish Referee* also picked out the Ayr midfield: *"The three half-backs are a strong trio and Logan for such a feather-weight does remarkably well."*

The local press finished off the match report with the following: *"When the team returned to Ayr about 9:30 quite a demonstration took place at the Townhead station. The players themselves were quite jubilant over their victory."* The following season Clyde joined the Scottish Football League and finished in mid-table, an entertaining campaign for the fans during which the goals flowed freely at both ends of the pitch, as it had in this cup tie.

This game was Jimmy's 'coming of age', a tough match against a top team, away from home, in front of a big crowd, Jimmy must have realised that he COULD mix it with the better players.

In November, the fourth round saw the first visit of a Scottish League club to Somerset Park in the shape of Heart of Midlothian. The Ayr team was to be the same as the one that played so well in eliminating Clyde.

That was: Steel (goal), Hamilton and Edgar (backs), Jack, Christie and Logan (half-backs), Russell, Feggans, Ross, Cunningham and Hamilton (forwards).

The fourth round tie began in the same fashion as the Clyde game, both teams taking it in turns to attack the other. It was Ayr who struck first with a goal from Ross but from that early jubilation, it was the League outfit that took control and equalised midway through the first half, grabbing a second just before the interval to lead 2-1. Early in the second half Hearts scored again to make it 3-1 so it looked bad for the home side, who nevertheless threw everything at their opponents and a fine run from Hamilton helped Ross reduce the arrears to 3-2.

It didn't last long as Hearts re-instated their two-goal lead with a disputed goal. Initially it appeared that the referee had given a free kick to Ayr, which they took quickly, had advanced to the half-way line when he suddenly indicated a goal had been awarded to Hearts which incensed the crowd.

The game was hectic and once again Ayr eroded the deficit as Hamilton finished off a good cross from Feggans. Then, Russell of Hearts rushing through on goal clashed with the Ayr keeper Steel who lay motionless on the ground after the incident. Some spectators nearby, already incensed by the disputed Hearts goal, got inside the ropes and soon, all around the park, others followed their example. Several fights broke out and Russell, the offending player was surrounded and roughly handled so during the confusion he made his escape and took refuge in the grandstand. There a sympathiser loaned him a hat and coat and suitably disguised, he reached the safety of the clubhouse.

The Ayr players and three policemen moved the visiting players into the clubhouse. Once the scene had calmed down, and Steel had received treatment, the game resumed, with Hearts playing with ten men. But they held fast and prevailed 4-3. It was a close call and Hearts, having scraped past Ayr by the narrowest of margins, went on to win the Scottish Cup at (the second) Hampden Park (now Cathkin Park) with David Russell, who had hidden incognito in the Ayr grandstand playing his part in the 1-0 win over Dumbarton in the final.

Master of disguise David Russell – Heart of Midlothian

The **Ayrshire Cup** was to prove significant – but not for any results. Ayr had eliminated Newmilns and Skares Thistle in the first two rounds before losing 5-3 to Hurlford at Somerset Park in the third round. In that December tie, in the absence of regular centre-forward Ross, Jimmy Logan was moved up front from the half-back position he had been occupying.

The effect was astonishing, Jimmy scored after only five minutes and was a constant threat, causing a local journalist to write, "*In front Logan was the Lion of the team. He is the best centre Ayr have had for many a day.*" While another wrote: *"Go on, ye'r dooin' fine,"* Logan. *The right man in the right place this time, if he only continues to play such splendid games as he has been doing lately.*

Amidst all the positive news about Jimmy's performances came the dreadful news on January 11, 1891 that his girlfriend's father, the Ayr FC trainer, William Munro had died. A terrible blow for William's family, Jimmy and the club.

After a 5-3 win over Stevenston Thistle, the *Ayrshire Post* of January 30, 1891, said:

"Logan was the mainspring of the Ayr front rank, and the way he shoots for goal now is a treat to witness. He gave Chalmers some stingers to stop on Saturday, and no fewer than four of the five goals scored for Ayr came from his foot."

In February 1891, a journal called *Sport* announced that Logan deserved a place in the forthcoming international trials. Word of his ability was spreading far and wide and it was not long before a Sunderland agent made an unsuccessful attempt to lure him south with the offer of good wages.

The Scottish Football Association appointed the following seven gentlemen, to act as the International Selection Committee (often referred to in the press as the Selection Seven):

| Mr Thomas Park of Cambuslang FC and President of the SFA | Mr George Sneddon of the East of Scotland Association and Vice President of the SFA | Mr John Campbell Treasurer of the SFA | Mr Thomas Lawrie of Queen's Park FC | Mr Robert Harrison of the Ayrshire Football Association | Mr Archibald Sliman of Battlefield FC | Mr Hugh Currie of the Vale of Leven FC |

These were the seven men who would decide if Jimmy's recent good form warranted a place in the trials for the Scottish international team. The International Selection Committee met in Glasgow on Tuesday, February 17, and chose the following four teams to play trial matches on Hampden Park, Glasgow on Saturday, February 28:

WHITE TEAM: Goal: Baird (Irvine), Backs: Whitelaw (Vale of Leven) and McKeown (Celtic), Half-backs: McQueen (Leith Athletic), Brown (St. Mirren) and McBain (St. Mirren), Forwards: Taylor (Heart of Midlothian), Buchanan (Abercorn), **Logan (Ayr),** Scott (Heart of Midlothian) and Bruce (Vale of Leven).

RED and WHITE TEAM: Goal: Connell (Port Glasgow), Backs: Walker (Inverness) and Collins (Cambuslang), Half-backs: Hamilton (Hurlford), Clelland (Royal Albert) and McLaren (Celtic), Forwards: Coupar (Dundee Our Boys), Thomson (Third Lanark), Butter (Our Boys), Keillor (Montrose) and Gourlay (Cambuslang).

BLACK and WHITE TEAM: Goal: McLeod (Dumbarton), Backs: Reynolds (Celtic) and Smellie (Queen's Park), Half-backs: Marshall (Rangers), McPherson (Heart of Midlothian) and Lochhead (Third Lanark), Forwards: Watt (Kilbirnie), Rankine (Vale of Leven), Johnstone (Third Lanark), McPherson (Rangers) and Bell (Dumbarton).

BLUE TEAM: Goal: McCorkindale (Partick Thistle), Backs: Adams (Heart of Midlothian) and Gow (Rangers), Half-backs: McMillan (Dumbarton), Boyle (Dumbarton) and Hill (Heart of Midlothian), Forwards: Gulliland (Queen's Park), Clements (Leith Athletic), Dowds (Celtic), Richardson (Hurlford) and Baird (Heart of Midlothian).

Jimmy was therefore included in the international trials; his recent outstanding form had clearly reached the ears of the Selection Seven. The SFA, through the Selection Seven proclaimed that, as a condition of selection, that all players chosen for the trial matches and absenting themselves without a valid excuse shall forfeit their chance of international honours.

It needs to be reiterated here that this season, 1890/91, was the first of the Scottish Football League. In the past, the SFA had been able to choose players for trials and international matches without any interference from anyone, but now, for the first time, the newly formed Scottish League was about to flex its muscles.

The League stepped in and quoted their rule XI which read, "Each club shall play its full strength teams in all matches unless some satisfactory explanation be offered to the committee." 27 of the 44 players selected for the trials were from the ten League clubs (i.e. Dumbarton, Rangers, Celtic, Cambuslang, Third Lanark, Heart of Midlothian, Abercorn, St Mirren, Vale of Leven and Cowlairs). The players from clubs not in the League, such as Jimmy Logan from Ayr FC, were unaffected by this ruling so prepared for the trials as best they could.

The trials descended into farce with the Black and White team having nine of their eleven players from League clubs, the White team having seven and the Blue team also having seven, the Red and White team had only four players from the League clubs.

Would all the League players withdraw? Would the clubs insist they did? In the end only seven players from the League took part in the trials, with the other twenty players turning out for their clubs. The ruling also caused problems between some of the clubs in the League. An example of this was Celtic.

They were due to play Hearts on the same day as the trials and both clubs agreed to play their full strength teams in the League game. It only became apparent close to the kick-off that Hearts had allowed half-backs McPherson and Hill to travel to Hampden Park to participate in the trials. This upset Celtic. Hearts had not stuck to the agreement between the two clubs. It also angered the Celtic players who felt they had forfeited the chance of an international 'cap' unnecessarily.

The International Selection Committee were left to replace almost half of their initial 44 selections with players who were immediately regarded by some of the press as 'second-class men' as they were not originally chosen. This farcical situation could only help the cause of players like Jimmy Logan.

Eventually, after much chopping and changing, even on the day of the trial, the much revised teams looked like this:

BLACK and WHITE TEAM: Goal: McCorkindale (Partick Thistle), Backs: Walker (Inverness Caledonian) and Hepburn (Alloa Athletic), Half-backs: Marshall (Rangers), McPherson (Heart of Midlothian) and Hill (Heart of Midlothian), Forwards: Watt (Kilbirnie), Rankine (Vale of Leven), **Logan (Ayr),** Richardson (Hurlford) and Keiller (Montrose).

BLUE TEAM: Goal: Maird (Irvine), Backs: Reid (5th KRV[5]) and Paul (Dykebar), Half-backs: McQueen (Leith Athletic), Brown (St Mirren) and K. McBain (St Mirren), Forwards: Gulliland (Queen's Park), Clements (Leith Athletic), Buttar (Our Boys), Boyd (Mossend Swifts) and Barker (Linthouse).

WHITE TEAM: Goal: Gold (Our Boys), Backs: O'Kane (Arbroath) and Dewar (Glasgow Wanderers), Half-backs: Hamilton (Hurlford), Clelland (Royal Albert) and W Sellar (Queen's Park), Forwards: Cowpar (Our Boys), Buchanan (Abercorn), Baird (Albion Rovers), Skea (Arbroath) and Berry (Queen's Park).

RED and WHITE TEAM: Goal: Connor (Airdreonians), Backs: Bennet (Clysedale) and Watt (Kilbirnie), Half-backs: Craig (Our Boys), Scott (Albion Rovers) and Frame (Royal

---

5 The 5th Kirkcudbrightshire Rifle Volunteers Football Club was a football team based in Dumfries, Scotland. The club was founded in 1879 and played their home games on their drill field, Palmerston Park in Dumfries.

Albert), Forwards: McIntoch (Linthouse), Anderson (Battlefield), Bowie (Linthouse), McInnes (King's Park) and Lambie (Queen's Park and Corinthians).

In the end just six players from the League took part in the trials, they were Marshall (Rangers), McPherson and Hill (Heart of Midlothian), Rankine (Vale of Leven), and Brown and K. McBain (St Mirren).

The Saturday of the trials was a particularly unpleasant day for football in Glasgow with a raw wind, accompanied by heavy rain, keeping spectators to less than a thousand.

The first game, featuring Black and White v Blue kicked off at 2:40 with 800 or 900 spectators watching comical football in the mud. They entered into the spirit of the difficulties the players were experiencing by enjoying every little blunder or mishap, hearty side-splitting laughter was frequently indulged in.

Result: The Black and Whites beat the Blues 7-2.

The second game, after a delay to let the hilarity die down, saw the White team take on the Red and White team. It was another 90 minutes of toil and struggle in appalling conditions.

Result: Red and Whites beat the Whites 5-2.

The matches were uninteresting, of a poor quality and it was unlikely to have been of any value to the Selection Seven in the choosing the forthcoming international teams.

Cathkin Park – site of Jimmy Logan's first international trial on February 28, 1891 Previously this ground was the second Hampden Park and home of Queen's Park FC who moved there in 1884 until the late 1890s. Third Lanark took over occupancy in 1903 and renamed it Cathkin Park. Third Lanark went out of business in 1967 and Cathkin Park is now a public park where football is still played. Although overgrown, much of the original terracing is still evident

Cathkin Park in better days

The second international trial match took place at Tynecastle Park, Edinburgh, home of Heart of Midlothian, on Saturday, March 7. The SFA selectors met on Monday evening to pick two final trial teams to play a further match. It was agreed not to include those players who did not play in last Saturday's trials and who had not sufficient reason for not turning up. The following are the two teams and reserves:

BLUE TEAM: Goal: Wilson (Vale of Leven), Backs: Arnott (Queen's Park) and Smellie (Queen's Park), Half-backs: Begbie (Heart of Midlothian), Kelly (Celtic) and Hill (Heart of Midlothian), Forwards: Watt (Kilbirnie), Berry (Queen's Park), Sellar (Queen's Park), Dunlop (St Mirren) and Baird (Heart of Midlothian).

WHITE TEAM: Goal: Gillespie (Queen's Park), Backs: Ritchie (East Stirlingshire) and Gow (Rangers), Half-backs: Marshall (Rangers), McPherson (Heart of Midlothian) and Robertson (Queen's Park), Forwards: Gulliland (Queen's Park), Rankine (Vale of Leven), McMahon (Celtic), Richardson (Hurlford) and Keillor (Montrose).

Reserves: Goal: McCorkindale (Partick Thistle), Backs: Sillars (Queen's Park) and Hepburn (Alloa Athletic), Half-backs: Johnstone (Abercorn), Brown (St Mirren) and McBarn (St Mirren), Forwards: McIntosh (Linthouse), Buchanan (Abercorn), Buttar (Our Boys), Boyd (Mossend Swifts) and Barker (Linthouse).

Jimmy Logan was not named in either team or the reserve players listed as stand by players.

SCOTTISH FOOTBALL ASSOCIATION.
INTERNATIONAL TRIAL MATCH,
At Tynecastle Park, on SATURDAY, 7th March.
Kick-Off at Four o'clock prompt.
Admission 6d. Ladies Free; Stands 6d. extra each person.
Membership Tickets not available.
Special Service of Cars run close to Entrance Gate.

A newspaper advert for the second international trial at Tynecastle Park

Exactly half of the 22 players chosen to play in the trial were from football clubs in the League (Hearts four, Rangers two, Celtic two, Vale of Leven two and St Mirren one).

The League sent out an edict stating that: *"Any member of a League team assisting at the international trial match in Edinburgh would be disqualified by the League and would, of course, be debarred from assisting his club in League engagements."*

Athletic News said: *"This has set the heather on fire in stern earnest."*

All the League players were contacted by their clubs and the situation explained. The players from St Mirren, Rangers and Celtic withdrew from the trials. The six players from Vale of Leven and Hearts made the decision to attend the trial and try to gain international honours.

Once again late amendments to the trial teams took place, including bringing in Jimmy Logan to replace McMahon the Celtic centre-forward. All of the bizarre happenings at the trials, both at Hampden Park and Tynecastle Park had worked in Jimmy's favour with so many of the League's best players now out of contention for selection. There was to be one more fact that would also help Jimmy gain selection for Scotland.

Three teams had to be selected to face England, Ireland and Wales. Traditionally these would be three **different** teams – a different team to face each country. Even if the 33 international players were chosen from the original 44 trialists the odds were definitely in Jimmy's favour but with so many of those outstanding players now unavailable, his chances of selection had become even better.

Changes were taking place right up to the kick-off as the League players continued to withdraw. The trial took place with the amended teams looking like this:

BLUE TEAM: Goal: Wilson (Vale of Leven), Backs: Arnott (Queen's Park) and Smellie (Queen's Park), Half-backs: Begbie (Heart of Midlothian), Macpherson (Heart of Midlothian) and Hill (Heart of Midlothian), Forwards: Watt (Kilbirnie), Berry (Queen's Park), Sellar (Queen's Park), Richardson (Hurlford) and Baird (Heart of Midlothian).

WHITE TEAM: Goal: Gillespie (Queen's Park), Backs: Ritchie (East Stirlingshire) and Hepburn (Alloa Athletic), Half-backs Gemmell (Glasgow Thistle), McQueen (Leith Athletic) and McLaren (Celtic), Forwards: Gulliland (Queen's Park), Rankine (Vale of Leven), **Logan (Ayr),** Robertson (Partick Thistle) and Keillor (Montrose).

The game was a slow one and by no means in keeping with the importance of the match. The four Hearts League players and most of the other strong players were in the Blue team and they ran out worthy winners by four goals to two.

Being in the international trials had certainly raised Jimmy's profile and when the Ayrshire selectors were required to select a team to represent the county against Renfrewshire at Greenock Morton's Cappielow Park on Saturday, March 14, the week before the international, Jimmy was picked.

Finally, on Tuesday, March 10, the three Scottish international teams were announced:
The team to play England at Ewood Park, Blackburn on April 4 1891:
Goal: James Wilson (Vale of Leven), Backs: Walter Arnott (captain) (Queen's Park) and Robert Smellie (Queen's Park), Half-backs Isaac Begbie, John McPherson and John Hill (all Hearts of Midlothian), Forwards: Frank Watt (Kilbirnie), Willian Berry (Queen's Park), William Sellar (Queen's Park), Gilbert Rankine (Vale of Leven) and David Baird (Heart of Midlothian).

The team to play Ireland at Celtic Park, Glasgow on March 28, 1891:

Goal: John McCorkindale (Partick Thistle), Backs: Richard Hunter (St Mirren) and William Paul (Dykebar), Half-backs: Thomas McMellan (Dumbarton), James Cleland (Royal Albert) and James McLaren (captain) (Celtic), Forwards: James Low (Cambuslang), Robert Clements (Leith Athletic), William Bowie (Linthouse), Thomas Waddell (Queen's Park), James Fraser (Moffat).

The team to play Wales at the Racecourse Ground, Wrexham on March 21, 1891:

Goal: George Gillespie (Queen's Park), Backs: Archibald Ritchie (East Stirlingshire) and James Hepburn (Alloa Athletic), Half-backs: Matthew McQueen (Leith Athletic), Andrew Brown (St Mirren) and Thomas Robertson (Queen's Park), Forwards: William Gulliland (Queen's Park), Robert Buchanan (Abercorn), **Jimmy Logan (Ayr),** D. Richardson (Hurlford) and Alexander Keillor (Montrose).

So, in an amazing turn of events, Jimmy Logan had progressed from starting the 1890/91 season in Ayr's reserve team, the Strollers, then moving up to the first team and by March being named for his county, taking part in international trials and being selected for his country as a Scottish international player.

The *Ayrshire Post*, well aware of the agents approaching Jimmy with good offers to turn professional carried the following just a couple of days after the international teams were announced: *"Logan has been selected to fill the centre position in the team chosen to oppose Wales tomorrow week at Wrexham. Have you to pass Sunderland on the way home to Scotland?"* So it was common knowledge that Jimmy and Sunderland were in talks – had Jimmy been been advised to wait until he was an international player in order to get a better deal when the English agents came calling?

A few days later a specially convened meeting of the Scottish Football League was held in Glasgow with the purpose of considering the cases of those players who had, in defiance of the League's edict, played last Saturday in the international trial match at Edinburgh.

After full consideration, they permanently suspended the following players from playing in any League matches:- Wilson and Rankine of the Vale of Leven club and Hill, Baird, McPherson and Begbie all of the Heart of Midlothian club.

The players named had all been chosen to face England, traditionally, the strongest team available was always selected for this fixture.

Saturday, March 14, saw Jimmy playing for his county against Renfrewshire at Cappielow Park. It was beautiful weather, firm turf and a good crowd of spectators had turned up to see the game.

An early picture of a game taking place on Cappielow Park

The teams were as follows:

Renfrewshire: Goal: Connell (Port), Backs: Paul (Dykebar) and Hirst (Arthurlie), Half-backs T. Steel (Neilston), McKinnon (Port) and Blair (Morton), Forwards: Brown (Morton), Gibson (Dykebar), Carswell (Arthurlie), Neil (Port) and A. Steel (Neilston).

Ayrshire: Goal: Baird (Irvine), Backs: Todd (Kilbirnie) and Orr (Kilmarnock), Half-backs: Hamilton (Hurlford), Campbell (Kilmarnock) and Donachie (Stevenston Thistle), Forwards: Watt (Kilbirnie), Lowe (Kilbirnie), **Logan (Ayr),** Richardson (Hurlford) and Cunningham (Ayr).

Ayrshire took the lead after only 15 minutes when Watt scored and they went further ahead when Jimmy Logan scored after fine work from Watt. From then on it was Renfrewshire who took a grip on the game and by half-time it was two goals apiece. The second half continued as the first had ended with Renfrewshire on top and the final score reflecting their dominance; Renfrewshire 6 Ayrshire 3.

The *Ayrshire Post* previewed the international game at Wrexham:

"Scotland's first International Association game falls to be decided against Wales tomorrow at Wrexham. Special interest will be directed to the team from this district seeing that Logan of Ayr is the centre man. It is to be hoped that it will give his name another lift up the ladder, and help the land o' cakes team to pull off a handsome victory. By the bye, I notice that Logan has been offered £100 for his services."

By the time the Wales v Scotland game came around, Wales had already lost 7-2 to Ireland and 4-1 to England in the British Home Championships and despite losing 14 of the previous 15 meetings (the other was a 0-0 draw) to Scotland, they were confident of a first ever victory over the Scots. After all they had witnessed the selection farce and conflict between the Scottish FA and League bodies and believed that this was a much weaker team visiting Wrexham.

The Scottish team left Glasgow at two o'clock on the Friday afternoon, the day before the game, to travel the 240 miles to Chester, where they spent the night, arriving at about 8pm that evening. On the morning of the match, on Saturday, March 21, the team drove the remaining dozen or so miles in their horse-drawn carriage to Wrexham's Racecourse Ground.

In preparation for the game, an extra stand, which held about 1,000 spectators, had been erected. The kick-off was fixed for 3:30pm. The ground was in splendid condition but the weather was dull and cold as approximately 4,000 spectators, described as the largest crowd ever seen at the North Wales ground, assembled in anticipation.

Elsewhere, on the same day, while the Ayr striker Jimmy Logan was representing his country, his team-mates were uncharitably and comprehensively beating a Deaf and Dumb English International Team 11-3 at Somerset Park. In the English FA Cup Final at the Kennington Oval, Blackburn Rovers were beating Notts County 3-1.

There were two late changes to the Scotland team. Goalkeeper Gillespie was unable to play and was replaced by John McCorkindale of Partick Thistle. Forward Richardson of Hurlford had 'taken the English shilling' by joining Derby County and his place was taken by Robert Boyd of Mossend Swifts.

The Racecourse Ground, Wrexham in 1910

The Turf Hotel stood at one corner of the pitch with the changing rooms adjacent to it from where the players of the two teams would have stepped down a wooden staircase and across the paddock area and entered the field with their chests puffed out with pride.

The two teams that day were as follows:

Wales:
Goal: J Trainer (Wrexham and Preston North End), Backs: S Powell (Summerhill and West Bromwich Albion) and D Jones (Chirk and Bolton Wanderers), Half-backs: Arthur Lea (Wrexham), Humphrey Jones (Bangor and Queen's Park) and C. Parry (Llanellin and Everton), Forwards: J Davies (Chirk), W. Owen (Chirk), W H Turner (Wrexham), J C H Bowdler (Rhayader and Wolverhampton Wanderers), W Lewis and (Bangor and Crewe Alexandra)

Scotland:
Goal: J McCorkindale (Partick Thistle), Backs: Archibald Ritchie (East Stirlingshire) and James Hepburn (Alloa Athletic), Half-backs: Matthew McQueen (Leith Athletic), Andrew Brown (St Mirren) and Thomas Robertson (Queen's Park), Forwards: William Gulliland (Queen's Park), Robert Buchanan (Abercorn), **Jimmy Logan (Ayr),** Robert Boyd (Mossend Swifts) and Alexander Keillor (Montrose).

Umpires were: Messrs G Sedden (vice-president of the Scottish Association) and G H Jones (of the Welsh Association). Referee was Mr C Crump (vice-president of the Football Association).

**The Scotland team pictured before the game against Wales in Wrexham
Back row (players only): Tom Robertson, William Gulliland, Archie Ritchie, James
Hepburn and Matt McQueen.
Front row: Robert Buchanan, Alexander 'Sandy' Keillor, Andrew Brown, John
McKorkindale, Robert Boyd and Jimmy Logan**

The match report from the Wrexham Advertiser went as follows:
At 3:45 the game began with Logan kicking off for Scotland. A free kick for hands was immediately granted to the visitors, but Humphrey Jones cleared. The Welsh forwards then made for their opponents' quarters, but Ritchie secured and returned. After the ball had gone the wrong side of Trainer's uprights, McCorkindale had to kick away a swift shot from Turner. Play was carried on for a bit near the Scotch goal, but Davies at last sent the ball out of play. From some nice passing by the Welsh centre and right wing a corner resulted, but the ball, after bobbing about in the goal mouth, was sent behind. Humphrey Jones stopped Keillor and Boyd when making for the Welsh goal and sent the ball on to Owen, who sent into the Scotch goal. Hands followed but the ball was safely got away. Buchanan and Gulliland got away and the latter sending the ball into the goalmouth, Logan heading through, five minutes after the start, Trainer just touching the ball with his hands. A free kick for hands was granted to the visitors near their opponent's goal, but the ball was sent out of play. D.Jones stopped the scotch left wingers and landed the ball down the field. Turner got possession and passed to Bowdler and skilfully dodging Ritchie he equalised for Wales amidst loud cheering. Wales were now playing up finely and the Scotch defence was severely taxed from a long shot by Parry the Welsh forwards looked dangerous, but Ritchie cleared and Logan made tracks for Trainer. Humphrey Jones, however pulled him up and returned the ball to the other end, where Davies sent out of play. The Scotch forwards now had a run down and Trainer had to save a shot by Logan. The play was then taken to the other end where Lewis shot into goal, but McCorkindale was on the alert and sent the ball away. From a scrimmage in front of the Scotch goal the ball was just kicked outside the upright. In meeting the kick-off Parry, the Welsh left half-back, received a severe blow on his forehead and the play had to be stopped, but was resumed in a few minutes without Parry, who,

however, came on five minutes afterwards. By combined play among the Scotch forwards the ball was taken down the field and Trainer had to punch away a sharp shot. A free-kick for 'hands' relieved the pressure and the ball was taken to the other end, where Ritchie achieved a grand save. Two corners for Wales followed in quick succession, but both were safely got away. Ritchie, standing on the goal line, again saved when the goalkeeper was out of his goal. Soon afterwards Hepburn gave a corner, but it was cleared and Boyd and Keillor got away with the ball and Trainer had to kick away a shot by the former. Parry, at the other end sent the ball with a huge kick into the Scotch goal, but McCorkindale caught and kicked away. The ball was, however, returned and Turner securing, passed to Owen and that player being in a good position, banged the ball past the Scotch custodian, placing the Welshmen ahead. McQueen was noticeable for stopping the Welsh left wing. Bowdler, one of the Welsh left wingers, was slightly hurt and play was suspended for a few minutes. When play was again resumed, Gulliland made several brilliant runs along the right wing, but the Welsh defenders fought hard and Trainer had to run out to stop a shot. Brown secured the return and sent into the goal, where Trainer brought off a marvellous save. Keillor got away, but was pulled up for being off-side and the Welsh forwards had a go, Davies shooting into goal, but Ritchie saved. Bowdler and Lewis came down the left wing by means of some accurate passing but Bowdler's shot just went over the cross-bar. The visitors' left wing then got away, Keillor crossing, Gulliland got possession of the ball but sent wildly over. Half-time was then called.

Half time: Wales 2 Scotland 1.

After the interval the game was resumed, the Scotchmen at once began to press, but D. Jones saved twice beautifully. Lea sent on to Davies, who put a swift shot into goal, but the custodian was ready and he neatly accounted for it. The Scotch forwards came down the field by some pretty passing. Boyd finishing by sending in a low shot but Trainer cleared. A free kick was granted to Wales in the centre of the field but Ritchie headed away and D. Jones next stopped the Scotch attackers in fine style.From a run by the Welsh forwards Bowdler sent into the mouth of goal but Hepburn headed away. Owen met but sent over the cross-bar. From a throw-in near the Welsh goal Logan seemed to have a chance of scoring but he sent the ball wildly over the bar. A free kick for a foul was given to Scotland, but Lea cleared. The ball was, however, returned and Trainer had to throw away. Still keeping up the pressure, Buchanan was a long shot equalised for Scotland. Soon afterwards Parry was again injured and had to leave the field the Welshmen playing the last half hour with ten men. After Trainer had saved from a shot by Logan, Wales had a look in and they were granted a corner. Brown cleared and the Scotch left pair got away but Powell pulled them up and returned the ball. After Davies had had a try at McCorkindale, Robertson sent into the mouth of goal with a long kick, but D Jones headed away. The ball was returned but passed out of play. Brown secured from the goal kick and landed the ball into the goal. Trainer was engaged in picking the ball up, when Boyd came rushing up and kicked it out of his hands through the goal, thus placing Scotland ahead. From the kick-off Humphrey Jones stopped Logan and sent on to Bowiller, who at once made for the Scotch goal. Ritchie deliberately fouled him but the free kick came to nothing. Play was now carried on in the Scotch quarters. From a cross by Owen, Bowdler got possession and having eluded Ritchie, looked like scoring but McQueen came rushing up and robbed him. From a corner, Owen equalised for Wales out of the scrummage that followed amidst loud cheering. Trainer immediately afterwards had to clear and as Turner was making for his opponents' quarters, he was fouled by Brown, but Robertson cleared. The ball was soon returned and Davies shot into the mouth of the goal, Bowdler heading in but McCorkindale saved. From a run down by the Scotch right wingers, Buchanan sent into the goal with a bouncing shot. Trainer picked up but mulled it and before he could recover possession Boyd had scored a fourth goal for Scotland. Scotland scored again but the goal was disallowed for off-side. There was only now a few minutes to play and the Welshmen strove hard to draw level but failed and 'time' was called.

Full time: Wales 3 Scotland 4.

After the game the two teams and the officials enjoyed a tea together at the Wynnstay Arms Hotel. Mr T E Thomas, chairman of the Welsh Association was presiding and during his speech he complained about the conduct of the English clubs in their refusal to release some of the Welsh players that plied their trade in the English League, to play for Wales. Mr Parks and Mr Snedden replied on behalf of the Scottish Association.

The Wynnstay Arms Hotel in Wrexham c.1895 where the Welsh and Scottish teams and officials enjoyed tea after the game

With Scotland also beating Ireland 2-1, the Home International Championships would be decided at Ewood Park, Blackburn, on May 4. England beat Scotland 2-1 and so claimed the title for 1891.

The final table:

	Pl	W	D	L	F	A	Pts
England	3	3	0	0	12	3	6
Scotland	3	2	0	1	7	6	4
Ireland	3	1	0	2	9	10	2
Wales	3	0	0	3	6	15	0

The 1890/91 season seemed to go on for ever. There was the **Kilmarnock Quoiting Association Timepieces Football Competition** – apparently a football competition would attract more spectators than a quoits competition and therefore the possibility of raising more much needed funds for the Quoits Association. This was a competition where four teams in the Kilmarnock area (Kilmarnock FC, Kilmarnock Athletic, Hurlford and Annbank) were invited to play in a two semi-finals and a final with all games taking place on Kilmarnock's Rugby Park.

The winners receiving timepieces from the organisers, with hopefully some profits going into their coffers as well. Because Jimmy's profile had been raised and he was now a Scottish international footballer he was invited to play as a guest for Kilmarnock, as it may improve their chances of winning, but more importantly as far as the Quoits Association were concerned, it may add a few more to the number of paying customers attending the games.

The first semi-final took place on Wednesday, May 6. The half-time score was 2-1 to Kilmarnock but the second half saw Hurlford doing much more of the attacking and *'rough play to an alarming extent.'* The result was still in doubt with both teams having chances until Jimmy Logan picked up a loose ball and fired in a shot to give Kilmarnock an unassailable 3-1 lead.

The game was described by the *Glasgow Evening Post* as *'one of the fastest and roughest games played in Ayrshire this season.'* The same newspaper, under the pseudonym of the 'Referee' also reported: *'The Killie team sought support from Ayr in Logan – the coming man. I never saw the youth before – but when I saw the young colt scamper up the field I singled him out at once as one playing with unusual dash and spirit, supported by talent. Logan has a great day before him.'*

The second semi-final was played on Saturday, May 9, but was a much more one-sided game which saw an easy 6-0 victory for Annbank over the local team. The final, played on Saturday, May 30, saw an even contest won eventually 2-1 by Annbank. After the game, the two teams and officials retired to the Bakers' Arms where they received their timepieces.

At a meeting of the SFA on Tuesday, May 5, a resolution was carried that a general amnesty be declared to all players who were already suspended for professionalism, or who, being at present in England, may return between May 5 and August 2. All players at present under suspicion were by resolutions were 'whitewashed' by the meeting.

Then there was the **Ayr Charity Cup**. Eight teams entered with all games played on Somerset Park and it turned into a nightmare for the organisers as three of the four first round (or quarter finals) resulted in draws and new dates had to be found in the clubs' busy schedules.

Eventually, the final was between Ayr, who had knocked out Kilbirnie and Kilmarnock and Hurlford who had 'seen off' Newmilns and Annbank.

The final eventually took place on June 20 and was an even and physical affair with Goudie (Hurlford) and Govan (Ayr) sent off for their pugilistic display. A single goal from a goalmouth scramble was enough to give Ayr the trophy 1-0 and after the game the trophy and medals were presented to the winning Ayr team with Dr. Naismith, president of the Ayr club, receiving the trophy on behalf of the club.

More importantly perhaps was the fact that it was a large attendance and the Ayr Charity Cup committee were able to hand over a cheque for £90 to the Ayr County Hospital – a total of £530 since the competition began seven years earlier.

Finally there was the **Ayr Swimming Club Timepieces Competition** – not just any old timepieces but marble clocks! Swimming clubs in those days did not take place in swimming pools – but in the sea! The Ayr swimming club were keen to raise funds to erect a building near the sea for changing rooms and other facilities so they decided to follow the lead of the Kilmarnock Quoits Association and stage a football competition for local teams in the Ayr area with games being played at Somerset Park where people could be charged as they enter – unlike a swimming event where it is much more difficult to put a fence around the sea!

Six teams were invited – Ayr Parkhouse, Ayr Athletic, Ayr FC, Kilmarnock Athletic, Kilwinning Monkcastle and Annbank. In the first round Ayr Parkhouse would play Ayr Athletic and Kilmarnock Athletic would play Kilwinning Monkhouse Monkcastle with Annbank and Ayr FC receiving a bye into the semi-finals.

Ayr Parkhouse won comfortably 8-1 and Kilmarnock were victorious by 3-2. In the semi-finals Annbank brushed aside Kilmarnock 7-1 while in the other, the clash of the local rivals, proved to be an exciting game in front of a large crowd. After only nine minutes Logan got hold of the ball in his own half and sped off towards the other end. Despite two or three fierce tackles being made he managed to stay on his feet and escaped with the ball still at his feet and went on to beat the Parkhouse keeper to put Ayr a goal ahead. Half-time saw Ayr in the lead 2-1. Play was even and 'end to end' in the second half. At 3-3 Logan went on another fine run to the Parkhouse goal and at the last moment laid the ball back to Feggans, who steadied himself before scoring to put Ayr 4-3 ahead. The final goal of the game was scored when Jack the Ayr half-back rushed in to the goalmouth putting both the ball and the defender into the back of the Parkhouse net for a 5-3 win and a place in the final.

The final took place on Saturday, June 13, but after a bruising contest it ended 2-2 so had to be replayed a fortnight later. In that second game Annbank were narrow victors by 3-2. After the match the teams and some of the spectators and members of the swimming club assembled in a room over the 3 Boat Vennal Inn where Mr Thompson, on behalf of the swimming club, expressed thanks to those football clubs who had so kindly come forward to take part in the ties and invited any of the footballers to join the swimming club on Saturday afternoons during the summer where they would be made very welcome.

A clock was then presented to each man who had played in the final, after which the company adjourned downstairs, where host William Smith provided a substantial and well deserved tea. Finally, on June 27 the football season came to an end in Ayrshire.

On July 16, Jimmy's sister, Janet Harkins gave birth to a daughter named Elizabeth Logan Harkins.

On July 8 an important ceremony took place in the town. It was the unveiling of the Robert Burns statue.

The unveiling of the Ayr Burns statue on July 8 as it appeared in the local press

During that summer the English football agents still circled around the local players like vultures with a Sunderland agent interviewing Logan, Feggans and Hamilton all of Ayr FC.

With the memorial to the national bard complete, negotiations between Sunderland and Jimmy Logan were also completed and the Ayr centre-forward signed, so joining the SFA's 'blacklist' of Scottish professional footballers.

At the end of the 1890/91 season the Scottish Referee newspaper made the following comment: *"Should Logan remain with his native team? He is a power among them and his power being admitted and acted on, showed that it is a grand thing when an eleven has a man they can look up to and depend on. This young player guided the field. In mute silence his orders were attended to and as a result Ayr played better games this season than I have seen them do for years."*

The statue and Jimmy's football career had run a strange parellel. His time with Ayr FC began in the summer of 1887, coinciding with the announcement of the statue fund. He had played in football games where the profits were donated to the statue. By its completion and unveiling in the summer of 1891, his time with Ayr FC was also over. Sunderland was his next port of call.

How the Burns statue looks today

1891/92 season saw Ayr FC join their first league – the Alliance[6] – but Jimmy wasn't there to experience it. He had turned professional.

---

[6] *The Alliance League was formed in time for the 1891/92 season (champions were Linthouse). The original members were: Airdrieonians, Ayr, East Stirlingshire, Morton, Kilmarnock, King's Park, Linthouse, Northern, Partick Thistle, Port Glasgow Athletic, St Bernard's and Thistle.*

CHAPTER SEVEN

July 1891 - November 1891

A professional footballer with Sunderland

JIMMY Logan arrived on Wearside in the summer of 1891 at the end of Sunderland's first season in the Football League. At that time their home ground was on Newcastle Road.

The Newcastle Road Ground c.1890
(Notice the pitch markings with the six yard 'rings' around each post and the twelve yard line across the pitch)

Position of the Newcastle Road ground from an 1897 map

Sunderland had moved to the Newcastle Road ground in 1886 and stayed put for 12 years until 1898[7]. A high wall surrounded much of the ground and a 1,000-seater grandstand was built on the north side of the pitch and terracing was eventually installed around the other three sides. The club's headquarters became the Royal Hotel on North Bridge Street, half-a-mile from their ground. The players would change at the hotel and travel onwards for the home matches, arriving by 'brake.'[8]

Later on in their tenancy they used tents in which to change until a final solution was found when they purchased number 37 Ellerslie Terrace, over the road from the ground. This became the club's office where committee meetings were held. The house next door was also bought and this became a billiards and card room for the players who would also get changed there and walk over the road into the ground.

In 1889 a clubhouse was built, the ground admittance was increased to a shilling. It was now the best stadium in the North East and boasted a capacity of 15,000. It recorded the highest-ever attendance at an English football ground in January 1891 when 21,000 spectators witnessed the first round FA cup-tie against Everton with some fans sat on the roof of the stand.

Aston Villa, runners-up in the League's first season, visited Sunderland on April 5, 1890, and were comprehensively beaten 7-2, with the founder of the Football League and Villa Chairman William McGregor, to remark that Sunderland had 'a talented man in every position'. A nickname was born and Sunderland became known throughout the land as 'The Team of all Talents'.

Of course it did their chances of election to the League a power of good when a man with such influence as McGregor was impressed with the quality of the team.

Normally the bottom four teams in the Football League were all required to retire and seek re-election at the AGM but at the end of the 1889-90 season Villa and Bolton Wanderers finished equal on 19 points so it was decided that neither should apply for re-election which meant that only the bottom three teams, Notts County, Burnley and Stoke, applied.

The teams wanting to join the League were: Bootle, Darwen, Grimsby Town, Sunderland, Sunderland Albion, Newton Heath and the three 'retiring' clubs Burnley, Notts County and Stoke. Representatives from each club attended the meeting and each stated their club's case. The result was that Notts County and Burnley were re-elected but Stoke[9] were not. Sunderland replaced them for the 1890-91 season.

As can be seen from the map over the page, up to this point all the teams in the Football League since its inception in 1888 had been from either the North West or the Midlands. Thus some clubs questioned the wisdom of inviting a team from the North East to join, the question of travelling expenses incurred being of paramount concern.

When Sunderland put forward their case for election they did point out that while other clubs would be making one long journey to Wearside, Sunderland would be making many more long trips in the opposite direction. By way of a compromise, they offered to pay towards the travelling costs of their opponents and that did the trick. This would have been a substantial sum of money at the time estimated between £10-£15 for each game played at Newcastle Road, a commitment of around £165 before the season had even got underway – such was the desire of the men running Sunderland to succeed in the Football League.

---

[7] *In 1898 Sunderland FC vacated Newcastle Road and moved to Roker Park. The Newcastle Road ground was used for housing.*
[8] *A brake was a horse-drawn carriage used in the 19th and early 20th centuries.*
[9] *Stoke played in the Football Alliance the following season but returned to the Football League after a one year absence.*

With League football established in Scotland, the legalization of professionalism was pushed higher up the agenda. It was approved at the SFA'S annual general meeting in 1892 sowing the seeds of Old Firm dominance.

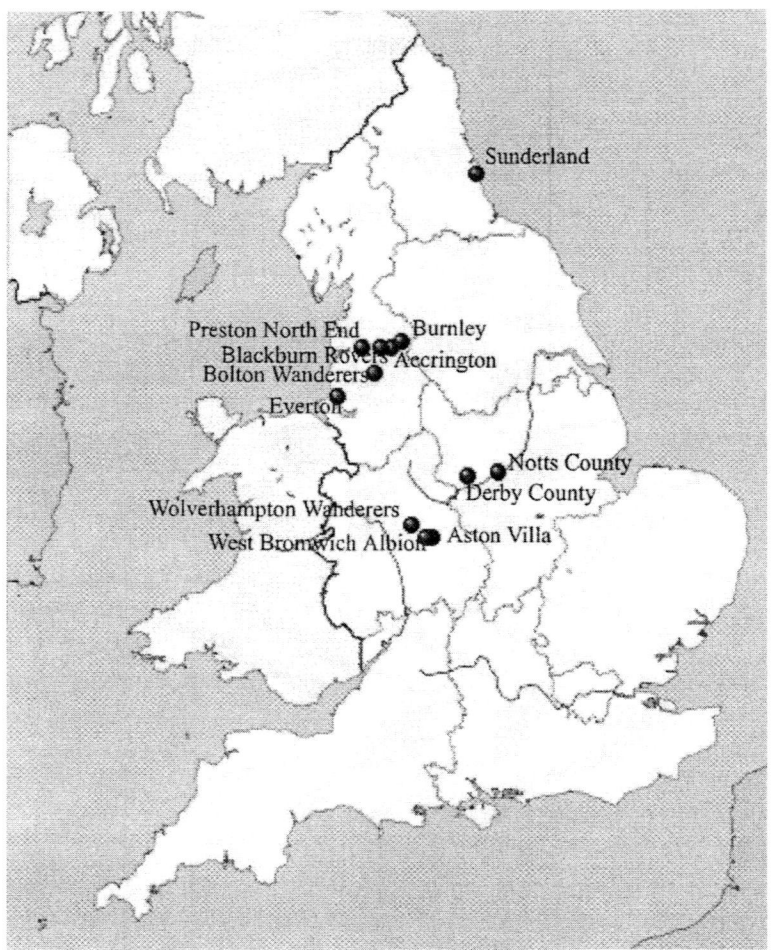

Map showing the location of the clubs for season 1891/92

Jimmy was one of only three new signings by Sunderland during the summer of 1891. He would have felt quite at home in the 15-man squad. Twelve of them were born in Scotland, including five from Jimmy's home county of Ayrshire. One other was born in Northern Ireland so it meant only two Englishmen started the season in the Sunderland squad.

Although Jimmy's signing was reported in Scottish newspapers at the end of July, way back in March the papers were carrying accusations that he had 'accepted the English shilling' and that he was already in receipt of pay from the Wearsiders.

Sunderland had finished the 1890/91 season 7th in the table having two points deducted for playing John Doig, their new goalkeeper, also known as Ned, before his registration was fully complete, without which they would have finished fifth. They also reached the FA Cup semi-finals.

With the addition of their three new players, Donald Gow a full-back from Rangers, James Hannah a winger from Sunderland Albion and Jimmy Logan a centre-forward from Ayr FC they were hoping for even better things.

The arrivals of these new men boosted the head count of internationals in Sunderland's ranks to eight - Thomas Porteus of England plus John Doig, Donald Gow, Hugh Wilson, John Auld, John Murray, James Hannah and Jimmy Logan all of Scotland.

50

Before the start of the 1891/92 season the colours of the Football League teams were published in the press as follows:

Accrington	Red
Aston Villa	Claret and light blue
Bolton Wanderers	Red and white quartered jerseys and black knickers
Blackburn Rovers	Light blue and white
Darwen	Salmon jersey and white knickers
Derby County	Cardinal and white shirts in halves and black knickers
Everton	Ruby shirts, blue trimmings and dark blue knickers
Notts County	Black and white stripes, black knickers
Preston North End	White shirts, blue knickers
Stoke	Amber and black shirts and blue knickers
Sunderland	Red and white shirts
West Bromwich Albion	Blue and white striped shirts, white knickers
Wolverhampton Wanderers	Old gold and black shirts quartered and black knickers

Sunderland 1891/92
Back row (left to right): Tom Porteous, Hugh Wilson, Ned Doig, James Dalton, Will Gibson, John Murray and T. Norris (referee)
Front row (left to right): Sam Tyzack (treasurer), Jimmy Hannah, David Hannah, John Middleton Campbell, Jimmy Millar, Jock Scott and Tom Watson (secretary)

With the 1891/92 season fast approaching, Sunderland's first practice took place at their Newcastle Road enclosure on Thursday, August 13. It was now that Jimmy probably began to realise the step up the football ladder he had made when between 5-6,000 fans turned up just to watch the players practice, with the three new men a particular the focus of their attention. A match was played between two teams composed of Whites and Reds with Jimmy at centre-forward for the Reds. The Whites won 1-0 but the local press said of Jimmy *"... it will suffice here to say that he fully satisfied the most exacting critics and promises to be a real acquisition to the club."*

A second match took place on Tuesday, August 18, at the same venue. Jimmy and Wilson were absent due to a trip they had undertaken to Middlesborough.

Two days later, Jimmy was centre-forward for Whites in a third game which his team won 1-0. The local press reported *"Unfortunately the players on the wings did not give him many opportunities to shine but when he had a chance the neat and well-timed manner in which he passed the ball evoked frequent expressions of approval."*

A fourth game, on Tuesday, August 25, went ahead despite a heavy deluge of rain which did not deter fans either, a crowd of over 2,000 turning up to watch. Jimmy was centre-forward for Reds who won 3-1.

There was a new rule regarding penalty-kicks which was enforced during this game. Murray fouled one of the Whites and Millar was entrusted with the kick. The ball was placed on the penalty line with no one allowed to intervene between the player taking the kick and the goalkeeper. In the event, Millar shot wide. Although he did not get on the scoresheet, the local press were still positive towards Jimmy with: *"... whose style of play greatly pleased the critics."*

The following day the club organised an excursion for players and some officials and friends to Barnard Castle. Anyone else wishing to accompany the group were invited to apply for tickets which were available from the secretary, Mr Tom Watson, at the club house at 37, Ellerslie Terrace, Monkswearmouth.

The final practice game took place on Saturday, August 29, with Jimmy at centre-forward for the Reds, who beat the White team by six goals to one. Two friendlies were scheduled for the following week, against the visiting Canadian team on Tuesday, September 1, and Newcastle West End the next day before the more serious League games began on Saturday at home to Wolves.

The Canadians had toured the UK previously in 1888, a successful trip that encouraged this repeat performance. It had been arranged with players from the Western Football Association in Canada but a number of the squad had withdrawn at short notice.

As a result, players were recruited from American clubs in New England with whom the WFA had close ties. Though travelling under the banner of Canadian tourists, of the 19-man squad nine were actually Americans. They had been staying at the Grand Hotel on Bridge Street and trained at Newcastle Road.

When the Sunderland team was announced Jimmy was in at centre-forward, a pleasing recommendation for the new boy.

The gates opened at 4:30, an hour before the advertised kick-off time, but there were no queues at the entrance gates because the majority of working men would not be released from their various toils until 5pm at the earliest. The attendance built slowly but steadily.

The pitch was in good condition for the impending season and marked out in accordance with the laws of the game, including the new penalty line. The Canadians entered the pavilion at 5:15pm to change for the game.

Spectators were now pouring through the gates to see Sunderland's first competitive game. Just before 5:30pm the visitors entered the field, throwing the ball before them amid a warm round of applause. The teams lined up and it was Logan who, at 5:35pm, set play in motion.

Fifteen minutes in, a well delivered corner invited Jeffrey to head between the posts to put the Canadians ahead. Sunderland then had the better of things. A throw-in found Campbell and in conjunction with Logan, they travelled the entire length of the field before Logan's drive was saved by Garrett, the Canadian goalkeeper. Minutes before half-time, good work by Campbell set Logan free and the Ayr youngster made easy work of beating Garrett to restore parity at 1-1. A moment later, Scott passed into the visitors' goalmouth, both Campbell and Miller challenged for the ball which ended up in the net. It was unclear which of the pair got the final touch. Half-time: Sunderland 2-1 Canada.

Sunderland began the second half as they had finished the first, on top. Prolonged applause was generously given to Garrett as he dealt with two fierce shots, the first from Logan and then from Auld pulling off two outstanding saves.

The Canadians broke away down the right wing and the ball was passed to Senkler who shot and despite the efforts of Doig a goal resulted, 2-2. Sunderland responded and a good run by Campbell ended with a quality cross into the goalmouth where Logan met it with his head, only for the ball to crash against the post and be scrambled away.

The pressure on the Canadian defence intensified and after some neat passing between Logan and Hannah, the latter beat Garrett with a fine shot. Final score Sunderland 3-2 Canadians.

Afterwards, the two teams and officials dined at the Grand Hotel on Bridge Street, which had been HQ for the tourists during their visit to Sunderland.

The Grand Hotel on Bridge Street

After the meal and much discussion about the game a series of speeches took place, including one from the Sunderland secretary Mr Tom Watson, followed by musical entertainment. They were not finished there. All the players then moved on to the Palace Theatre on High Street West where seats had been reserved for them in the dress circle.

The Palace Theatre as it looked around 1950. It was demolished in 1973

The Palace Theatre was a new theatre that had only opened a month earlier on August 3. A review of the programme that night went as follows: *"Cee-Mee and his beautiful children' who were a family of gymnasts who performed their act 'in close proximity to the roof of the building' and were 'top of the bill'. 'Mr Jess Parker deserves special mention for his display of forward and backward jumping'. 'Miss Clara Bell a soprano ballad vocalist of many pleasing attributes'. 'Mr Will Hebden a comic and descriptive vocalist'. 'Miss Bella Willing, a comedienne'. 'Mr Harry Walton a comic character vocalist'. 'Mons. Nello adds considerably to the entertainment as a feet equilibrist'. The Keene and Reeves Combination in their original musical sketch, Chips in Japan' and finally Messrs O'Connor and Brady, eccentric comedians, vocalists and dancers complete the programme."*

Cee Mee

Mons. Nello

At 1:30 pm the following day the Canadians left the Central Railway Station for their next stop, at Middlesborough Ironopolis. In all they played a total of 58 games in 135 days - the first on August 22, 1891, and the last on January 4, 1892. A demanding tour and hardly surprising that their record showed: Played 58, Won 13, Drawn 14, Lost 31.

The evening after the Canadian game, Sunderland travelled to St James' Park to take on Newcastle West End. The team contained nine of the team that had played the previous day – just skipper John Auld and striker John Campbell were rested for the game, replaced by John Murray and John Smith. Both sides agreed to reduce the game to 40 minutes each half.

Tom Watson and the rest of the Sunderland officials took an early train to Newcastle while the players arrived just after five o'clock with their journey by brake from the station to the ground arousing plenty of interest amongst local football fans. At six o'clock the West End team, wearing red and blue, were first onto the playing area, closely followed by the Sunderland team in white and dark blue. Jimmy kicked off at 6:10pm for another Tyne/Wear derby rivalry, the sort that has endured to this day.

West End were members of the Northern League and the gulf in ability was apparent immediately in what turned out to be an uneven contest, ending in an 8-1 win for the visitors. Jimmy terrorised the defence throughout and netted five of the goals.

Upon signing, he had been fixed up with digs in Zetland Street in Monkwearmouth, which was less than a mile from Newcastle Road. Before the 1891-92 season was underway the local press sent a reporter to his 'comfortable lodgings in Zetland Street' as they were described in the interview with the incoming striker.

The houses where Jimmy lodged in Zetland Street as they look today

Here is the rest of the article:

"Logan at once showed himself ready to answer any questions that might be put regarding his football career. He is 22 years of age, 5ft 8in high and 11st 4lb in weight. He was born at Troon in Ayrshire a county which not only gave a poet to Scotland, but was the nursery of some of the best footballers now before the public. Logan began to play for Arden Villa, a junior team in the town of Ayr, six years ago and he remained with them for two years, during which time he filled all positions from goalkeeper to forward, but chiefly half-back. He next joined the Ayr club and was altogether with them for about four years. He was first captain and centre-forward of the second eleven and in that capacity took part in the Scottish second XI cup and the Ayrshire second XI cup competitions in both of which he was on the side of the vanquished. Next season he took no part in football for the first three or four months, but was then placed on the Ayr first team as left half-back and went through the Scottish cup ties until the club was knocked out by the Heart of Midlothian. The club, however, won the Ayr Charity Cup, defeating Hurlford in the final by one goal to nil and Ross having left, Logan was shifted to centre-forward. The Scottish trial games for the international came on when Logan had been centre-forward for Ayr for only four weeks. He was, however, assigned the same position in both the trial matches at Glasgow and Edinburgh and he was entrusted with the same post of honour for Scotland against Wales at Wrexham, the result of which was in favour of Scotland. Logan signed on for Sunderland

about three weeks ago. He states that he is very much pleased with the town and the club. He is a fine able-bodied young fellow, single and very abstemious in his habits."

Sunderland hosted Wolverhampton Wanderers on Saturday, September 5, 1891, their first League game of the season. Despite Jimmy scoring five in his previous outing, when the team was announced, Jimmy wasn't in it. John Campbell was in at centre-forward, a major blow to the young striker after such a promising pre-season.

In front of about 8,000 spectators, it was even during a first half that ended two-apiece but Sunderland seized the initiative thereafter and won 5-2, Campbell claiming two and Jimmy Miller a hat-trick.

A week later Sunderland were at Preston North End. Jimmy would probably have had mixed feelings when he saw the team selection, delighted because he was in but a joy that may have been tempered by the news that he was starting on the right wing!

Special trains were run from all the areas surrounding Sunderland and just before kick-off there were nearly 7,000 spectators in the ground. After only five minutes Preston's Drummond picked up the ball, beat Auld, dodged between Porteous and Oliver then completely beat Doig with a fast low drive amidst the most boisterous cheering.

Shortly afterwards Sunderland gained a corner and in the ensuing goalmouth scramble Miller fired a shot into the net for the equaliser.

The game was only eight minutes old by then. Preston were now well on top and a rare break was ended when Logan shot wide of the target followed by the half-time whistle. 1-1, honours even.

Preston settled first after the interval and a number of shots rained down on Doig's goal but a head or a foot always appeared to block the ball and if that failed Doig denied the attackers.

Eventually, a free kick for hands was sent in by Drummond, with all 11 Sunderland men behind the ball but despite desperate defending, Gordon guided it into the net. With only six minutes remaining Gallagher received the ball from Drummond and centred Towie who eluded Porteous, and beat Doig amidst a tremendous cheer for Preston, who won 3-1.

Soon after that game Wearside bid farewell to left-back John Oliver. He made the short trip to Teesside and joined Middlesbrough Ironopolis, mainly because Donald Gow had taken hold of the left back position.

After disappointing on the wing at Preston, Jimmy was omitted from the next three matches against Bolton Wanderers, Aston Villa and Everton. In between those three League games Jimmy did play, in two friendlies against Newcastle East End and Middlesbrough – playing as a central striker and scored in both games.

Saturday, October 17, 1891 saw a reserve game take place on the Newcastle Road ground between Sunderland A and Trafalgar. The interesting fact about the fixture was that goal nets were used for the first time on that ground. The *Sunderland Daily Echo and Shipping Gazette* described one of the goals as follows: *"The point could not be disputed, for the ball was in the net."*

With the team off to a poor start, winning only two of their first five games, and with James Murray having returned home to visit his ill father, Jimmy was eventually, on October 17, recalled to play West Bromwich Albion away at Stoney Lane – this time on the left wing!

Albion took an early lead when Bassett gained possession and sent in a cross which beat Murray and before Doig could claim the ball McLeod was there first and drove the ball between the posts. Sunderland responded immediately and Millar sent in a powerful shot that Roberts in the Albion goal tried hard to save but was beaten by its pace. Then Campbell made a good run ending with a cross to Logan who shot the ball hard against the post. A minute before half-time Bassett put in a shot which should have been kept out by Murray and Doig but it sailed straight into the goal to give a half-time score of Albion 2-1 Sunderland.

On commencement of the second half Albion started the stronger but gradually Sunderland eased their way into it and three shots threatened the Albion goal without success. Finally, Scott scored and then a minute later Logan latched on to a loose ball and fired a powerful shot that Roberts blocked but couldn't hold, Scott tucking away the rebound. Logan then raced away from the Albion defenders only to see his shot safely dealt with by Roberts. Campbell completed the scoring with two goals the second being a clever overhead kick. Final score: Albion 2-5 Sunderland

That was to be Jimmy's second and last League appearance for Sunderland. On Friday, November 6, his name appeared in the reserves, or Sunderland A as they were known. They were to oppose Newcastle Science and Art, a team of ex scholars of the Science and Art school in Newcastle. Sunderland A played their league games in the Northern Alliance but when they trotted out at Newcastle Road Jimmy was absent – he had refused to play.

Clearly there had been a falling-out between player and club. Jimmy was not prepared to play 'second fiddle' to anyone. He had signed for Sunderland to be their centre-forward and he was therefore unhappy with the situation. Before the end of November, Jimmy had walked out of the club, his digs and the town and returned home to Ayr.

The following appeared in the press:

"FREE-LANCE, writing to the Scottish Referee, says that J. Logan, who came from Ayr to join Sunderland, has returned home. After making a capital impression, Logan appeared to fall off in his play, and was voted slow for a man who won his Scotch International cap against Wales. Consequently he has not been tried for some time past in the first team. He failed on Saturday to put in an appearance for the reserves, and it was reported that the committee had discharged him for disobedience. Such, however, is not the case. They mutually agreed to separate, and so Logan returns home after a brief stay on Wearside."

Jimmy's time at Sunderland was a strange and frustrating one. He had made two appearances in the League – one on the right wing and one on the left. He was never really given a chance in the first team in his proper position of centre-forward because John Campbell, who was at Sunderland the previous season, had made the centre-forward position his own with consistently good performances and regular goalscoring. Campbell, after all, breached the 30-goal mark that season and the following one as Sunderland retained the title. However, in Jimmy's defence, when selected in the friendly games in his more natural central position he played six matches and scored NINE times – what more could he have done?

After he had walked out, Sunderland were champions by May and in the next three years they repeated the feat twice, finishing runners-up once. In 1895, after topping the table again, they faced Scottish champions Hearts and won 5-3, thus claiming that Champions of the World title.

Truly, they were earning that other title bestowed upon them by McGregor as the Team of all Talents.

CHAPTER EIGHT

November 1891 - June 1892

Suspended by the Scottish FA

AYR FC membership of the newly formed Scottish Alliance League had been ratified for the 1891-92 season. Local fans were now enjoying regular football of a good standard and it also maintained their position as the No.1 team in Ayr as rivals Ayr Parkhouse were in the more parochial Ayrshire League.

As soon as Jimmy was back, late in 1891, he applied to the SFA for reinstatement as an amateur as other returning ex-professionals had done. But at their meeting on January 5, his request was refused and he was handed the standard 12-months ban from all football in Scotland. The ban ran from the date of the application so he was destined to sit out virtually all of 1892 on the sidelines.

The *Scottish Referee* newspaper commented as follows:

"I visited Ayr lately and had a look at Logan, the 'prodigal son' who has returned to the fresh breezes of his native home. I don't think he is looking so well. The 'clog' being on, he will be unable to play for Ayr, a matter to be regretted."

On Saturday, January 9, 1892, Jimmy's mind was taken off his football problems, at least for a short time, as he married his girlfriend Mary Munro, the daughter of the late Ayr trainer William Munro, at the Kelvin Registration Office, 173 Shamrock Street in Glasgow. Jimmy, aged 21, was now a confectioner (journeyman[10]), having joined brother John in his business. On April 6 the couple celebrated the birth of their first child, a son, also called James Logan.

At this time Scottish football was in a mess. Though still supposedly amateur, rumours were rife of players receiving payments. Since the Scottish League's formation in 1890, winning had become even more crucial and stories emerged of undeclared payments. One example of this was the case of Daniel Doyle and Alexander 'Alec' Brady.

Daniel Doyle

Alexander 'Alec' Brady

---

[10] *A journeyman was a skilled worker who has successfully completed an official apprenticeship qualification in a particular trade or craft. Journeymen are considered competent and authorised to work in that field as a fully qualified employee. They earn their journeyman's license by education, supervised experience and examination. Journeymen were paid each day. The word "journey" is derived from journée, meaning "day" in French. Each individual trade guild generally recognised three ranks of workers: apprentices, journeymen, and masters. A journeyman would need to become a master to run their own business.*

Both men were professional footballers for Everton but were lured away by 'amateur' Celtic with the promise of even more money than they were earning with Everton. In fact, Doyle was to be provided with a public house from Celtic that would give him between £4 and £5 each week on top of the money the club were paying him for every match he played.

In January 1892, the *Glasgow Evening Post* summed up the thoughts of many:

"When will the Scottish Football Association put an end to the mockery of amateurism which exists under its jurisdiction? The present condition of affairs is an insult to common sense, a disgrace to the Association which permits its continuance and a perpetual cause of irritation to the bona fide amateurs who play football north of the Tweed.

If the Scottish Association wishes to have the credit of being sincere, let it either take steps to expel the many professional clubs in its ranks or let it declare itself a professional association. To allow the present state of affairs to continue is to perpetuate a scandal which must seriously injure not only the game but the morale of those who take part in it.

It is useless to argue that no cases of professionalism have been brought to the notice of the S.F.A. Committee. The Doyle case and the very existence of the Celtic Club give the lie direct to such an assertion. It is well known to the Association that the Celtic Club is directly or indirectly paying its members and it is equally certain that many other clubs are also infringing the rules relating to amateurism."

During 1892 Jimmy's father James purchased 38 Union Avenue in Newton-on-Ayr and moved the family there.

The house on Union Avenue as it looks today. Jimmy's family lived with his parents while he was away playing football in England

After what must have seen like an absolute age to Jimmy, on Tuesday, May 3, 1892 the annual meeting of the SFA was held in the City Hall in Glasgow where Mr McLean, the Ayr FC representative moved (with maybe just a hint of self interest) that an amnesty be granted to all registered professionals applying for reinstatement between the dates of May 3 and September 1, 1892 inclusive and that a free pardon be granted to all players presently under suspension.

The motion was carried by a large majority and Jimmy was once again free to play football in Scotland.

The SFA also reiterated, with a vote of 104 to 78, that 'no professionalism shall be countenanced, allowed or legalised.' The meeting also decided that for the first time, international players, linesmen and the seven members of the selection committee should all receive caps to mark the Scottish international games.

After the previous amnesty, in August 1891, 115 players took advantage and were re-instated as amateurs and since then 22 registered professionals had made application for reinstatement but were dealt with in accordance with the rules and so most had received a twelve months ban.

Keen to get Jimmy involved in the remainder of the season, Ayr wasted no time in arranging a game for his benefit - Jimmy would be well short of match fitness since his last outing had been back in the middle of November for Sunderland A!

The evening after the ban was lifted, Wednesday May 4, Ayr Strollers played Ayr Juniors at Somerset Park. Jimmy was making his first appearance after the successful commuting of his suspension having served five of his twelve months ban. He was instantly back in the thick of it, heading the only goal of the first half and as the Strollers continued to have the better of the game they ran out 3-2 winners. An observer from the *Ayrshire Post* commented about Jimmy: *"His foot has lost very little of its cunning and he was very dangerous whenever he got near the Juniors' goal."*

Three days later it was straight in at the deep end as the first team entertained King's Park in the penultimate Alliance League game of the season. A large crowd saw Ayr get the better of their opponents in a 4-2 win despite Jimmy's penalty being saved by the visiting goalie.

The following Wednesday they were in action again, in a friendly against Stevenson Thistle at Somerset Park. Although he didn't score, Jimmy created the first Ayr goal when he laid the ball into the path of team-mate Loudon to finish with a fine shot into the net. Ayr won 2-1.

Ayr played hosts to Kilmarnock in their final league game three days later, the match falling on the annual Curd Fair Saturday Holiday[11] so a big following of Killie supporters were present. Jimmy had a number of chances but failed to take any of them, probably a result of a lack of match fitness. Ayr led 1-0 for most of the game but a goal for Kilmarnock with almost the last kick made it 1-1. Five days later Ayr's season concluded at Somerset Park with an uninspiring and tame 2-2 local derby draw against Ayr Parkhouse.

---

[11] *Curd Fair Saturday was a public holiday in May in Kilmarnock in Ayrshire, on which the population formerly resorted to neighbouring farms to eat curds and cream.*

CHAPTER NINE

July 1892 – September 1892

A brief return to Ayr FC

DESPITE rumours that hinted at English clubs wanting to lure Jimmy Logan south for another try at professional football, he began the 1892/93 season as an Ayr FC player. After just a single season in the Scottish Football Alliance, Ayr resigned their membership along with several other clubs. They briefly entered the more local Ayrshire League but at the next meeting withdrew and instead decided not to be in a league at all but return to filling their fixture list with friendlies on the home and away basis in addition to the Scottish, Ayrshire and Charity cup competitions.

Jimmy was with his family in Newton-on-Ayr for the close season and working for his brother John as a confectioner – but football was never far away from his thoughts. During the summer, many of Scotland's clubs had organised sports days as part of the never ending pursuit of funds to keep their clubs afloat. Celtic, Hearts, Clyde, Cambuslang, St Mirren and the more local Ayrshire clubs such as Newmilns, Beith, Dalry and Hurlford etc, all ran advertisements in the sporting press advertising their athletics meetings and football competitions.

As Jimmy's status was now returned to that of an amateur he must have felt he was ok to participate in these football competitions – but he would be wrong and there would be repercussions.

The Ayr players went through their usual pre-season practices choosing sides amongst themselves while others, including Jimmy, travelled to Mauchline for a 5-a-side competition there – where Kilmarnock Athletic beat Lanemark in the final - all to get themselves as close to match fit as possible before their first game against Hurlford on August 6.

As it turned out, their season started well with wins over Ayrshire opponents Hurlford 4-2 and the Scottish Football Federation[12] champions Arthurlie 2-0 followed by a 3-1 defeat by Port Glasgow. The first three games were played without Jimmy but he returned for the next one against the current Scottish League champions Dumbarton, with one local scribe likening his comeback to the return of the 'prodigal son', helping obtain a commendable 1-1 draw. This prompted the *Scottish Referee* to write: *"It will please many lovers of football pure and pretty to hear that the gentle Logan is again at the game – that on Saturday last he tutored his men as only he can against the Dumbarton and came off with flying colours. The rejected of Sunderland I take to be a football gem. He is not a rash, rushy player, but a footballer of skill, of brains and who believes that unity of quiet yet smart and clever action can defeat the headless raids so common in modern football."*

Next up was Beith in the Scottish Cup first round. Jimmy was at the centre of all the goalmouth action but his shots were just off target or well saved by the Beith custodian. A fine team display had Ayr 3-1 ahead at the interval then midway through the second half Ross twisted his knee and was forced to leave the field reducing Ayr to ten men. Five minutes from time, Jimmy also had to retire from the playing area after an accidental injury. With nine men, Ayr hung on to claim a deserved 3-1 victory.

---

[12] *The Scottish Football Federation was an association football competition formed in 1891 which ran for just two seasons. In 1893 it was absorbed by the Scottish Football Alliance when that league lost all but one of its members to the Scottish Football League's new Second Division.*

Two goals from Jimmy in an exciting 5-4 victory over Stephenson Thistle in a friendly game set the team up nicely for the third round of the Scottish Cup at Wishaw Thistle. Unfortunately, things went badly wrong in a poor team performance in a 6-0 defeat as they crashed out of the competition.

To make matters worse for Ayr, the sporting newspapers were carrying the story of Jimmy Logan and full back George Russell's impending departure to Birmingham, both having signed for Aston Villa. Villa had paid £30 for Jimmy but Sunderland received the fee as they still held his registration. The pair's exit prompted this entry in the local press from someone who was clearly not going to miss them:

"Young Fullarton, who took up Russell's position on Saturday, is a strong fearless player and had he had the necessary amount of training even Russell would not put him in the shade, so that Ayr should not miss the runaway much; while Feggans, who is not much of a shot at goal, as a worker, far surpasses Logan, who cannot and never could, stand a fast game out."

George Russell – Aston Villa

Jimmy's final game for Ayr was a derby with Ayr Parkhouse for the unofficial title of 'Champions of Ayr' and the bragging rights for the supporters that went with it. It was to be played away at Beresford Park. Parkhouse were fresh from an outstanding victory over Greenock Morton while Ayr were still smarting from that 6-0 cup thrashing at the hands of Wishaw Thistle.

A large crowd attended and the ensuing encounter did not disappoint them. In an exciting 'end-to-end' tussle Jimmy was back to his best, a real handful for the Parkhouse defence as Ayr cantered to victory 7-2. Jimmy scored twice. He headed south once more, with his head held high.

CHAPTER TEN

October 1892 – June 1893

Jimmy joins Aston Villa

FOR the start of the 1892-93 season a new Second Division was formed for the Football League which included the absorption of the rival Football Alliance. Alliance clubs Nottingham Forest, The Wednesday (later, in 1929, they became Sheffield Wednesday) and Newton Heath (later Manchester United) were added to the new First Division, and Darwen were reallocated to the new Second, bringing the First Division total to 16 clubs. With the addition of Northwich Victoria (from the Combination), Burslem Port Vale (later Port Vale, from the Midland League) and Sheffield United (from the Northern League), the Second Division started with 12 clubs, as Alliance club Birmingham St George's disbanded at that point. The bottom clubs of the lower division were subsequently required to apply for re-election to the League at the end of each season.

Jimmy Logan and George Russell arrived in Birmingham on Friday evening, October 7, and were met by club secretary George Ramsay. Jimmy had signed for Villa earlier but he would not be eligible to play for the first team until October 12.

Aston Villa Secretary George Ramsay[13]

It was straight into action the next day as the reserves had a fixture in the Birmingham and District League at home against Wolverampton Wanderers. The game was evenly contested though Russell showed signs of nerves, missing his kick on more than one occasion. Jimmy, on the other hand, was in superb form culminating in him hitting the only goal just a few minutes before the end. He was off to the proverbial flyer. Unfortunately, this reserve team game played at Perry Barr on October 8 was scratched from the record as Wolves later protested against Jimmy and Russell being on the pitch because neither had been registered the requisite seven days before the game. The protest was heard and the match was ordered to be replayed at a later date.

---

[13] *George Ramsay was a player for Aston Villa (1874-1882) before he became Secretary/Manager (1884-1926). His tenure as Manager was the most successful in Aston Villa's history with his record of six League Championships and six FA Cups.*

Aston Villa, let us remember, were one of the original 12 clubs that formed the Football League in 1888/89 and had firmly established themselves in that sphere. Jimmy joined in October with the club having finished fourth the previous 1891/92 season. They were regarded as a well run club and the accounts published in the summer showed a healthy surplus at the bank of £756.

Their campaign had started well with three wins in the first three League games but then it slumped markedly with five successive defeats. At Sunderland John Campbell was the resident centre-forward but at Villa there was no such player claiming that position as his own.

In fact the opening six weeks had seen three different players tried at centre-forward so there was a real opportunity for Jimmy to stake a claim for a regular starting place in the central striking role.

Villa's home games were then at Wellington Road in the Perry Barr area of the second city, having moved there in 1876. Initially, with no spectator facilities, players changed in a nearby blacksmith's shed, and a hayrick was kept on the pitch, which had to be removed prior to each game. The ground was gradually improved, a grandstand built on the eastern touchline followed by two pavilions built on the western one behind the southern goal line.

Aston Villa playing at Perry Barr during the 1892/93 season

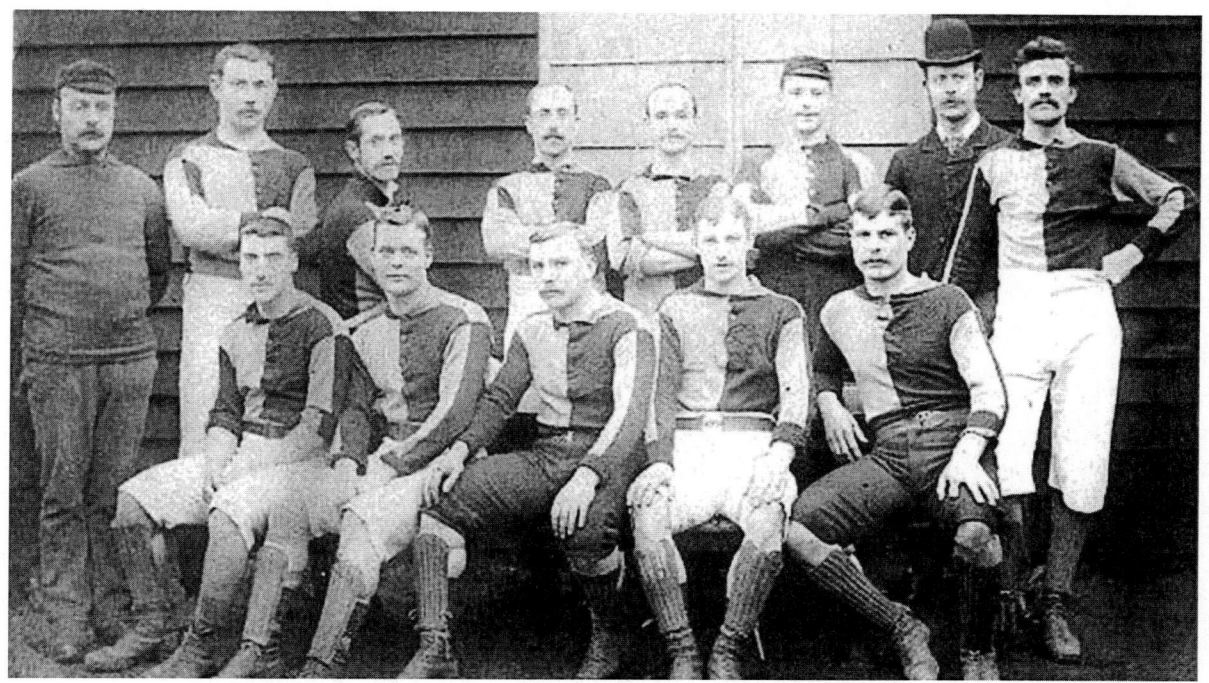

The Aston Villa team that Jimmy Logan joined in October 1892
Back row: Gorman, Dickson, Albert Brown, Thomas Clarkson, George Burton,
Jimmy Warner, Archie Hunter, John Devey
Front row: James Cowan, Frank Coulton, Gersom Cox, Allen, Dennis Hodgetts

Jimmy's next game arrived the following Thursday afternoon, October 13, a trial match at Perry Barr between two sides selected from the first and reserve teams to assist the selection committee to judge better the respective merits of the players. There were several hundred spectators present, many eager to focus attention on the latest recruits.

The teams were as follows:

'A' team: Benwell (goal); Evans and Baird (backs); J. Brown, Cowan and Dowds (half-backs); Athersmith and A. Brown (right wing); Logan (centre); Devey and Hodgetts (left wing).

'B' team: Roberts (goal); Ramsey and Russell (backs); Skea, J. Davis and F. Burton (half-backs); Hare and Paton (right wing); Fleming (centre); L. Campbell and Woolley (left wing);

Some capital play was witnessed by both sides and the final result was a 4-3 win for the A team and although the goalscorers were not named, Logan was described as follows; *"Logan is certainly an acquisition to the Villa displaying resource and dash which quite pleased the members of the committee."*

Two days later, he made his first team debut – at Perry Barr against Nottingham Forest in a single goal victory, scored by Albert Brown the Villa inside-right. A number of chances fell to Jimmy but it wasn't his day as his shots were saved or went wide of the target.

Two more games followed, a 4-1 defeat at Preston then an emphatic 6-1 win at home against Derby though Jimmy failed to trouble the scorers in either game.

A jolt to the system awaited him however, as a meeting of the Football Association Council on December 12, 1892 at London's Chancery Lane would bring Jimmy's season to a juddering halt. He was suspended for four weeks for playing football in the close season. At this time the FA were keen to prevent players from turning out during the summer months, either in unaffiliated competitions or with suchlike clubs.

Jimmy was sidelined for the games against West Bromwich Albion, Nottingham Forest, Newton Heath, Preston North End and The Wednesday.

On his return from suspension he was given a run-out in the reserves to blow away the cobwebs of inactivity on Saturday, December 3, against Stourbridge at Perry Barr. The teams went for goal from the first kick with opportunities in both goalmouths. Eventually, Villa came out on top 7-4 courtesy of goals from Hare, Campbell (3) and Logan (3) – cobwebs well and truly blown away!

A week later he resumed his League career in a home game against Blackburn Rovers before about 8,000 spectators. A solid performance earned Villa a 4-1 success.

GREAT WESTERN RAILWAY.

GRAND LEAGUE FOOTBALL MATCH
ASTON VILLA v. BLACKBURN ROVERS.

ON SATURDAY, DECEMBER 10, a CHEAP HALF-DAY EXCURSION to BIRMINGHAM, will leave GREAT MALVERN at 12.10 p.m., Malvern Link 12.15, Bransford-road 12.25, Henwick 12.30, WORCESTER (Foregate-street) 12.35, Fernhill Heath 12.45, Droitwich 12.50, KIDDERMINSTER 1.10, and Stourbridge Junction at 1.30 p.m.; returning at 11.45 p.m.

For full particulars see Bills.

HY. LAMBERT, General Manager.

Over his next six games against Derby County, Bolton Wanderers, Notts County, The Wednesday, Sunderland and Newton Heath Jimmy hit a purple patch scoring seven goals in six games

The first round of the FA Cup was staged on Saturday, January 21. Villa had been drawn away at Darwen's Barley Bank ground, which actually belonged to Darwen Cricket Club, football being permitted during the winter months. An exciting 5-4 game ended in Darwen's favour.

Despite that first round exit, Villa were entered in the Bass Charity Vase, a competition founded in 1889 in Burton upon Trent to raise funds for medical and hospital charities. The impressive trophy was donated by the Bass Brewery, or more specifically Lord Burton and his brother Mr Hamar Bass. The first final was played in 1890 and was won by Derby County, who retained it for the next two years. With nine teams entered, the draw that took place on Tuesday, February 7, looked like this:

Preliminary Round:

| West Bromwich Albion | v | Stoke |

Quarter Finals:

Burton Wanderers	v	Aston Villa
Burton Swifts	v	Wolverhampton Wanderers
Derby County (holders)	v	The Wednesday
WBA or Stoke	v	Notts County

66

Aston Villa Reserves finished the season as champions of the Birmingham and District League (equal points with Wolverhampton Wanderers) and it was a tradition that the champions would play a Select XI from the rest of the teams in the League.

This game took place on Monday, February 13, at Perry Barr in front of about 1,000 spectators with all proceeds going to the league.

Jimmy was chosen at centre-forward but it was the Select XI who took the lead after just ten minutes. Jimmy's only shot in the first half was well saved by goalkeeper Wilkes. Though a goal down at the interval, Villa were more in control in the early part of the second half and Jimmy sprinted up the field before laying the ball off to Woolley out wide and when he centred there was Jimmy in the middle to equalise. The Select XI replied strongly and scored twice to go 3-1 ahead. Then it was Villa's turn to retaliate and they drew level once more but with a draw looking likely, their opponents scored late on for a 4-3 win.

A week later there was a change from the pressure of League football for the first team when Notts County visited Perry Barr in a match for the benefit of Warwickshire County Cricket Club. The Notts team included ex player, board member and Nottinghamshire CCC player William Gunn, by then aged 34. In front of about 5,000 spectators Villa ran out 6-2 winners (Jimmy's only goal being disallowed for offside) and after the match the two teams were entertained to tea at the Colonnade Hotel by the members of the cricket club's committee who thanked the two teams for their kindness in arranging the game which raised over £140 for Warwickshire CCC. Alf Shelton, one of the Notts County players and an England international, responded on behalf of the football club and wished Warwickshire CCC all the best for the future.

The Colonnade Hotel, New Street, Birmingham c.1880

The top English amateur team Corinthians had arranged to play their annual match with Queen's Park on Saturday, March 11, but the famous club were involved in the final of the Scottish Cup that day and had to withdraw – so Villa, who had a free Saturday, were invited to step into the vacancy, which they duly did, at the Kennington Oval. A one-sided match saw the Villans record a crushing 7-2 victory. Athersmith (2), Devey (2) and Logan (3) were on target.

Next up, Villa eased past Burton Wanderers at Derby Turn with a narrow 2-1 victory in the quarter-final of the Bass Charity Vase on Wednesday, March 15.

Back in League action and the return fixture with Notts County arrived on March 18 – but once again Jimmy was too ill to play in the game. It was not detailed exactly what his problem was but it was bad enough to keep him out of the last five League games of the season against Notts County, Accrington, Wolves, Burnley and Accrington again. It must have been a hugely frustrating time, just as he was hitting his best form, with 7 goals in six games, so whatever the ailment, it was a severe and debilitating one.

Incidentally, although Jimmy was a sickness absentee for that Notts County match, he was so anonymous in the region that the report in the *Nottingham Evening Post* included him in the starting line-up, regularly mentioned in dispatches as being all over the pitch and missing chances. Still, a case of mistaken identity by football reporters was an enduring tradition that carried on long into the 20th century! For Jimmy, though, his reputation in Nottingham would later change quite dramatically.

Villa eased past Burton Swifts in their own backyard at Peel Croft in the semi-final of the Bass Vase on Wednesday, April 19, goals from John Devey, Jimmy Logan and Albert Brown earning them to a comfortable 3-1 win to meet the holders Derby County in the final. This was Jimmy's first game back after illness, his next coming on the following Saturday against Wolves in the Birmingham Senior Cup final played at the neutral Aston Lower Grounds.[14]

In front of 12,000 spectators, Villa lost 3-1 with Jimmy 'out of touch' after his lay off. Whenever chances came his way his shots were either, poor, high, or wide of the mark.

Then came the final of the Bass Charity Vase on Wednesday, April 26, at Burton where Villa met Derby. There lurked a twist in the tale, however, of a highly competitive game. At the final whistle the score was 2-2, skipper John Devey having bagged both Villa goals. When the referee called the two teams together for extra-time, Derby simply refused to take part. With little other option, the organising committee presented the trophy to captain Devey and Aston Villa!

The Bass Charity Vase won by Aston Villa in 1893

---

[14] *Aston Lower Grounds would eventually become Aston Villa's current home – Villa Park.*

A week later, Jimmy and Villa's final game of the season was in a Charity Football Festival, once again at Aston Lower Grounds. The first game for the 'large' crowd was between Birmingham Boys and London Boys with the latter putting on a dazzling display to beat the local lads 7-1. The 'top of the bill' fare pitted Villa against Small Heath with Villa winning an entertaining game 3-2.

Jimmy had gone from being a player in good form before his illness to one who was now 'rusty' and in need of games to sharpen himself up – but time had run out, at least for this season.

CHAPTER ELEVEN

July 1893 – September 1893

An on-field argument ends his time at Villa

FOR the second successive season Aston Villa had finished fourth in the Football League, but their ambition to do better still burnt fiercely. In the summer of 1893 out went some of the peripheral figures such as Robert Roberts, Peter Dowds, Louis Campbell and William Evans and in came five players to strengthen the first team: William Groves a wing-half and John Reynolds a right-half both from West Bromwich Albion, James Elliott a full-back from Middlesbrough Ironopolis, James Welford a full-back from Birmingham St. George's and Stephen Smith an outside-left from Hednesford Town.

| William | John | James | James | Stephen |
| Groves | Reynolds | Elliott | Welford | Smith |

Jimmy must have been relieved to see there were no central strikers in amongst the new players. The reason for that was because secretary George Ramsay felt confident that with Charlie Athersmith, John Devey, Charles Hare, Dennis Hodgetts and Jimmy Logan he already had sufficient firepower in the team.

The usual trial games were played in order to help the committee decide on the team for the opening game of the season against West Bromwich Albion at Perry Barr on Saturday, September 2. When the starting XI was announced, Jimmy was selected at inside-right with skipper John Devey alongside at centre-forward.

During the summer months much time, effort and money had been spent on Wellington Road including the erection of a 4ft-high iron fencing all around the field perimeter in order to prevent encroachment during matches and the habit of fans rushing over to the other side of the ground at half-time, which was damaging the pitch. As well as the ground now looking in excellent condition, the fencing also meant less policemen were required and the club reducing costs on match days.

On what was reported to be a beautifully fine day, in front of about 14,000 spectators, Villa opened their season at Perry Barr. However, kick-off scheduled for 3:30pm, was delayed 15 minutes owing to the late arrival of the referee, Mr. J. J. Bentley.

The game was vigorously contested for some considerable time, but at length Villa began to get the upper hand and the dashing Athersmith proved mighty troublesome for the Albion backs. Thirty-five minutes passed without any score, but then Villa made a prolonged attack on the Albion goal. Reader, the Albion netminder, put out two shots, the first by Athersmith and the second by Hodgetts, but the ball was again sent in and Nicholson knocked it down. A penalty kick was given and Reynolds, who had never failed to score under such circumstances, gave Villa the lead. The Albion now played better and before half-time Geddes scored from a centre by Norman.

The second half opened in Villa's favour but the players could not break through the Albion defence and the latter's forwards at length forced a corner kick. It was well taken by T. Perry and Cowan had the misfortune to head the ball through his own goal. Soon afterwards John Devey equalised from a free kick taken by Hodgetts and the home team took advantage. Devey scored again but the goal was disallowed because Hodgetts had impeded Reader. Three minutes remained when Woolley scored again and Villa claimed the points in an exciting game 3-2. According to the press, forwards Woolley, Hodgetts and Devey all played well, while the weakest link was Logan.

When the team for Saturday, September 9, was announced Jimmy was back in his preferred position of centre-forward, with Devey moving to inside-right, which would have pleased him, especially as the game was back at his former club Sunderland.

Aston Villa travelled north on the eve of the match, arriving at their hotel, The Empress on Union Street on Friday night. By coincidence, Sunderland's rivals, Sunderland Albion, were formed in a meeting there on Tuesday, March 13, 1888.

An image of the Empress Hotel in Sunderland from a 1906 yearbook

This was Sunderland's first home game of the season and the kick-off was planned for 3:15pm. Villa were first to enter the field in their chocolate and blue jerseys, white pants and 'untanned leggings'. Sunderland soon followed in their red and white stripes but each player also wore a black badge on his arm as a sign of mourning for Thomas Jenkinson, a Sunderland A team player who had died a few days earlier.

Just before kick-off a ceremony took place, the unfurling of a flag presented to the club by Mr James Speeding of Roker in recognition of their success of being League champions in 1892-93. The flag was 9ft x 6ft, white with a red border. In the centre was the name of the club in red letters together with the words 'League Champions 1892-3'. The flag sat ready atop the pole and was duly unfurled by Viscount Castlereagh, eldest son of the Marquis of Londonderry, accompanied by his cousin Lord Helmsley and Mr George Childs, the secretary of the Sunderland Conservative Association. The party had driven to the clubhouse from Seaham Hall on the day of the game. On the appointed time a few vigorous pulls on the rope by Viscount Castlereagh and the flag was unrolled into the breeze, amidst a round of applause from the spectators.

It must have been a time of very mixed emotions for Jimmy, returning to the Newcastle Road ground he had graced so often and seeing the 'Champions' flag being unfurled at the club he had walked out on.

Did he know young Thomas Jenkinson from his time at the club? The answer is, most likely. When Jimmy refused to play in the Sunderland A team to face Newcastle Science and Art, Jenkinson was also in the side that day. They were the same age, 23, and they lived on adjoining streets in Monkwearmouth, probably walking to the ground together on numerous occasions.

Almost 10,000 people gathered at the Newcastle Road ground to see the champions against Villa. The weather was pleasant and the ground in excellent condition. In no time at all Villa were 1-0 ahead with a goal from Hodgetts but Campbell 'equalised' for Sunderland soon after, only for the goal to be disallowed for offside.

Exciting play followed with each goal being threatened in turn but neither side could score; they reached half-time with Villa still ahead. From the restart the home team attacked relentlessly and though the Villa defence stood firm it was eventually undone when Millar succeeded in heading the equaliser. With no more scoring the game ended 1-1, a good result for Villa away at the home of the champions.

Two days later Villa were at Perry Barr for the visit of Stoke in bright, clear weather in front of a crowd of about 8,000 spectators. Stoke scored through a Dickson header after only two minutes play. After that Villa pressed continually and it wasn't long before they equalised through Hodgetts from a free kick. Villa went into the lead a few minutes later when Logan received a pass and 'beat the Stoke custodian with a beauty'. Then dextrous headwork by Chatt and Davey enabled Woolley to put the Villa further ahead. No further scoring in the first half: Villa 3-1 Stoke.

Midway through the second half Hodgetts headed neatly to Woolley in the goalmouth and the latter scored before the Stoke goalkeeper Rowley could get anywhere near the ball. One more goal from Hodgetts before the final whistle brought a full-time score of 5-1.

The following Saturday Villa travelled to Goodison Park to take on Everton. In the most modern football ground in the country and in front of 20,000 spectators, Villa kept the same team which had played in the three previous games – with Jimmy at centre-forward and captain John Devey alongside him at inside-right.

Villa had the wind in their favour and attacked first resulting in Hodgetts missing a good chance. Fifteen minutes later Everton took the lead from a free kick by Stewart. This was followed soon after by a second goal from Bell after good work by Southworth. Elliott crossed and Southworth picked up the loose ball and scored to put Everton three goals to the good.

The game was going badly from a Villa point of view and tempers were fraying, resulting in an on the field argument between Jimmy Logan and his captain John Devey[15]. This was not a good idea as John Devey was highly respected and a well established player at the football club. As skipper, he was the club's representative on the field of play and a member of the selection committee – so not a man to upset. Half-time was reached with the score still 3-0. Villa fought hard to get back into the game and scored twice through Woolley and Athersmith, but another goal from Walker meant the game finished 4-2 to Everton.

_____

[15] *Devey was one of Aston Villa's greatest ever captains. Under his captaincy, they won the League championship five times and the FA Cup twice. A skilful inside right/centre-forward and an England international, he played for Villa for eleven seasons making over 300 League and FA Cup appearances and scoring 186 goals. After retiring in 1902 he was an Aston Villa director for the next 32 years.*

A week later came the return fixture at Perry Barr, which was much anticipated. Aston Villa made three changes, Elliott, one of the full backs had wrenched his knee, Chatt was unavailable and Jimmy was dropped after yet another poor performance though of more significance was his on-the-pitch argument at Everton with captain Devey, to whom he had demonstrated disobedience.

In 1893 the club captain's authority during matches was as good as the management and Villa had recently reorganised and implemented a policy of strict discipline. As vindication perhaps, Villa took revenge by virtue of a 3-1 win over the Merseysiders.

A few days later on Tuesday, September 26, Jimmy started in a friendly against Wolves at Molineux where a visiting team containing six reserves were beaten 4-1. This disappointing game would be Jimmy's last for Aston Villa.

According to the local press Jimmy had been 'at loggerheads' with the Aston Villa committee for some time and the club had made it known that Jimmy was available for transfer. Preston North End had shown interest in signing him previously so a Scottish agent, acting on Jimmy's behalf, contacted Deepdale and a number of other clubs to see if they would be interested in signing him. Preston confirmed their interest and Mr Tom Houghton was sent by his directors to Birmingham to set up the deal. Mr Houghton arrived at Birmingham only to find that they were not the only club in the hunt for Jimmy, who had already signed for Notts County.

Once again he was leaving a club in mid-season; and once again the club he was leaving, first Sunderland, now Villa would progress to be Football League champions by the season's end. Thus far Jimmy had always climbed upwards on his career ladder. Now he was descending a rung, to Division Two.

The Aston Villa team (after the departure of Logan) that went on to win the League Championship in 1893/94
Back row (players only): John Baird, William Dunning, James Elliott,
Middle row: Charlie Athersmith, Robert Chatt, John Devey, Dennis Hodgetts, Albert Woolley
Front row: John Reynolds, James Cowan, George Russell

CHAPTER TWELVE

1893

Jimmy's father buys a whole street in Newton

The financial benefits of being a Master Mariner (or captain) for the last twenty years or so were clearly beginning to pay off for Jimmy's father James. Having already purchased a new family home in Union Avenue in 1892 he then, in 1893, purchased 49 McCall's Avenue just a couple of streets away from Union Avenue.

The idea was that it already had a workshop for the confectionery business and a cottage (which James named after his current ship, *Dunreggan*) for son John and his family to live in and have the business on site – which is exactly what happened, with Jimmy also working there whenever he was in Ayr.

James though wasn't finished there; on October 10, 1893 he purchased all ten cottages on Britannia Place, literally just around the corner from 49 McCall's Avenue. Janet McClelland had sold the land to James Murray Ferguson (proprietor and publisher of the *Ayrshire Observer and Galloway Chronicle*) on November 1, 1888. Mr. Ferguson had been given two years to erect properties on the land that measured just over an acre but the agreement with James Logan said that he had one year to erect properties 'where not already done so'. Thus James may have been purchasing an unfinished set of properties.

Britannia Place, the row of ten cottages purchased by James Logan in October 1893

The second cottage on the right is 49 McCall's Avenue, owned by James Logan back in the 1890s and where John Logan ran his confectionery business. The road on the left of the photograph is Britannia Place which was also owned by James Logan.

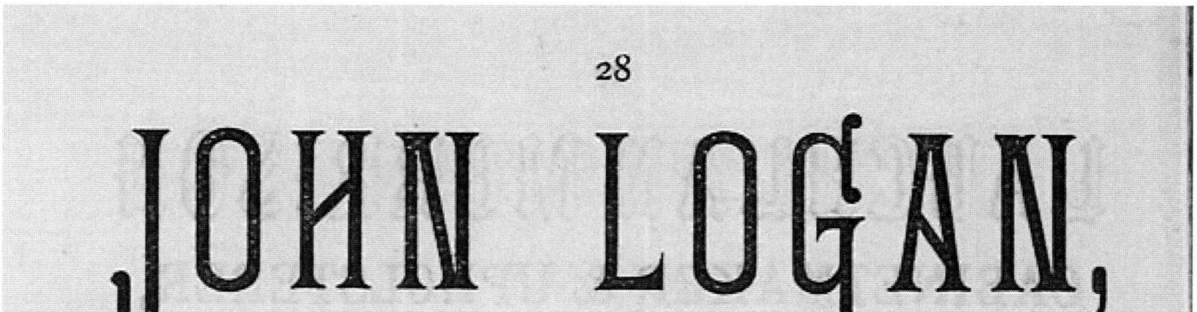

28

JOHN LOGAN,

Newton Confectionery Works,

⚹ AYR. ⚹

PRICES ON APPLICATION.

John Logan's confectionery business which was operated from 49 McCall's Avenue

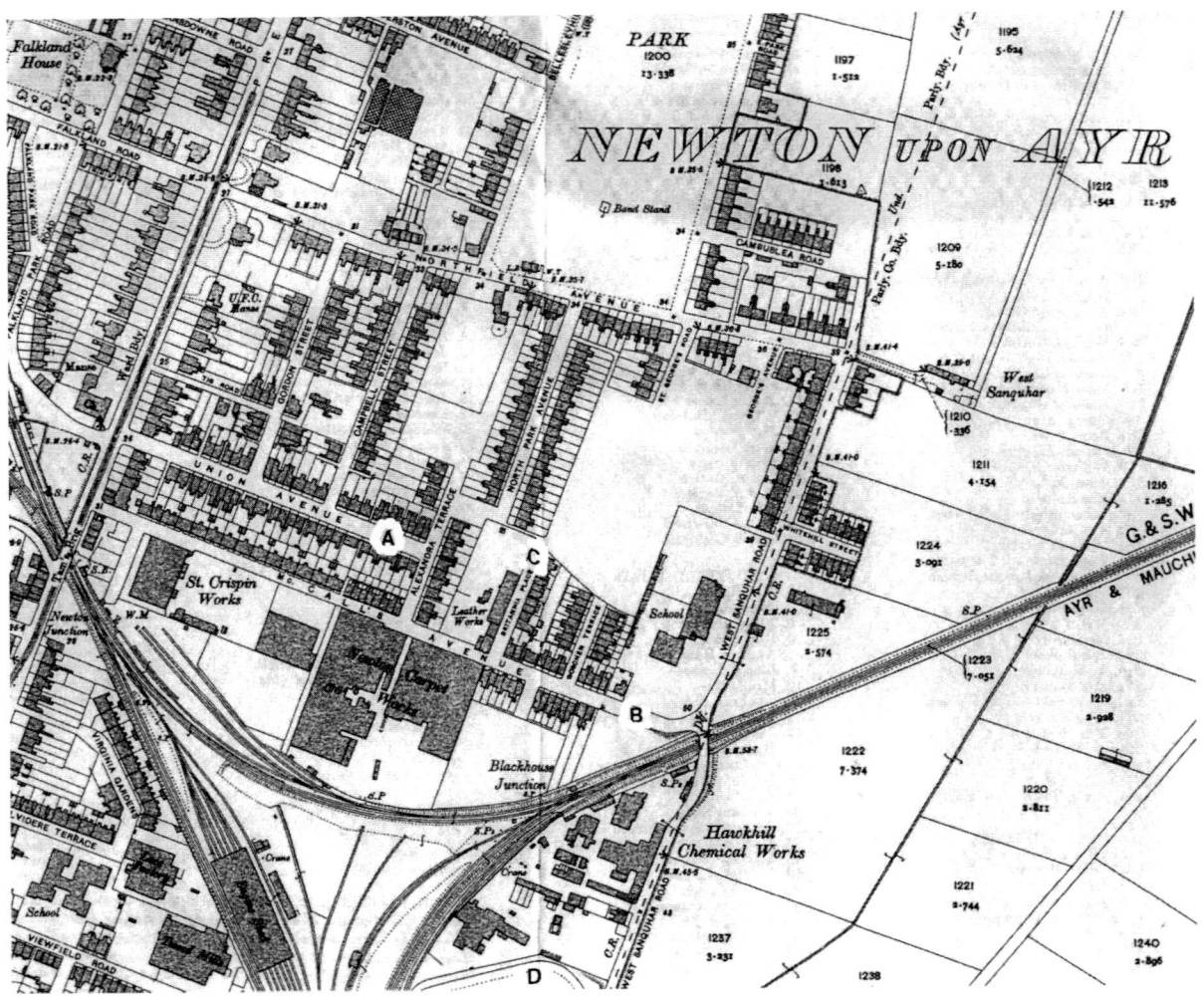

Newton-upon-Ayr from a 1908 map

The map shows:

A   Union Avenue – the family home being at number 38

B   McCall's Avenue – number 49 being the home of brother John and the confectionery business Newton Confectionery Works.

C   Britannia Place – all ten cottages were purchased by Jimmy's father James in 1893

D   Just shows the edge of Somerset Park, the home ground of Ayr FC

CHAPTER THIRTEEN

October 1, 1893 – December 31, 1893

Down into the Second Division to join Notts County

The 1892/93 season had ended with Notts County having their first taste of relegation, demoted as they were from Division One. The implications were serious. Notts were sliding into debt, a number of the directors resigned and the remaining board even considered withdrawing from the Football League and joining the Midland League. There were, after all, the obvious benefits of more local derbies and less travelling but in the end common sense prevailed and planning began for Division Two. It was important that Notts bounced straight back to the First Division.

The following players from the previous campaign were offered contracts on reduced terms for 1893/94: George Toone, John Hendry, Theo Harper, Alf Shelton, David Calderhead, Charles Bramley, James Oswald, Dan Bruce, and Tom McInnes. All the players accepted reduced terms except James Oswald (the club's top scorer for the last four seasons) who decided to leave rather than accept reduced wages and returned to Scotland. This left the club short of a centre-forward so at the board meeting on June 26 it was recorded that Aston Villa FC would be contacted to see if it was possible to bring their centre-forward Jimmy Logan to Notts County.

New players coming into the club included George Kerr an inside forward from Kilmarnock and Arthur Watson, an outside-right from Mansfield. Inside-forward Dan Bruce became the stand-in centre-forward and the team began the season well, winning their first four games and drawing the next.

It was well known that the Villa had a surplus of first-class forwards so when Mr. Sibert, a Notts director, went over to Birmingham and approached them on the subject of Jimmy Logan, the Villa executive signified their readiness to release him. A number of other clubs were also in the process of trying to sign him, including Preston North End and Newton Heath. Mr. Sibert, however, was successful, and returned to Nottingham with the necessary signed documentation.

Notts County had been required to pay a transfer fee of £15 while Jimmy received £10 down and £3 per week for the playing season.

Jimmy signed for Notts County on September 28, 1893 and arrived having missed their first five games. At that stage the table showed that Notts were well placed to regain their top flight status:

The top of League Division Two as at 4th October, 1893:

		Pl	W	D	L	F	A	Pts
1	Burslem Port Vale	7	7	0	0	30	7	14
2	Burton Swifts	7	5	0	2	24	13	10
3	Small Heath	7	5	0	2	19	13	10
4	Liverpool	5	4	1	0	11	2	9
5	**Notts County**	**5**	**4**	**1**	**0**	**9**	**3**	**9**

News of his transfer from Aston Villa is difficult to unearth but early in October the *Birmingham Daily Post* did carry the following entry tucked away under the unflattering heading of SCRAPS – hardly the back page news it would be these days.

SCRAPS.—Mr. W. Southworth, the musical director at the Prince of Wales Theatre, is the brother of ...an Southworth, the Everton centre forward. Mr. South-worth himself is by no means ignorant of the ... and practice of the game.—J. Logan has been transferred to Notts County.—Thomson of the Villa in .... to Newton Heath.—Warner, late of Newton Heath and Aston Villa, was keeping goal for the Walsall Reserves on Saturday.—The Old Edwardians open their .... at the County Ground on Saturday against ...... Moseley will play the Marlborough Nomads.—Reynolds and Groves can sing a good song.—Ather ... will probably be playing again next Saturday.—Ned Dougall from Denny, is expected at Stoke.

Jimmy was fixed up with lodgings at 55 Muskham Street – a short walk of less than a mile to the Trent Bridge ground.

Muskham Street today. The house where Jimmy lodged, like most of the road, has been demolished.

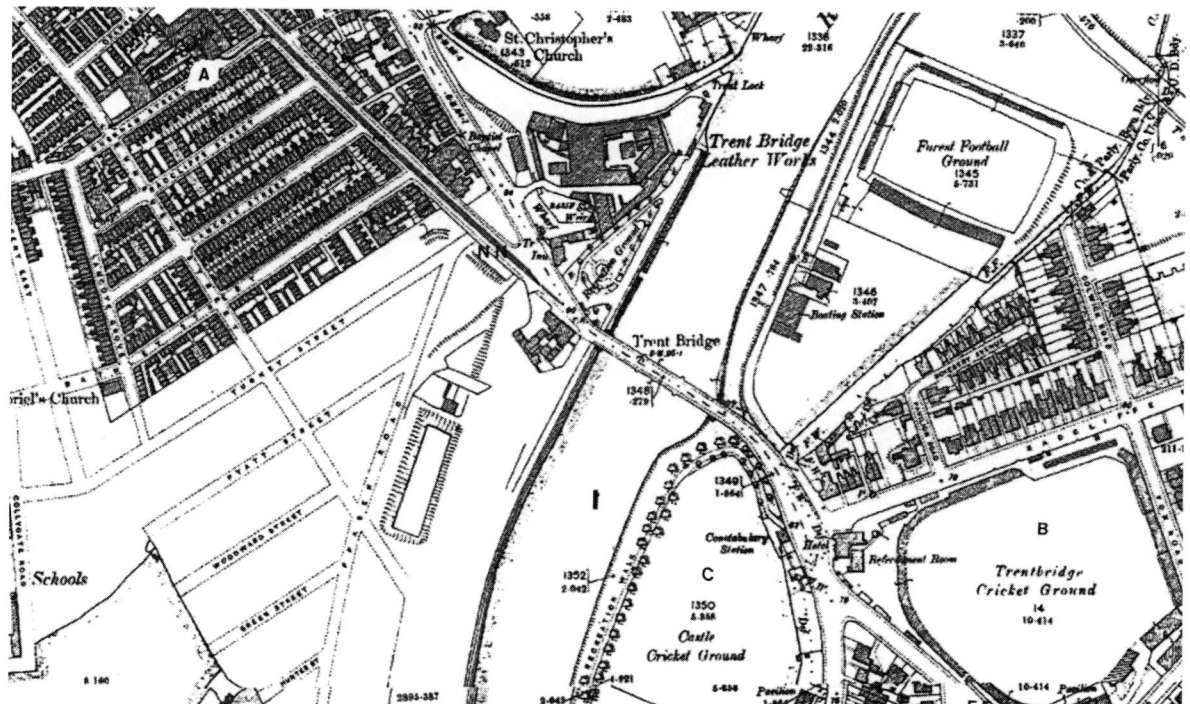

The map shows:
   A) Muskam Street where Jimmy lodged while playing for Notts County FC.
   B) Trent Bridge cricket ground where Notts played their home games.
   C) Castle cricket ground[16]

Jimmy signed too late to play in the 1-1 home draw with Liverpool on September 30, so his debut would be in a friendly against West Bromwich Albion at Stoney Lane on Monday, October 2.

A football match taking place on Trent Bridge cricket ground in 1910.
Fox Road is to the right side of the pitch and Radcliffe Road is behind the far goal

---

[16] *The football pitch on the Castle Cricket Ground was only usually used at the start and end of the football season when the Trent Bridge cricket ground was being used by the cricket club. Located to the south of the city centre and east of Queens Drive, Notts County FC first played on the Castle Cricket Ground in 1880 but only used it intermittently for matches after their move to Trent Bridge. The cricket ground was lost around 1900 when the land was used initially by the Great Central Railway, later for housing and now the site of the council offices.*

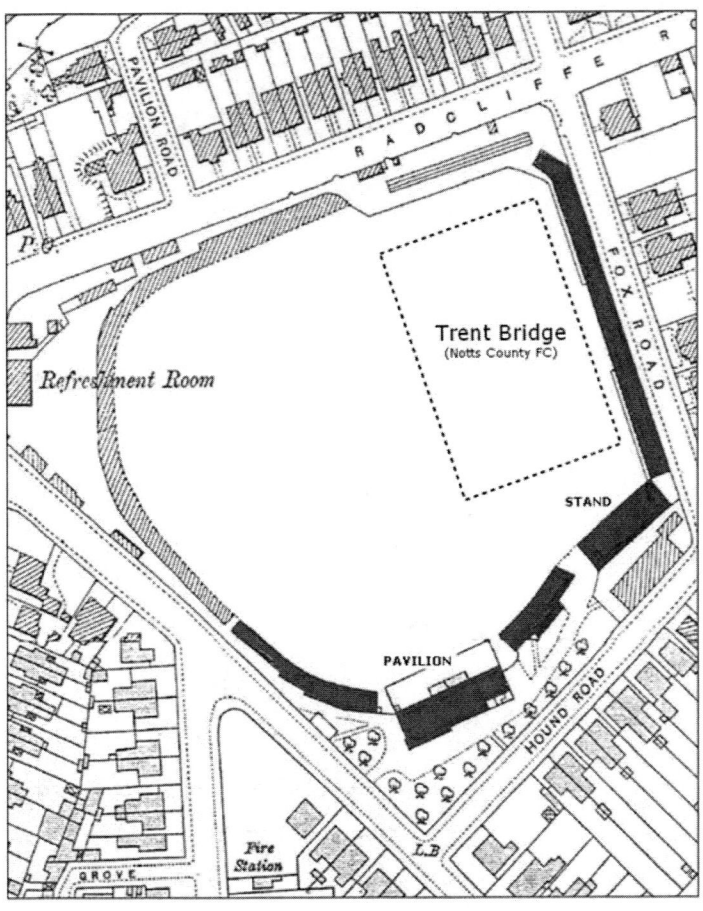

Part of a 1901 map showing the Trent Bridge cricket ground with the approximate position of the football pitch

It was an inauspicious start. After an hour Albion were ahead 2-0 and while Notts kept plugging away in search of a goal to get themselves back into the game, Albion stood firm to clinch victory by that margin. As he began the process of settling in with his new team-mates, Jimmy's Division Two debut came three days later at home to GrimsbyTown.

In the first half the Notts forwards were attacking consistently but could not penetrate with Whitehouse, the Grimsby goalkeeper, in excellent form. After a scoreless first half, Notts resumed with great determination and Bruce crossed the ball into the centre where Logan made light of a difficult position with a lovely left-footed screw shot that completely beat Whitehouse. It was his first goal for Notts, greeted by tremendous applause.

Notts got a free kick for hands against Frith. Calderhead took the kick and passing to Logan, that player shot hard and low through a forest of legs into the net, amidst more delighted applause. Again and again Notts attacked now and the Grimsby goal was being bombarded. Whitehouse saved wonderfully, time after time, one shot after another. But this could not continue forever and Bruce added a third before the final whistle.

Two goals against Grimsby would be the start of a fine run of scoring for Jimmy with four against Chatham (friendly), two against The Wednesday (friendly), one each against Newcastle United and Grimsby and then three against Burslem Port Vale – thirteen goals in six matches!!! Safe to say Jimmy had settled in well.

The local press had positive things to say about the new centre-forward too:

Against Chatham – "*Without in any way awarding undue praise to Logan, it must be confessed that he has made a wonderful difference to Notts. He possesses that ability so necessary in a centre-forward, the power to keep his wings in touch with each other and the knowledge of when and how to shoot. Whenever the ball went to him on Saturday he despatched it straight to the desired goal, and no better proof of this can be afforded than the fact that he obtained four of the seven points.*"

Against The Wednesday – "*...thanks to Logan's untiring energies and unselfish passing, the Notts five were kept in something like touch with each other...the two goals which Logan scored were really splendid efforts...*"

Against Newcastle United – "*...a similar compliment was paid to Logan who scored the second goal with a dashing kick that seemed as though it would drive the ball through the back of the net.*"

Against Burslem Port Vale – "*Logan, in a pack of players, forced his way through by sheer strength and with a fine shot, which Frail failed to hold, put on the sixth goal.*"

Notts County's initial outlay of £15 on Jimmy Logan was looking like money well spent.

On Monday, October 23, Mr Deplidge, the chairman of directors, generously provided a trip to the Dukeries[17] for the players, directors and officials of the Notts Football Club. The party travelled to Mansfield on the 9.35 train from Nottingham. Mr George Shepperson supplemented the generosity of Mr Deplidge by providing a couple of horse drawn carriages which met the party at Mansfield and transported them via Welbeck, Clumber, and Thoresby to Edwinstowe and back again to Mansfield. There were 29 gentlemen in the party including directors: R. Deplidge (chairman), T. E. Harris, A. Sibert, J. Shepperson, H. Heath, W. J. Bramley, H. Vann, R. Coppack (treasurer), W. T. Bramley and T. Featherstone (secretary). Also in attendance were Mr E Booth (Lion Hotel), Mr J. Wooley, Mr Rufus Sisson, Mr James Burrow, and the following players: David Calderhead (captain), Harry Daft, George Toone, Alf Shelton, Dan Bruce, Archie Osborne, John Hendry, Arthur Watson, Sam Donnelly, Jimmy Logan, George Kerr, Charles Bramley, Tom McLean, Bobby Jardine and Henry Kirk (trainer).

Robert Deplidge (Chairman)

Tom Featherstone (Secretary)

Tom Harris (Director)

---

[17] *The Dukeries is an area of the county of Nottinghamshire so called because it contained four ducal seats. It is south of Worksop, which has been called its "gateway". The ducal seats were: i) Worksop Manor: a home of the Dukes of Norfolk, ii) Welbeck Abbey: seat of the Dukes of Portland, iii) Thoresby Hall: seat of the Dukes of Kingston (later of the Earls Manvers) and iv) Clumber House: seat of the Dukes of Newcastle (since demolished).*

After a charming drive through the woods in bright sunshine, the party enjoyed lunch on the lawn near Welbeck. Later the party enjoyed a ramble through the woods before meeting their transport and being taken to the Royal Oak Hotel at Edwinstowe for tea where various speeches and toasts took place. A couple of hours were then spent singing with Messrs Harris, Booth, H Kirk and George Kerr, whose Scottish songs were extremely popular, were the principal contributors, accompanied by Mr Featherstone on the piano, before the return journey was made arriving back in Nottingham soon after nine o'clock after a very pleasant trip.

The Royal Oak Hotel, Edwinstowe c1910 on the day of a visit by the Duke of Portland.
(Courtesy of the Edwinstowe Historical Society and www.picturethepast.org.uk)

How the same building looks today

With the 6-1 win over Burslem, Notts headed the Division Two table, a point ahead of Liverpool, Burslem, and Small Heath. Jimmy Logan's Notts County career had started with a bang, to put it mildly.

Tight at the top: Division Two, October 27, 1893:

		Pl	W	D	L	F	A	Pts
1	**Notts County**	**9**	**7**	**1**	**1**	**23**	**10**	**15**
2	Liverpool	8	6	2	0	22	6	14
3	Small Heath	10	7	0	3	31	20	14
4	Burslem Port Vale	10	7	0	3	34	24	14
5	Burton Swifts	9	6	1	2	27	15	13

Notts' next home game, against Middlesborough Ironopilis was significant because the team were photographed before the game.

Notts County FC 1893/94 (the team that played against Middlesbrough Ironopolis).
Back row: Harris (Secretary), Sam Donnelly, Theo Harper, George Toone, David Calderhead, John Hendry, Bramley (Director), Featherstone (Director)
Middle row: Arthur Watson, George Kerr, Jimmy Logan, Dan Bruce, Harry Daft.
Front row: Charles Bramley, Archie Osborne

The Ironopolis team arrived in the morning and put up at the Lion Hotel, the Notts County headquarters. Notts were without their left half Shelton, his injured eye had improved a little but it would have been dangerous for him to play as an attempt to head a ball might have resulted in further serious damage. Osborne went to centre-half, while Calderhead, the Notts captain, took Shelton's place at left-half.

Watson sprinted off down the right wing with the ball before putting in a cross to the centre and Logan and Upton, the back, raced to get it. Upton missed his kick and Logan pushed the ball into Watson's path who fired in a powerful shot at Ord who parried the shot. Logan, Watson and Ord all chased the loose ball and all three went down in a heap and it was the nimble Logan who was on his feet in an instant and had the ball safely into the net five minutes from the start of the game.

The remainder of the first half saw the Notts forwards continue to pound away at their opponents but could not add to their single goal lead, mainly due to the excellent display of Ord in the Ironopolis goal. The second half saw more chances created by the Notts forwards but desperate play and a large slice of luck kept them out but it could not last forever and following up a hard shot from Bruce, Daft made no mistake and scored Notts second goal of the game.

Logan, beat Oliver the full-back and sprinted forward with only Ord to beat. Ord ran at Logan but the latter side-stepped him and fired in a shot at the empty goal, only for Watson to sprint in and apply the final touch to put the ball into the net. Immediately after this the whistle went for the last time. A good display by Notts and only an outstanding performance by Ord in the 'Washers' goal prevented Notts from running up a much higher score.

Jimmy was once again singled out by the local press – "*Logan was playing superbly in the centre and keeping his wings well together...Logan was ever on the qui vive*[18] *and getting on the ball very quickly he made some dashing and tricky runs, having hard lines on more than one occasion.*"

Notts then had a 'blip' in their season losing consecutive games for the first time against mid-table Lincoln City and away at undefeated Liverpool. The following appeared in the *Nottingham Daily Express*:

In the evening after the game several of the Liverpool team were strolling round the town and getting rather elated over their success over Notts. Hannah undertook to enter a lion's den in a travelling menagerie. A five pound bet was made with some of his companions and Hannah won it by remaining in the den for over a minute.

Trent Bridge was the venue for the return League match against Northwich Victoria which took on a 'must-win' fixture if Notts were going to maintain their promotion push. The same team that was so unluckily beaten on Saturday at Liverpool turned out. Northwich began the game with only ten men as Guest, the full-back, had missed the train and hoped to join the game later!

Notts got straight to the visitors end at the outset and pressed relentlessly and it wasn't long before they took the lead. After a good run down the left wing Daft put in a shot and Bruce managed to deflect the ball into the net using his knee followed shortly afterwards by a good shot and goal high up into the net by Logan only three minutes after the previous goal. Redfern on the right wing got clear away and Harper had to give away a corner to stop him.

From the corner the ball was well placed and Finnerhan scored for Northwich. Guest, the Northwich full-back, who had missed his train, now put in an appearance amidst much laughter – it seemed that many people in the ground had not even noticed he was missing! Watson tricked Sumner and got in a grand centre which Bruce met and with a great shot, put the ball an inch above the crossbar. It was the last act of the first half, with Notts leading 2-1.

Straight after the restart Notts resumed their attack on the Northwich goal behind which many Notts fans had now congregated, and Kerr soon made the crossbar rattle with a scorching shot. Notts were awarded a throw-in and Harper came up amid cheers to take it. Straight as an arrow he sent the ball into the mouth of the goal and a great cheer announced that Bruce had scored a third goal for Notts. The ball was kicked into touch by Northwich and

---

[18] *A state of heightened vigilance or alertness.*

once again cries of 'Harper' arose from the Notts fans. He came up smiling and once more landed the ball clean into goal. Hornby beat it out.

Logan lay watching and popped the ball back again scoring a fourth goal for Notts. After a run down the wing Watson scored a fifth goal. Following this another throw in fell to Notts on the right and Harper was again appealed to by the crowd. He again responded to the appeal. And from his throw Logan scored a sixth goal. Notts were still attacking when the whistle went for the last time.

A fantastic 6-1 win but the team's inconsistency reared its head again when a 1-0 defeat away at Burslem Port Vale followed.

In between games, at the weekly Notts board meeting on November 27, it was agreed that in future, no smoking would be allowed on the train during the journey to matches.

The following night the United Midland Counties League met at the Clarendon Hotel, Derby and Notts County's place in the competition was confirmed.

Back in League action, under normal circumstances Notts fans would have been confident of a home win over Burton Swifts but after three defeats in their last four games against Lincoln, Liverpool and Burslem Port Vale, Notts badly needed a win to boost morale, not least because Burton were only three points behind them – and with three games in hand.

The Notts flag was flying at half-mast and the players all wore black armbands in recognition of the death of Mr Arthur Williams. Mr Williams was one of the original directors when the football club's limited company was formed in the summer of 1890. He was also elected as their first chairman. Mr Williams was a solicitor in the firm Hunt and Williams aged only 45 and left a wife and six children. The club board confirmed they would send a letter of condolence to the late chairman's widow Mrs Arthur Williams.

Harper was unavailable after injuring his right ankle in the Burslem game. The always reliable captain, Calderhead, therefore went back in the Mansfield man's place, Bramley coming into the team again in his favoured position of right-half and Osborne going to centre half.

Early in the game, and in the absence of Harper, Bramley put in a long throw into the Burton goalmouth which Watson and Logan chased and while Logan tackled Bury, Kerr scored a lovely goal with a swift low shot after about ten minutes play. Good work from Logan before he gave the ball to Daft and he scored with a good shot. Daft put in another scorching shot, which Hay beat out but nimble little Watson got the ball and in a twinkling had it into the back of the net scoring the third goal for his side. Half time arrived after a good first half for the Notts men and a 3-0 lead.

Burton started the second half well but Notts eventually took the upper hand again. A good run and centre by Watson saw Logan send the ball out to Daft, who headed it back across goal and Kerr scored a fourth goal.

The Swifts were by no means done and Dewars seized the opportunity and fired in a terrific shot from long range, which completely beat Toone and scored a fine goal for Burton. Ekins received the ball in an offside position with only Toone in front of him. He centred and Munro put through, the referee allowing the goal. Notts quickly struck back and after a clever dash by Watson, Logan neatly scored a fifth goal. As soon as the ball was kicked off Logan collared the ball and dribbling from the centre right through all the Burton men, scored a magnificent goal unaided amidst tremendous applause. Soon afterwards the whistle went for the end of the game, with the final score of 6-2 to Notts County.

Top of the Division Two November 30, 1893:

		Pl	W	D	L	F	A	Pts
1	Liverpool	13	9	4	0	35	9	22
2	Notts County	16	10	2	4	40	18	22
3	Small Heath	13	9	0	4	38	25	18
4	Burslem Port Vale	12	9	0	3	36	24	18
5	Burton Swifts	13	8	1	4	41	27	17

Although Notts sat in second spot and occupied one of the all important top three berths, Liverpool had three games in hand while Small Heath, Burslem Port Vale and Burton Swifts, the three clubs immediately below them, could all overtake Notts if they won their games in hand.

The next game was against Newcastle United at St James' Park. The Notts executive had made arrangements for the 11 Notts players to leave Nottingham on the Friday, December 8, by the 1.56 train, timed to arrive at Newcastle at eight o'clock in the evening, but some of the players were unhappy with this arrangement and felt they should be allowed to travel on Friday evening. This was another example of the indiscipline present within the first team players at that time. Some of the players were even at the platform but refused to travel until Saturday morning, the result being that the Friday train contained only seven of the players chosen for the Newcastle game, instead of the full team.

Having already beaten Newcastle 3-1 at Trent Bridge earlier in the season Notts were optimistic of another success. Unfortunately the Notts team were clearly not at their best, maybe the troubles on the journey up to Newcastle were on their minds and a 3-0 defeat ensued.

At the weekly meeting of the Notts board on Monday, December 11, the members deliberated on the actions of the players who failed to catch the arranged Friday train to Newcastle at the weekend. Their decisions were that Toone be suspended for one week for disobeying directors' orders and that Bruce and Osborne be suspended pending their report to the directors why they also refused to go to Newcastle. It was also decided that a match committee be formed consisting of directors Bramley, Gilbert, Thomas and Harris, to meet the secretary at 8 o'clock in the evening the day prior to each match. This committee would also draw up a new code of rules for the players aimed at improving the discipline within the club.

Boxing Day saw another meeting of the two Nottingham rivals – and another good crowd. When the kick off took place at a quarter past two, 12,000 spectators lined the Trent Bridge enclosure and colours distinguishing the supporters of the rival clubs were freely displayed. Both sides were represented by their full strength side with a surprise return to action for Watson on the right wing and the only other significant change for Notts was the change of Bramley being brought in to replace Osborne at right half.

For a while the game was confined to midfield exchanges. Toone had then to beat away from a splendid long shot by Higgins, and then Forest were awarded a free kick because of Calderhead's robust charge on one of the Forest forwards. Scott dealt with the free kick and putting the ball well into the Notts goalmouth, McInnes headed dangerously at goal but Harper just managed to head the ball over the bar to safety. It was now a fast paced 'end to end' game. It became apparent that Calderhead had hurt one of his knees in an encounter with Collins, but after a short while he was able to resume. From yet another Forest attack Hendry conceded a corner and half time break was signalled.

On resuming, the exchanges were very even. Forest attacked but they were quickly repulsed and Harry Daft returned in fine style. He tricked Ritchie beautifully on two occasions and succeeding in crossing the ball into the centre where Logan *'met the ball with a flying shot'* and opened the scoring for Notts. After the goal Forest had the better of things as they went in search of the equaliser and after a few minutes Higgins, shooting to a corner of the goal, scored the equaliser. Forest continued to have the best of matters and in the final minute an attempt by Higgins grazed the top of the cross bar, but the game finished in a 1-1 draw.

At the weekly Notts board meeting on Wednesday, December 27, Mr Tom Featherstone found it necessary to resign his position of honorary Secretary to the Notts Football Club due to the role requiring more time than he had available due to his other commitments. Mr Tom Harris took over the role on a temporary basis. Mr Joseph Goode, an ex-athlete, began his new role as the trainer of the Notts team.

Joe Goode

On Saturday, December 30, Notts went to Burton's Peel Croft accompanied by a good crowd of their supporters to play the return League match with Burton Swifts. Notts had won the first game 6-2 earlier in the season and so were optimistic of obtaining another positive result.

It was unfortunate for Notts that two of their most reliable and best players, Calderhead and Shelton should be 'hors de combat[19]' for this important match but in the game against Forest both were hurt and neither would be able to take part, Wilkinson and Osborne had been called into the team to replace them. It was also expected that Watson would make a

---

[19] *Out of action due to injury*

return to the League team after his illness, especially after his two outings in the friendly game against Forest and also for the Mansfield side against the Corinthians, but at the last moment it was found that Watson would not be able to play, the morning's fog having rendered him unable to take the field. Kerr, therefore, was chosen to partner Donnelly on the right. The team only just arrived at the ground in time, having to rush from the station to the ground in horse-drawn cabs and a cart!

In the first few minutes Notts found themselves under pressure from the Burton attack when Ekins and Birch threatened the Notts goal and Toone had to run out for 20 yards to assist the backs only to completely miss the ball, but Hendry recovered well and cleared the ball upfield.

Bramley put the ball into the Burton goalmouth and in the confusion that followed Furniss badly miskicked and Logan was onto the loose ball 'in the blink of an eye' and drove the ball into the net to give his side the lead half an hour from the start of the game. The goal proved to be the only score of the first half.

Notts restarted and a good shot by Daft had to be dealt with by the Burton keeper. Logan got hold of the ball and after dribbling half the length of the field, beating both full-backs as he went, scored in a very similar fashion as he had at Trent Bridge against the Swifts. This second success was loudly cheered by the numerous Notts supporters who had made the trip to Burton. Notts by now were doing practically all the pressing. As the end of the game approached, the home goal had some extraordinary escapes, as the Notts attacks continued on the Burton goal until the whistle went for full time, with Logan's two goals being the difference between the two sides.

Peel Croft[20] – the home of Burton RUFC for over one hundred years

---

[20] *In 2017, it was announced that Burton RFC will be moving to a new stadium in nearby Tatenhill, with Peel Croft being demolished and replaced with a retail park*

CHAPTER FOURTEEN

January 1 1894 – March 15 1894

The FA Cup gets under way

A MEETING of the Football Association Council on Wednesday, December 20, at Chancery Lane, included the draw for the first round of the FA Cup. From the original 155 entrants, 133 took part in the qualifying rounds until only ten teams survived and entered the draw for the first round proper. Those 22 clubs who had received a bye up to this point were included in the draw, so from the original 155 entrants it had now come down to the last 32:

Aston Villa	v	Wolverhampton Wanderers (holders)
Derby County	v	Darwen
Grimsby Town	v	Liverpool
Leicester Fosse	v	South Shore
Middlesbrough Ironopolis	v	Luton or Sherwood Foresters
Newcastle United	v	Sheffield United
Newton Heath	v	Middlesbrough
Nottingham Forest	v	Heanor Town
Notts County	**v**	**Burnley**
Preston North End	v	Reading
Small Heath	v	Bolton Wanderers
Stockport County/Crewe Alexandra	v	Burton Wanderers
Stoke	v	Everton
Sunderland	v	Accrington
West Bromwich Albion	v	Blackburn Rovers
Woolwich Arsenal	v	The Wednesday

After the Burton Swifts game on December 30 Notts' senior players appear to have been given a few days off. They had played four games in nine days over the Christmas period and were probably a little weary. The next two games were friendlies against Kettering and West Bromwich Albion and the club saw it as an opportunity to give some of the fringe players match action. Since he joined Notts in October, to the end of December, Jimmy had played 23 times (missing only two friendlies against Loughborough and Corinthians) and had scored 21 goals – so a few days off, probably back in Ayr at the family home would no doubt have been most welcome.

Notts' next game was in the League against Rotherham Town at home and the club knew they couldn't afford to slack off if their ambition of gaining promotion was to be realised. Despite being well on the way to recovery Calderhead and Watson were still absentees in order to ensure they were fit for the forthcoming FA Cup tie with Burnley. Harper was also missing due to his injured knee he received in the Forest game. Despite the loss of three senior players the team won 4-2 with the goals coming from Kerr and Bruce (3).

At the Notts board meeting on Monday, January 15, it was revealed that Mr Pratt, the proprietor of the Star and Garter Hotel at Hazelford Ferry near Bleasby, had offered his facilities for the team's training during the build up to their FA Cup tie which was accepted.

A week before the Burnley tie Notts were at home to Walsall Town Swifts in Division Two but were not able to field a full strenth side with Harper and Logan both missing, but

Calderhead, Shelton and Watson all returned. The outcome was a 2-0 victory for the Magpies with Shelton and Bruce getting the goals.

On the Saturday evening after the match, the Notts team were sent to Hazelford for a week's training in preparation for the cup.

The Star and Garter at Hazelford Ferry near Bleasby as it looked c1907

The Hazelford Residential Home as it looks today

Although it was a tough-looking fixture against First Division opponents, the good news was that they came out of the hat first and would therefore have home advantage and a much anticipated contest at Trent Bridge. At the time, Notts were third in Division Two, Burnley were perched fourth in the First Division.

Trainer Joe Goode was with the team, aiming to have the players in perfect condition for the important clash. At the start of the week Harper had looked unlikely to start but thanks to Goode's excellent work, he reported fit to play so the team would be selected from a fully fit squad. Burnley had also been away for the week preparing for the game. Their committee decided to send the team to Derby the previous Friday and they left by the 2.23 train. They remained in Derby until Saturday morning when they journeyed on to Nottingham.

Burnley FC 1892/93
Standing L-R Hillman, Crabtree, Nicol, King, Espie, Mullineaux, Midgeley (Committee), Hill, Lang, Parker (Committee)
Sitting L-R Buchanan, McNab, Bowes

There was a surprise for Notts fans just before kick off when the amateur Arthur Henfrey, the English international from Corinthian, was unveiled and took his place amongst the forwards in the Notts team with George Kerr being left out. The Notts directors had kept the secret very well. Corinthian were arguably the greatest amateur club of all time, comprised of outstanding players, mainly former public schoolboys, who declined to turn professional in order to continue their careers, often in London and the south, while remaining amateurs.

The weather was fine but a strong wind blew the length of the pitch from the Pavilion goal and Notts, winning the toss, took advantage of it. There were 8,000 spectators at the game and the match was commenced amid great excitement and a huge cheer went up as the players of both teams stepped on to the field. Espie, the Burnley centre forward kicked off but it was Notts who were first to attack as Daft progressed well down the left wing. Hill was immediately penalised after kicking Hendry in the back. A free kick was given to Notts and this was quickly followed by a second for a trip on Bruce. This was nicely worked and Bramley got in a scorching shot which was just wide. Two free-kicks followed for rough play against the Notts players. From the free kicks Notts attacked desperately and Henfrey almost had the ball past Hillman, Lang saving at the expense of a corner. Watson took the corner and sent in a quality centre and the ball was worked about near the Burnley goal until Logan pounced onto the loose ball like a flash and scored with a magnificent shot amidst tremendous cheering seven minutes from the start. The Nottingham Evening Post described the goal as *"Logan shot one of the best goals scored at Trent Bridge this season."* This early success lifted Notts greatly and they attacked repeatedly, Henfrey and Watson making a fast run with the latter crossing the ball into the goal-mouth resulting in Daft going within an ace of scoring but the ball was just wide of the post.

Notts continued to do most of the pressing with Crabtree having an outstanding game in the Burnley defence and on one occasion he stopped a multitude of opponents, one after the other, and was deservedly applauded for it. The Notts' half-back line of Bramley, Calderhead and Shelton were the dominant figures in the game at this stage defending well but also using the ball well to prompt the attackers forward. Henfrey was only just too high with a shot and in a subsequent attack Logan followed with a similar shot but then going out on the wing he crossed the ball and Henfrey, running through, shot quick and low, the ball almost slipping into the net through Hillman's fingers. Still Notts pressed and Daft looked bound to score until Espie lunged at him 'savagely' and brought him down. There were loud cries for Espie to be sent off but the referee gave a free kick and cautioned Espie. From the free kick Hendry fired over. Lang had to kick out of the ground a minute later to stop Henfrey and some desperate defending took place near the Burnley goal but the defence held firm and Notts could not beat Hillman. Burnley improved and came more into the game. Nichol sprinted away and after a clever run got past Hendry and centering beautifully and Espie had a grand opening but shot wildly over the bar. Espie then sprinted the length of the field, past Hendry, leaving him yards in the rear. He had no one but Toone to beat and shot hard and low. Toone dived all his length and saved the ball by the tips of his fingers and Hendry recovered his position in time to get the ball away. It was a wonderful save and the crowd cheered tremendously. Abortive runs to each end were made and then the referee signalled half time with Notts ahead by the slenderest of margins.

Logan restarted the game but it was Burnley, now with the wind in their favour, that had much the better of the early exchanges in the second half. Burnley pressed and from a weak kick by Harper the ball was crossed by Hill and Nichol scored as the whistle went for offside and the goal was disallowed. A long shot was put in and after Toone had cleared it Espie charged him into the net. He was penalised for this and once again spoken to by the referee but a minute later he nearly scored with a tremendous shot which just shaved the top of the bar as it flew over. Notts were now seldom getting into their opponents half as Burnley continued to press and Hendry and Nichol got to loggerheads with the result that Mr Gough had a fatherly talk to them and awarded Notts a free kick which came to nought.

The cheering was now immense and in a rare visit into the Burnley half Henfrey was loudly applauded for a fine attempt to score his shot only just missing the bar from a Logan centre. Burnley took up the running again and Harper cleared a shot by Turnbull before Nichol put in a grand shot along the ground which went across the goal and just wide. A free kick to Burnley followed. Crabtree placed the ball finely and Hill lying up against the post headed through but once again the referee disallowed it for offside. Still Burnley continued to press, but the Notts defence were all working desperately hard to keep the Burnley forwards out.

Crabtree rushed at Daft apparently tripping him inside the penalty line and the referee awarded a penalty kick to Notts giving them an opportunity to score a second goal and earn themselves a little breathing space. After considerable hesitation Bruce took the penalty and as Hillman advanced out of his goal Bruce lashed the ball against the cross-bar, and the ball bounced back into play and despite the utmost efforts Notts could not scramble the rebound home. Then in midfield Espie and Calderhead were seen kicking each other and the referee immediately ordered both players off the field. Logan moved back into defence to cover for the missing Calderhead.

Burnley attacked again and Toone only just stopped a splendid shot from close quarters right on the goal line. He fell in doing so and only just got rid of the ball before several of the Burnley forwards were upon him. There were claims from the Burnley followers that the ball had, in fact, crossed the line for a goal - but the referee thought otherwise.

Burnley were now having by far the best of things and were continually driving Notts backwards. Notts were missing the running up front of Logan since he dropped back to cover for Calderhead. Both teams were now tiring because of the continued frantic pace of the game – but both sides were determined to keep going. For the Notts fans it was now very painful to watch as Burnley continued to push forward in search of the equaliser while Notts hung on desperately and it seemed like every minute towards the end of the game was taking forever. The visitors had certainly been very unlucky not to score at least one goal in the second half.

The crowd were worked up to an extra-ordinary pitch of excitement and as time after time first Shelton then Logan, Hendry and Harper saved when goals looked certain the players named were cheered frantically. Shelton, Logan and Hendry were working themselves to exhaustion. Shelton played a giant and magnificent game in these moments of excitement and Logan threw his whole heart into his work into the duties of his new position and kicked, charged, headed and dribbled the ball out of danger into safer quarters splendidly. Hendry played in champion fashion his burly form being in the midst of the battle

At last came the welcome blast from Mr Gough's whistle. A tremendous roar went up from the Notts supporters and large numbers of the crowd rushed into the arena to pat and cheer the men who had played so well for their club and had contributed so much to the outstanding result.

Espie and Calderhead were expected to appear before the Football Association in the near future to receive their punishment. It would be a major blow if Notts were to lose the services of their captain Calderhead through suspension.

'Free Lance' in the *Burnley Gazette* had the following to say on the game: *"An awkward, stiffish wind placed the men under extra difficulties, but beyond that the Burnley team were, in my opinion, a long way the better of the two. During the first half, when the wind was against them, they had as much of the game as their opponents and in the second portion they were pressing almost the whole of the time, Hillman spending most of his time in midfield. Notts scored one goal in the first half, and Burnley replied with three when the wind favoured them, and for that, according to the remarkable rulings of the referee, a gentleman named Mr. Gough, Nottingham are placed in the second round. They lost by three goals to one and yet were credited with a victory of one goal to nothing."*

'Free Lance' also had access to the referee's report regarding the trouble between Espie and Calderhead. Mr Gough says: *"I beg to inform you that I had occasion to send two players, viz., Espie of Burnley and Calderhead of Notts off the field for deliberately kicking each other. I had twice previously cautioned Espie, the first time for tripping Daft and the second time for jumping on the Notts goalkeeper after the latter had cleared the ball from goal. Calderhead appears to have acted as he did after some provocation and no fault whatever could be found with his behaviour in the match up to the time of the above incident and the enclosed apology from him was received this morning."*

The Football Association Council met at their offices at 61, Chancery Lane in London to draw the second round of the FA Cup. The draw came out as follows:

Liverpool	v	Preston North End
The Wednesday	v	Stoke
Sunderland	v	Aston Villa
Newton Heath	v	Blackburn Rovers
Burton Wanderers	v	**Notts County**
Newcastle United	v	Bolton Wanderers
Nottingham Forest	v	Middlesbrough Ironopolis
Leicester Fosse	v	Derby County

At a Notts board meeting on Saturday, February 3, it was decided that the team would again spend most of the week before the cup tie at Hazelford Ferry. It was also decided they would stay there until the day of the game and then travel to Burton on the Saturday morning.

Before all that, however, another vital League game to deal with at home to Small Heath, who sat second in the table, one place above the Magpies. Notts were without Harper, Kerr and Calderhead. Kerr's absence was of a matrimonial nature: he was in Ayr getting married to local girl Lizzie Neil – a wool spinner. In the event, Notts won 3-1 with goals from Watson, an own goal from Jenkins and an outstanding shot from Logan which dipped just under the bar.

Once again the players and trainer Joe Goode spent the week preparing at Hazelford Ferry, travelling there on the Monday. They journeyed to Burton on the 12:20 train on match day. Excursions for Notts fans from Nottingham and surrounding areas to the brewery town would follow later.

A week's rest was of immense benefit to Harper and expressed himself as feeling better than he had done all season. Bruce, too, had recovered from the injury to his leg, and every man, with the exception of Bramley, was fit and 'sound as a bell', Bramley only suffering from a slight cold.

The Wanderers did not go away and had been under the charge of trainer Tommy Waterson, who had paid every attention to their requirements. It was reported that the Burton team were also in prime condition. Two of the Notts directors had attended a Burton Wanderers committee meeting in the hope of transferring the game to Trent Bridge, in vain as it transpired.

At the Notts board meeting on Monday, February 5, it was decided that the players would each receive £1 'talent money' (bonus) if they beat Burton. That may not sound much today but put in perspective against a weekly wage of around £3, then a 33% bonus was very welcome indeed!

Burton had already beaten Notts only a few months earlier, 2-1 at Trent Bridge in a friendly, and they had also seen off local neighbours and Division Two club Burton Swifts 4-0. They were in pole position in the Midland League and had yet to experience defeat in either league or cup. It would not be a stroll in the park for the Magpies, that much was certain.

The top of the Midland League Table - as at February 10 1894:

	Pl	W	D	L	F	A	Pts
*Burton Wanderers	13	10	3	0	46	11	21
Leicester Fosse	13	10	1	2	33	8	21
Loughborough	13	7	4	2	30	17	18
Grantham Rovers	12	7	3	2	24	15	17
Mansfield Greenhalgh's	15	7	2	6	38	40	16

*Burton Wanderers were deducted two points having played Isaac Moore against Leicester Fosse before receiving an acknowledgement from the League of his registration.

Notts had previously played at Burton in both League and Bass Vase matches, but this was the first time they had appeared there competing for the greatly coveted national trophy.

The pitch sloped from one side to the other and the space for spectators was very limited. Extra stands had been erected all round the field and everything possible for the visitors' comfort had been provided by the Burton committee.

There was a carnival atmosphere preceding the game, all round the ground were to be seen rattles and the well-known black and white badges and at frequent intervals was to be heard 'Play up Notts' - the 'battle cry' of their supporters.

Shortly after two o'clock the spectators began to arrive on the ground and by half-past two there was a big gate and as the remaining excursions arrived every available space appeared to be filled. The crowd of 6,000 spectators was, at that time, the largest number of spectators ever seen in Burton at a football match. There was an exceptionally large show of cards adorned with Play up Notts but very few from the Wanderers' fans. Amongst the visitors on the stand was the president of the Notts club Mr Deplidge while the entire Notts committee were accommodated with chairs on the same structure. The Nottingham press estimated that the special trains from Nottingham had brought around 3,000 supporters - half of the estimated attendance.

With Arthur Henfrey unable to make an appearance and Arthur Watson still unavailable Donnelly partnered Kerr with Bramley at right half-back. Rain fell sharply just before kick-off but it had stopped by the time the players entered onto the field.

Notts were the first to appear on the scene and they were received with deafening cheers. This noise then doubled as the home team followed close behind. From the kick off Arthur Capes did some good work and play was initially in the Notts half but after some good work by Shelton put Notts on the attack.

Draper missed his kick and like a flash Donnelly was onto it and put in a fierce shot which Brentnall saved at the expense of a corner. Shelton again stopped his winger and passed to Calderhead who released Logan who set off on a dribble and after beating Haywood he put in a good low shot from distance which just grazed the outside of the post.

Play remained all in the Burton half with the home team seldom crossing the half way line and the goal had some lucky escapes. Soon after, another attack by Notts saw Logan put in a good shot just over the bar. Hendry stopped Smallman and Logan darted away again before putting in a terrific shot which brought another good save out of Brentnall and he received generous applause for doing so.

The Notts backs Hendry and Harper were playing exceptionally well and the Burton forwards were finding it very difficult to get past them. From a pass by Calderhead, Logan was within only a few yards of goal but in trying to make sure of missing Brentnall, he sent outside amidst loud groans of disappointment.

Referee Mr Tillotson had a talk to some of the players on both sides who were playing extremely vigorously. Smallman ran the ball before passing to Adrian Capes but when that player looked like scoring he was stopped in his tracks. Then Notts took a free-kick immediately afterwards which released Logan, Daft and Bruce who all rushed into goal, and the ball went with them. Brentnall scrambled the ball out but Donnelly, true to his reputation as a 'man about goal' had the ball into the net in a twinkling about half-an-hour after the start of the game amid enthusiastic cheers from the visiting fans.

This success only spurred Notts on to greater heights and attack after attack threatened the home goal with Brentnall pulling off some remarkable saves. After about 40 minutes Notts swarmed in again and a goal was sure to have resulted, Logan making a beautiful shot when one of the backs fisted it out. A penalty-kick was at once given by Mr Tillotson and Logan had his revenge by scoring a grand goal for his side followed by deafening cheers from the Notts followers.

In the first half, Notts had kicked down the slope and with the wind at their backs allowing Burton just two shots at the Notts goal while their opponents had innumerable shots and corners. In the second half it would be Burton's turn to enjoy those benefits.

On restarting, a long kick by the homesters resulted in their first corner but Lowe put behind. Burton returned finely and a miskick by Hendry enabled Moore to shoot hard and low, the ball striking the post and after a desperate struggle Bruce scrambled the ball out of danger. Hendry was suffering from the effects of a collision and carried his right arm in his belt. This greatly weakened the defence and a series of hot rushes followed, on the Notts goal, Calderhead cleared once but Haywood returned with a dropping shot which Toone fisted away but Adrian Capes trapped the ball and scored with a lightning shot, which gave Toone no chance.

The deafening cheering which greeted this was terrific and play became more and more exciting. The home team were now playing with great determination and good combination of their own particular style. Their attacks were successfully repulsed, however and a fine burst by Notts resulted in Logan just missing the corner of the goal. It was lucky that the finish came when it did or the Wanderers would surely have equalised.

Mr Tillotson, however signalled the finish and a tremendous cheer arose from the Notts supporters when it was certain that their team were safely into the third round with a 2-1 win. During the game Hendry had received a hefty kick in the ribs but the club were hopeful that he would be all right to play again in a few days.

At a meeting on Monday, February 12, the Notts board decided to keep faith with their usual preparation for FA Cup games and send the team to Hazelford on Tuesday, February 20, before their quarter final tie. It was also decided that £3 'talent money' would be given to each player if they progressed to the semis.

Two days later, the draw was made for the last-eight stage though because of drawn games, eleven clubs still remained in the hat: Leicester Fosse of the Midland League, Liverpool and Notts County from the Second Division and eight First Division clubs.

The draw was as follows:

Bolton Wanderers	v	Liverpool
The Wednesday	v	Aston Villa or Sunderland
Nottingham Forest	v	**Notts County**
Derby County or Leicester Fosse	v	Blackburn Rovers or Newton Heath

What a draw for the Nottingham football fans! The following appeared in the Nottingham Daily Express: *"When the news of the draw for the quarter-final reached Nottingham, the headquarters of both clubs were in a state of sensational turmoil which could only be equalled by the agitation at Portsmouth or Plymouth if the British Government had declared war with Russia or France. The evening was passed in animated discussions at both headquarters of the chances of the teams."*

On Thursday, February 15 the Notts chairman invited the players, directors, county councillor Heath and members of the press to a long walk in Papplewick followed by dinner at the Lion Hotel. Present were directors Mr T E Harris, A. Sibert, J.W. Shepperson, R.Coppack, T.R.Featherstone and players Davie Calderhead, Alf Shelton, John Hendry, George Toone, Charles Bramley, Jimmy Logan, Archie Osborne, Frank Wilkinson, Sam Donnelly, George Kerr, Dan Bruce and Joe Goode the trainer. After the meal Mr T.E. Harris proposed the toast to the health of Mr. Deplidge. Mr Deplidge replied and complimented the team on their past achievements and also a few words of encouragement for the future. Everyone enjoyed the dinner and afterwards, at Mr Deplidge's invitation, the company adjourned to the Theatre Royal to enjoy the *The Forty Thieves* pantomime.

Although the FA Cup dominated the thoughts of football fans in Nottingham, for Notts there was still the task of reclaiming their place back in the First Division. The return match with Crewe Alexandra at Trent Bridge was the next hurdle to conquer if that ambition was to be achieved.

Notts had already beaten the Railwaymen 2-0 early in the season and the visitors had shown very little improvement in form since then. Hendry was out due to the injury he received against Burton and Kerr was left out in favour of Watson. Consequently, Calderhead once more played full back, with Osborne at centre half, Watson and Donnelly starting on the right wing.

The miserable weather entirely spoiled the attendance numbered only about 300. Jack Hendry's omission was the first major fixture he had missed since he joined the club in July 1890 – ending a run of 113 consecutive appearances (100 League, 12 FA Cup and one Test Match) – which included a 4-0 League defeat at Preston on March 31, 1893, where he played in goal after George Toone had missed the train!

The game was a very one-sided affair as Notts once again demonstrated their FA Cup form, running away to a 9-1 victory with goals from Watson (4), Bruce (2), Logan (2) and Daft.

After the demolition of Crewe, the magic of the FA Cup really took a hold. The competition and the imminent local derby clash in the quarter-finals was the talk of the town. Cup fever had arrived! Being in the First Division, Forest considered themselves to be the premier club and with an enormous amount of interest in the meeting it was expected that the attendance would probably be the highest ever known in connection with the Town Ground since it was taken over by the Forest executive.

Roughly estimated, there were between 15,000 and 18,000 spectators present and the most intense excitement prevailed. During the night there had been a heavy downpour of rain and this had rendered the pitch very wet and muddy in places. A rough wind prevailed from the

North-West and as Higgins, the Forest captain won the toss for choice of ends he elected to kick with it. This was a decided advantage as the wind blew nearly straight down the ground.

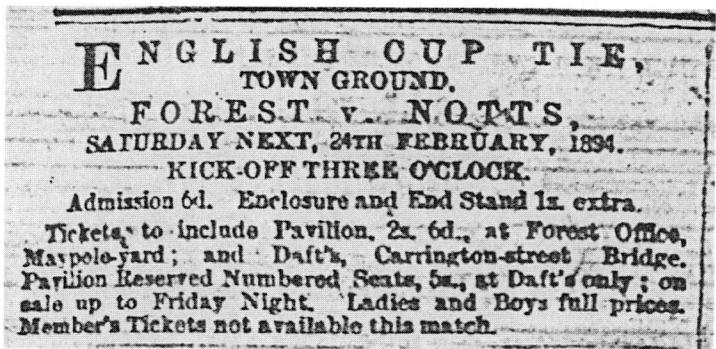

Advertisement in the local press for the quarter-final tie

In preparation for the game both teams spent the previous week away training, Notts at their usual, and now lucky, venue, Hazelford Ferry. Forest stayed at the Royal Hotel at Ashby-de-la-Zouch, only a short walk from Ashby station. It was described in the local press as having plenty of ground attached for football and running.

The Royal Hotel, Ashby-de-la-Zouch c1884

The Royal Hotel as it looks today

The main concerns for Forest had been that two of their players were doubtful for the game so their supporters were delighted to hear that McInnes, their left winger and Scott, their tenacious left back had both recovered from their injuries and would start after intensive treatment at the hands of Dr. Wharton Hood. This news meant that Forest would have their full team available for the game.

Over at the Star and Garter all the Notts players reported to be fully fit, confident and raring to go with even Harper's recently injured knee reported as being 'as sound as a brass bell'. So the Notts team would be a strong one. Calderhead would return to his usual position at centre half-back with Bramley and Shelton to right and left of him and Harper and Hendry were at full back so that they also had a full team.

On the day of the game the sun shone brightly. Although the match was advertised not to commence until three o'clock and the gates were not due to open until one o'clock huge crowds were gathering outside the ground most of the morning. More than half-an-hour before kick-off the ground to the casual observer was completely full. Not only were the usual stands packed but the extra banks capable of holding about 4,000 people were also jam-packed. Despite the best efforts of the organisers many people were unable to gain admittance to the ground. The tedium of waiting for the game to start was occupied by a band playing popular music of the day in the centre of the field. There was a real gala spirit to the occasion.

A match in progress at The Town Ground c1895 with the houses in Bathley Street visible behind the stand

The spectators arrived wearing their 'Sunday best' clothes and brought with them their best sense of humour so consequently the massed crowd was exemplary in patience and good humour. They jostled one another in the highest of spirits and cracked jokes as though they felt no anxiety at all as to the result of the match.

Club colours were as common as the proverbial blackberry. The enthusiasm even ran to huge flags which were borne aloft and carried around the ground to the delight or derision of the individual occupants. The windows of the adjacent houses were all thronged with spectators and in one very noticeable instance a skylight in a somewhat more remote terrace betrayed its owner's predilections by flaunting a flaring strip of red material which rippled in the breeze.

Every stand was filled and the hoardings and trees around the enclosure were even taken advantage of in order that a good view of the game might be obtained. The new stand erected at the Wilford Road end of the ground and the banking up that had been carried out there as well as in front of the large stand at the Arkwright Street end were fully utilised.

Here and there small masses of people swayed in slow rhythmic motion like a field of corn waving in the breeze. As time drew near to three o'clock the tense feelings of the spectators were manifest in the frequent outbursts of shouting which greeted the slightest display of partisanship. When the Forest men were seen making their way down the road leading to the field a sudden roar went up from the now very excited crowd.

A few minutes later the roar redoubled in volume as the well-known red-shirted forms of the Forest players were seen springing onto the turf. Almost immediately the striped Notts men followed and the shouts of the people and the noise of rattles was taken by the band as the signal to quit.

Roughly estimated, there were between 15,000 and 18,000 spectators present and the most intense excitement prevailed. During the night there had been a heavy downpour of rain and this had rendered the pitch very wet and muddy in places.

The referee, Mr Lithgoe, was not long in appearing on the field of play and Calderhead and Higgins having tossed to the advantage of the latter. A rough wind prevailed from the north-west and with a wave of his hand, the Forest captain indicated to his men that they might remain at the Meadow end and play with both the wind and sun in their favour. This was a decided advantage as the wind blew nearly straight down the ground.

At the start of play both sides were on edge and the ball spent more time amongst the spectators than it did on the pitch. Forest had the best of the early exchanges. After a good move by the Reds, Macpherson put in a good effort which dropped just over the bar. There was a sensational run the whole length of the field to the Forest end by Watson and Donnelly, Watson finishing up with a grand shot which Allsopp beat down and kicked away for a corner from which Watson placed the ball into the Forest goalmouth but Daft headed just wide.

Collins, however, returned it when kicked from goal and Toone failing to clear the ball dropped at Shaw's foot the little forward having the goal at his mercy when, from only a few yards from goal, he shot high over the bar to the intense disappointment of the Forest supporters. It became a rough game and one of the chief sufferers being Daft at the hands of McPherson. After 38 minutes play McInnes got hold of the ball and before Harper could get at him he had sent in a low shot whizzing into the Notts goal past the helpless Toone to the frantic delight of the Forest supporters.

Notts went after the equaliser with plenty of vigour and were almost immediately rewarded. Their first attempt was smartly repulsed but Calderhead again gave Logan the ball who, in turn found Bruce who darted out and ran right up to the Forest goal and even before the Forest cheers had died away easily beat Allsopp with a tremendous shot which hit the top of the net.

Cheer after cheer went up from the Notts supporters and the pace of the game went on faster than ever. After the two goals in quick succession defences then dominated the forwards of both sides for the remainder of the first half. Despite being in different divisions the two teams appeared to be very evenly matched. Half-time was then announced by a cheer from the crowd, the referee's whistle not being audible above the din of the spectators.

The Notts men were the first to reappear and they now had the benefit of the wind and the sun, which was still shining brightly, at their backs. Brodie restarted the game and Notts were first to get on top and shots by Logan and Bruce both sailed harmlessly over the bar. Calderhead placed the ball right into the goalmouth and a scramble ensued and although there were several attempts to force the ball home the Reds defence eventually succeeded in getting the ball away.

With ten minutes left for play and Notts attacking the Forest goal, Watson looked like scoring the winning goal with a grand shot but Allsopp punched it out and Ritchie completed the clearance. A good run by Daft from the centre of the field saw him beat both McPherson and Stewart before passing to Watson. This created a good opening for Watson but to the horror and groans of the Notts supporters he sent his shot wide of the goal. Soon afterwards the referee signalled time and the players retired for a brief rest before contesting the extra time with the score unchanged.

Some delay was caused in the commencement of the extra time with Forest maintaining that they had the right to again play with the wind having won the toss in the first instance. They were supported in their view by the referee and linesmen and accordingly kicked towards the Arkwright street goal so once again Notts returned to having the wind against them and also a dazzling sun in their eyes.

The excitement was intense and on all sides of the ground the crowd had forced their way over the perimeter ropes. With no score for either team the referee blew his whistle for change of ends. There were however still four minutes to go and on being informed of this by one of the linesmen, the ball was thrown up and the game resumed.

In the second half play was even with both defences dominant with few chances falling to either side. Shelton tripped Higgins and from the resulting free kick Stewart put well in with

Harper's clearance being dangerously close to heading through his own goal. With only two minutes left for play and Notts attacking down the left wing, Ritchie kicked the ball right out of the ground. Immediately on it being thrown in Stewart kicked it back out into the spectators. Almost as soon as it had been thrown back into play the whistle went for the last time with the score unaltered at a single goal apiece.

The draw for the semi-finals took place at Chancery Lane, London on Wednesday February 28. The five remaining teams were drawn as follows:

Notts County or Nottingham Forest   v   **Blackburn Rovers**
(at Bramall Lane)

Bolton Wanderers   v   The Wednesday
(at Fallowfield Athletic Ground Manchester)

So the two Nottingham clubs were now aware that whoever won the quarter-final replay would face Blackburn Rovers who were sitting second in the First Division and had won the FA Cup five times between 1883-84 and 1890-91.

With the other two semi-finalists sitting in the lower half of the First Division, Notts or Forest had certainly drawn the short straw by facing the club the others were hoping to avoid. Notts' league game with Walsall Swifts was postponed the following Saturday with the quarter-final replay scheduled in its place.

Meanwhile, over in Blackburn, when news of the draw was placed in the window of the offices of the local newspaper, *The Weekly Standard and Express*, it was met with huge cheers from the crowd waiting outside because they had avoided local rivals Bolton Wanderers which by popular opinion had cleared the way for an all Lancashire final.

Football League Division One as at February 28 1894

	Pl	W	D	L	F	A	Pts
Aston Villa	25	16	5	4	70	33	37
Blackburn Rovers	**23**	**14**	**2**	**7**	**54**	**35**	**30**
Burnley	23	13	3	7	48	36	29
Sunderland	23	12	4	7	55	37	28
West Bromwich Albion	26	12	4	10	59	55	28
Wolverhampton Wanderers	25	13	2	10	48	52	28
Everton	25	11	3	11	76	51	25
Nottingham Forest	22	11	3	8	46	35	25
Derby County	22	11	3	8	51	46	25
Sheffield United	26	10	5	11	41	56	25
Stoke	24	10	3	11	53	60	23
The Wednesday	**27**	**7**	**8**	**12**	**46**	**53**	**22**
Bolton Wanderers	**23**	**8**	**2**	**13**	**28**	**40**	**18**
Darwen	25	6	5	14	31	63	17
Preston North End	25	6	3	16	32	60	15
Newton Heath	20	4	1	15	17	43	9

After the stalemate at the Town Ground, both teams returned to their training headquarters with Notts at Hazelford and Forest at Ashby. The news coming out of the training camps was good. Both teams had recovered from the bumps and bruises received in the local derby and both teams were in good health. Notts' only worry was Bruce who had suffered from a cold early in the week but had recovered as the week progressed.

The morning of the replay was a beautiful one and it was clear from the spirits of both sets of supporters that their enthusiasm had not been dampened by the fact that the winners had to meet Blackburn Rovers in the semi-final.

That same morning the Notts executive were informed by letter that the FA Committee would be meeting the following Tuesday, March 6, at the Grosvenor Hotel, Manchester to discuss the issue of the sending off of Calderhead and Espie of Burnley and that Calderhead should attend, with not more than two witnesses both of whom must be from outside the club.

At a special meeting of the Notts board they decided to keep the information to themselves until after the game so as to ensure Calderhead was unaffected by the news. The Notts committee decided that Messrs F. W. Kidd and Grant be asked to go to Manchester as witnesses in Calderhead's case.

Notts were unchanged from the previous Saturday and entered the playing area at ten minutes to three, and they were received with loud cheers upon their appearance. Two or three minutes later the Forest players received an equally boisterous welcome. Higgins the Forest captain won the toss and elected to kick towards the Gamston Lane goal so Logan kicked off facing the sun but the wind was blowing across the pitch.

After only three minutes Logan got hold of the ball and sprinted down the pitch, beating both full backs, Ritchie and Scott, before letting loose a terrific shot which gave Allsopp no chance in the Forest goal to give Notts the lead and send the Notts supporters into a frenzy of cheering and applauding. From the kick-off Forest could make little headway with most of the play confined to the Reds' half of the pitch. Bruce came away with the ball before he passed to Donnelly who sprinted down the wing keeping the ball under close control before crossing to Bruce who put in a scorcher of a shot which struck the inside of the post and went into the net amid huge cheers from the Notts fans.

The Forest players appealed to the referee for offside and the cheering subsided as the referee went over to consult with his linesman but after their brief discussion the referee pointed to the centre and Notts had a second goal – and the Notts fans erupted into noise once again.

Almost immediately after the second Notts goal, a good cross from Daft was met well by Bruce but his fine header came back off the goal post. The game became a little rougher and was held up for a minute when Pike was injured in an exchange with Hendry, but he was soon up and running again. Very soon after it was Watson's turn to suffer as he was heavily grassed by McCracken.

Unlike the first game which was a very even affair, Notts had much the best of the play this time, though the Forest players continued to work extremely hard. Higgins, Smith and Pike but the trio of half-backs they were up against were just too good for them.

From a free kick Bruce sent in a really hard shot which took a slight deflection off one of the Forest players which was enough to send it past Allsopp in the Forest goal and so Notts registered their third goal in the 31st minute with the Notts supporters cheering even louder with every goal. At 3-0 to Notts street vendors were already seen moving amongst the spectators selling, at the charge of one penny, the 'In Memorial' cards marking the demise of Nottingham Forest.

On the restart, Notts were soon attacking again and a neat pass by Bramley enabled Donnelly to get in a good shot which struck the crossbar violently. Although Forest improved in the second half Notts were still the better side and they continued to have the best of the play and spent most of the time in their opponents half. From a Notts free kick Hendry sent in a good cross which Logan met and nodded back to Watson who sent in a scorcher of a shot.

Allsopp parried the shot but could not hold it and Donnelly pounced on the loose ball and had it in the back of the net before the keeper could recover, putting Notts four goals to the good.

After a rare spell of Forest pressure they were awarded a free kick which McCracken delivered invitingly into the Notts goalmouth and McInnes threw himself at the ball resulting both the ball and Notts keeper Toone ending up in the back of the net so scoring for Forest amid subdued cheering.

Spurred on by their success Forest attacked again and McInnes got past the Notts backs but knocked the ball too far ahead in doing so. A race was then on between Toone, McInnes and Higgins to get to the ball first. All arrived at the same time and all colliding together and going down in a heap. Toone was up quickly to clear the ball but both Higgins and McInnes took a few minutes to recover before they could continue. The whistle blew for the finish, leaving Notts worthy winners of the quarter-final replay 4-1.

Upon receipt of the Notts v Forest result, the *Weekly Standard and Express* in Blackburn published the following bookmakers' odds for the four semi-finalists to lift the cup:

Blackburn Rovers	Evens
Bolton Wanderers	5 to 2
The Wednesday	7 to 2
Notts County	**8 to 1**

The majority of the Notts players left Nottingham for their usual FA Cup training camp at the Star and Garter on Monday, March 5, where they would remain until travelling to Sheffield to meet Blackburn Rovers in the FA Cup semi-final at Bramall Lane on Saturday, March 10.

Unfortunately Notts were fearing the worst and trying to get used to the idea that they may have to cope in the semi-final without Davie Calderhead, their captain and centre-half, in their most important game of the season. The FA Emergency Committee which was to decide his fate after his sending off (along with Burnley's Espie), in the first round six weeks earlier, was finally going to sit and consider the case.

The match in question was played on January 27 and referee Mr Gough had forwarded his report to the FA immediately after the tie. After much delay, caused by a variety of reasons, the FA were at last set to adjudicate upon the matter on March 6 in Manchester.

David Calderhead as he appeared in English Sports in 1894

Calderhead was accompanied by Mr Kidd and Mr Grant, as the rules insisted, who witnessed the incident and who were prepared to give Calderhead an excellent testimonial.

Espie and his friends and the referee Mr Gough were also present. The referee's statement had been submitted to the committee in advance of the meeting. The culprits were then called into the room separately and called upon for an explanation of their conduct. This having been given, the chairman remarked that it was a pity that players of such ability as both men had proved themselves to be could not control their tempers when on the field of play.

Calderhead had one of the best reputations of any professional or amateur footballer playing at that time. The excellent character which Calderhead has won for himself would hopefully be taken into consideration by the committee.

After a period of due deliberation they announced their decision – and that was that the players having to leave the field at the time of the incident would, the committee thought, be a sufficient punishment for the players and so they decided there would be no further punishment but if they offended in future they would be very severely dealt with.

After such a long period of time had elapsed between the offence and the meeting, a suspension for Calderhead with such an important fixture only a few days away would, in the eyes of many Notts supporters, have been too harsh a punishment. They and his team-mates were delighted that the popular captain of the team would be in his usual place at centre-half against Blackburn.

So with Calderhead available, enabling both Blackburn and Notts to field their strongest teams, the stage was now set for the two semi-finals on Saturday. While Blackburn and Notts were due to meet at Bramall Lane, Bolton Wanderers and The Wednesday were to play their game on the Manchester Athletic Ground at Fallowfield. The kick-off in both matches was fixed for 3.30pm but history did not favour Notts having won only five of their previous 24 meetings with Blackburn.

The south Yorkshire weather was beautiful with the sun shining and apart from a wind blowing it was a good day for a football match. The streets of Sheffield were busy, particularly in the areas around the stations, with thousands of people leaving Sheffield in order to support Wednesday at Fallowfield while train loads of supporters were arriving from Blackburn and Nottingham to support their teams at Bramall Lane.

The Blackburn supporters were first to arrive and were particularly enthusiastic sporting the famous blue and white colours and loudly asserting their belief in victory for their team. Meanwhile the Rovers team who had left Blackburn by the 10:40 train, were met on their arrival in Sheffield and were taken away to a hotel and kept there quiet to prepare for the match.

An early picture of Bramall Lane

Everyone was in high spirits and even after one o'clock when rain began to fall the ardour of the enthusiasts was in no way dampened. The Blackburn supporters had matters very much their own way until between two and three o'clock when the special trains from Nottingham began to arrive and then a steady stream of people commenced to flow in the direction of the Bramall Lane enclosure, the black and white favours of the Notts fans also being much in evidence.

The accommodation was exceptionally good. The turf looked bright enough but it was certainly on the soft side and showers that fell between one and two o'clock had the effect of making it rather greasy on the surface but not sufficiently so to render the playing of a hard and fast game a matter of difficulty.

The gates were thrown open at an early hour and the Lancashire excursionists who were the first to arrive in Sheffield installed themselves in good positions and whiled away the time as best they could. By a quarter past two o'clock there was quite a large crowd present and people were then flocking into the ground as fast as their money could be taken at the many turnstiles which were available. By kick-off time, of 3:30pm, between 20,000 and 25,000 people were inside the ground.

Notts won the toss and the Rovers kicked off towards the Bramall Lane against a wind and bright sun. Early on the game was 'end to end' with Haydock heading wide of the Notts goal whilst Daft shot over the Blackburn crossbar. Logan appeared to have a good early chance of scoring but his shot, low and hard, was a foot wide of the post.

Aided by the wind, Notts attacked vigorously but the Rovers defence was equal to the task and kept the Notts forwards at bay. After a quarter of an hour's play Daft picked up a loose ball and raced forward before sending in a powerful 'daisy-cutter' shot which beat the diving Ogilvie to put Notts into the lead.

The goal was received by tremendous cheering by the Notts supporters. After the kick-off Notts continued to dominate the game, forcing two good saves from Ogilvie and then Bruce put in a good shot only for the whistle to go for offside. Donnelly was involved in a tussle with the Blackburn defenders only for him to receive a kick on the knee which caused him to limp. The Rovers came more into the game with Haydock sending in a shot which tested Toone but he was equal to the test. Only a minute later Haydock shot just over the Notts bar.

Daft made another run down the wing but was sent sprawling on the turf by a heavy challenge by Dewar. Logan raced away and centred only for Watson to shoot wide with an overhead kick. A breakaway by the Rovers with some neat passing resulted in a shot from Haydock which Toone forced round the post for a corner.

From the resulting set-piece there was a frantic goalmouth scramble before the Notts supporters broke into cheering as Calderhead strode from the ruck of players with the ball at his feet. For some time the Rovers defence had plenty to do but full-backs Brandon and Murray performed well on a number of occasions.

Notts surged around the Rovers' goal and Watson hit the best shot of the match which Ogilvie appeared to touch the ball just over the bar leaving the Notts players appealing for a corner. Instead of giving either a goal kick or a corner the referee blew for the end of the first half with Notts just having their noses in front with the single goal.

After an interval of six minutes the teams changed ends and Notts were first to attack but were driven back and Townley made a fine run along the left but when he got close up to the Notts goal he was stopped by Harper. The first twenty minutes of the second half was a fight on the part of Notts to secure a second goal but this was not achieved and as a consequence, aided by the wind, the Rovers began to take control of the game.

Blackburn Rovers circa 1895
Standing: E.H. Dodd (linesman), Hargreaves, Whitehead, Chippendale, Dewar,
Anderson, Turnbull, Cleghorn, J. Hunter (trainer)
Seated: Haydock, Brandon, Ogilvie, Murray

The only respite Notts were getting was the occasional break away by Daft or Logan which relieved the pressure for short periods. Following one of those runs by Daft, Bramley sent in a splendid shot that Brandon headed away. The Rovers pressure was relentless and pushed the Notts defence to the limit and despite outstanding performances from Calderhead and the backs, Harper and Hendry, Toone was called upon time after time to keep out Blackburn's forwards.

Toone conceded a corner and although accurately delivered by Townley, Chippendale headed over the bar. The Rovers were now dominating the game. For some time the Notts players kept strictly on the defensive. Under pressure Hendry conceded a corner. Chippendale took the kick and Brandon put the ball into the Notts goalmouth where Toone, who was showing the style that earned his selection for the England team, saved well only for Calvey to send the loose ball wide – a narrow escape for Notts.

The relief was only temporary as Blackburn returned once again to the attack. With only fifteen minutes left the only question on the lips of the supporters of both clubs was whether or not Notts could hang onto their slender lead. Corner after corner accrued to the Rovers but owing mainly to the wind they were difficult to direct and all were got away by the Notts rearguard. With only ten minutes to play, the Rovers, with defenders joining in the attack, attacked desperately but could not score.

The scene at Bramall Lane as depicted in the *Sheffield Telegraph and Star*

As the end drew near the excitement of the Notts supporters knew no bounds and every kick was greeted with uproarious applause and cries of 'Play up Notts!' The Rovers never relaxed their efforts and Townley had a final opportunity in the last few seconds but failed to connect well with the ball and the chance was gone and despite all their pressure they could not score and the result of a very exciting game ended moments later amid great applause and prolonged cheering from the Notts supporters:

In the *Northern Daily Telegraph*, "Free Kick" wrote:

The unexpected has happened and the favourites for the English Cup have been knocked out in the semi-final by a team which up to a little over a week ago was regarded as a rank outsider.

On Saturday despite the warnings given by our Nottingham correspondent almost everybody outside the lace capital believed the Rovers would pull the match off somewhat easily. I certainly thought they would win but I had not seen Notts County play this season and the game had not been going more than half an hour before I came to the conclusion that the Lambs stood a better chance of victory than the Rovers. Among the Notts players there was an utter absence of that nervousness which was so conspicuous the last time the two teams met in the English final. From the start they were cool and collected. Every man in the team was turned out in the best possible condition not one of them at the conclusion of the game having moved a hair. The Notts defence, however, was safe and sound. Toone had a lot more work to do than Ogilvie, but when the Notts forwards got away they were infinitely more dangerous than their opponents. Logan is a champion.

It was with tremendous joy and celebrations that the result of the game was received back in Nottingham. During the afternoon the news was eagerly awaited and when it became known that Notts had scored 15 minutes after the start of the game interest was heightened.

Both the half-time and final result were awaited with the greatest interest-
, crowds of excited people assembling in the vicinity of those places where telegrams were expected to arrive, such as the local newspaper offices, the Notts Club headquarters at the Lion Hotel on Clumber Street and on Carrington Street where the business premises of Harry Daft (R.P. & H.B. Daft – sports outfitters) and the Notts director and ex Notts player William Gunn (Gunn & Moore – sports outfitters) were to be found. All of these places were known to attach score updates to their windows when the appropriate telegrams were received with

some people rushing from window to window in order to be first with the news. Even at the Castle ground, where a rugby game was in progress, was buzzing with excited chatter about the cup tie.

The result was published in these premises shortly after five o'clock being only two or three minutes after the referee's whistle had been blown in Sheffield. Very soon after the initial announcement, a rush of 'news' boys were met by eager people on every side and the opening of the papers and the hurried glance at the match details was followed by wild demonstrations of delight of the victory.

After the match the directors of the Notts club with their chairman, Mr R. Deplidge, entertained the team to tea at the Wharncliffe Hotel there being present in all a company of about forty including many ladies, wives of the directors of the Notts Club. It was a most enthusiastic gathering.

The team and directors returned to Nottingham by the 6.40pm saloon special – a remarkable train, which included no fewer than 20 saloon carriages – the largest train of the kind ever sent out from Nottingham. The train arrived at the Midland Station just after eight o'clock and was greeted by a crowd of several thousand persons assembled on the long platform, the bridge also being crowded. The cheering was tremendous. With difficulty, players and directors made their way to a horse-drawn coach, which was driven to the Lion Hotel. Station Street was thronged so as to be almost impassable, and on arriving at Clumber Street the crowd was so great that it was not possible for some time to proceed further. Eventually the party found their way to headquarters, where an informal meeting was held under the presidency of Mr. T. Harris, the honorary secretary of the club.

The following report from the *Nottingham Daily Express* described the event:

There were present Mr Robert Deplidge (chairman of directors), Messrs Hy. Vann, A. Sibert, H. Heath, C. C., (directors), R. W. Coppack (hon. treasurer), 'Major' Lewis, C. Hibbert, E. Browne, F. Wharton, C. Gilbert, J. Woolley, J. Crane, E. C. Price, Kennedy, &c.

Mr E. Browne, in proposing the health of Mr. Deplidge, said that as an old official of the club he was delighted to see Mr. Deplidge and so many enthusiastic supporters present on such a very auspicious occasion. (Hear, hear.) He could honestly say that the best team had won that day (applause) and he was confident that Notts would now win the Cup (applause.) When that time came Mr. Deplidge would occupy a position that he had never held before.

The toast was drunk with musical honours.

Mr Deplidge, in responding said he felt very gratified at the compliment paid to him by Mr Browne and to the company for their cordial reception of his name. Of course they knew he was a sportsman (applause) and what he had done for the Notts club had been to him a source of sincere pleasure. (applause) He had been pleased at the receipt of numerous letters speaking in most complimentary terms of the team and of the directorate. His colleagues on the board of directors were deserving of every thanks for their hearty and unflagging support of the old club under such depressing times as they had had to pass through. (applause) He would, in conclusion, propose the health of the players and express the hope that their success might long continue and that they would not only succeed in bringing the cup to Nottingham, but regain their lost position in the First Division of the League. (applause) He would couple with the toast the name of David Calderhead the greatly esteemed captain of the team. (cheers)

Mr Harris said that their captain was very bashful when off the field and had asked him (the speaker) to respond on his behalf. (laughter) He wished to express thanks on behalf of himself and the other members of the team and to assure the company that every man had done his level best and would continue to do so and they would not rest content until they succeeded in bringing the cup to Nottingham. (cheers)

Mr Charlie Coulby spoke very highly of the recent performances of the team and hoped that the men would all escape injury, continue to play as well as they had been doing and that they would meet with well-deserved success. (applause)

The health of Mr T. E. Harris the honorary secretary, who has rendered such excellent services to the club was next enthusiastically drunk.

Mr Harris, in response, said he did not know of a club where more cordial relationship existed between directorate and players than was the case in the Notts club. (hear, hear.) The directors worked hard and well for the success of the club and the players did their utmost to place the club on a good footing again. He had never met a more agreeable, genuine and gentlemanly lot of players than those who were so splendidly carrying the old colours to fame and victory. (cheers) In every way their conduct was admirable and he was proud of them (cheers) Mr Harris announced that he had just received several telegrams congratulating the club upon their last grand achievement. Mr Louis Ford, of the West Bromwich Albion Club had wired:- "Hurrah! Heartiest congratulations – we hope you will win the cup." (cheers) Similar telegrams had been received by him from Mr. W. T. Thompson from the Manchester Prince's Theatre, from Mr Jos. Parlby (Ardwick), H. T. Whitworth (Wolverhampton), &c.

The health of Mr. R. W. Coppack, the hon. Treasurer, was next proposed by Mr. E. Browne, who said that there was no more valuable man in the club than Mr. Coppack, who , like Calderhead, though modest and retiring, had done an immense amount of work for the club. (cheers) Like Mr. Deplidge, Mr Harris and other gentlemen connected with the club, Mr. Coppack had had an anxious time. But he congratulated those gentlemen that their time of anxiety was now over. (cheers)

Mr Coppack, responding to the toast said that he had had a very anxious time as treasurer but like his colleagues, he had done his best for the club and he was willing to continue to do so. (cheers)

At the weekly Notts board meeting two days later a letter was read out from Lord Henry Bentinck inviting the team and officials to dinner after the FA Cup Final – this was accepted. The outstanding league game with Ardwick was re-arranged for Thursday, March 15.

Meanwhile in the other semi-final Bolton had beaten The Wednesday 2-1, thus reaching the FA Cup final for the first time in their history. The year of 1894 would see a new name added to the list of Cup winners.

After three successive Saturdays battling in the FA Cup, Notts finally returned to League action after almost a month. The battle was resumed when the cup finalists journeyed to Walsall to fulfil the return fixture with the Town club. As long as Notts were sufficiently recovered and suffering no ill effects from the severe struggle with Blackburn, there was every prospect of adding further to their tally. Having played the same number of matches as Walsall, Notts possessed a clear lead of 20, 33 to 13.

Notts left out Shelton and Watson, Osborne going centre half and Kerr partnering Donnelly on the right wing. After 17 minutes Logan scored with a 'beautiful' shot – but it wasn't to be enough. As the game progressed into the second half Notts were looking as if they had not yet got over the stiffness occasioned by the struggle with Blackburn and two late goals gave the points to Walsall.

CHAPTER FIFTEEN

March 15 1894 – July 31 1894

The FA Cup Final

IT was on Thursday, March 15, that the FA decided the 1894 FA Cup final venue. The choices were between Perry Barr (Birmingham), Molyneux (Wolverhampton), Bramall Lane (Sheffield) and Goodison Park (Liverpool). The FA Council elected for Everton's Goodison Park, kick-off 4pm. The officials for the final were selected as Referee: Mr C.J. Hughes of Cheshire and the linesmen were: Mr J. Howcroft of Redcar and Mr A. Scragg of Crewe

Notts met Ardwick on the Castle Ground in their return League fixture on the same March day. All circumstances considered there was every prospect that Notts could consolidate their top three position in Division Two. With Small Heath only a single point and one place below and Newcastle United two points behind them in the chase promotion, a good result was imperative.

Notts left out Watson and Donnelly, bringing in Elijah Allsopp a Worksop amateur on the right wing to partner Kerr and Shelton returned to the team. Within only four minutes of the start Logan had scored TWICE! This set the tone with further goals from Bruce, Allsopp and Kerr in a thumping 5-0 win for the Magpies.

At a special Meeting of the Notts County board at the Lion Hotel on Saturday, March 17, the club received a letter from Rangers asking to play Notts, in Glasgow, on April 30 – the board agreed to this subject to the financial offer being acceptable. The board also decided that after the League game with Lincoln City on Friday, March 23, the team would, immediately after the game, catch the train straight down to London to play Woolwich Arsenal in another League game the following day.

Two nights later another meeting of the board at the same location decided that since the Star and Garter was unavailable, the team would break with their so far very successful tradition of preparing at the Hazelford Ferry and instead go to the West Kirby Hotel in West Kirby before the FA Cup Final.

In order to keep the players fresh and in good spirits the Notts enjoyed a short sojourn at Ollerton, a village in the Dukeries, from Tuesday until Friday before making the trip to Lincoln and playing two games in two days.

The Lincoln players were reported to be in a very sombre mood having lost their trainer, Alf Bailey, who died suddenly, aged only 32 just a few days earlier.

The game was to commence at three o'clock but shortly after two o'clock the thronged state of High Street showed the keenness of the spectators to secure a good vantage point from which to view the contest. Excursion trains were run from Nottingham, Gainsborough, Grimsby and other parts of Lincolnshire and half an hour before the commencement of the game the grandstand on the south side of the John O'Gaunt's was filled.

There was a constant flow of spectators for the next half hour and every available position commanding anything like a view of the ground was occupied. The City players were on the ground first and their appearance elicited applause. Each player wore a black band round his arm in memory of the late trainer. By the time Notts put in an appearance it was estimated that 6,000 spectators or more were present. The Notts team were 30 minutes late but the crowd waited patiently. When the visitors came on to the ground at 3:30 they were cheered.

The entrance to the John O'Gaunts ground in 1891. The posters on the wall are for a game between Lincoln City Swifts (reserves) and Nottingham Forest on September 12, 1891

The archway entrance to the John O'Gaunts Lincoln High Street today.
(The football ground has long gone)

In a first half wherein Lincoln were the better team, Toone played exceptionally well to keep the game scoreless. In the second half it was Notts who took up the running and two goals from Daft secured the points for the visitors.

The train carrying the Notts team steamed out of Lincoln station about 5.30pm on its way to London to meet Woolwich Arsenal the following day. Having beat Lincoln, Notts were now on 37 points which was the maximum number of points that the chasing Newcastle and Grimsby could achieve so they were almost secure in the top three places. A single point at Arsenal the following day would guarantee that position beyond any doubt.

Notts journeyed to Woolwich to fulfil their return engagement in the best of spirits and fully determined to save themselves, as far as possible, for the final tie on Saturday. Arsenal had much the best of the opening exchanges and Crawford scored the first goal at the end of ten minutes play. Notts improved but could not score and went into the break a single goal behind.

In the second half the play was mainly in midfield but then Calderhead found Donnelly in the clear only for him to send his shot crashing against the cross-bar and back into play. Immediately afterwards it was Daft's turn to hit the crossbar but this time the rebound fell close to Logan who was quickly on to it ensuring the ball was snuggled in the back of the net before the Arsenal keeper had chance to move. Fairly even play followed with both defences on top but then Bruce sent in a long shot which completely beat Williams and scored the second goal. Notts had done just enough to win the points 2-1.

The Notts County players had clearly become celebrities as fans were now very keen to see the FA Cup finalists in action. Lincoln, whose average home gate was around the 3,000 mark, suddenly had a gate of double that when Notts came to town and similarly Arsenal, who averaged about 6,000, attracted a gate of 13,000 mostly to see the Magpies in the flesh.

Back at the Lion Hotel in Clumber Street on Saturday, March 24, a week before the big day, the Notts board accepted an offer from a Mr Lewis to drive the team to and from Goodison Park and the station on the day of the final.

On the Monday, the eleven Notts players who had played twice against Forest in the quarter-final and beaten Blackburn in the semi-final were taken to the West Kirby Hotel on the Wirral for a few days of gentle training. They were accompanied by Joe Goode, the trainer and Mr Deplidge, the club chairman.

On the left on the corner of Sandy Lane is the West Kirby Hotel c1911. The hotel was demolished and replaced by the Moby Dick public house in 1964

The same view up Sandy Lane as it looks today with the Moby Dick pub on the left

West Kirby was one of Mr Deplidge's favourite places, situated on the east coast of the Dee estuary with beautiful views across the river of Holywell, Mostyn and the Welsh hills. Just 12 miles from Goodison Park, it was an ideal training camp. The hotel in which they stayed was situated on a hill with a south-west aspect, sloping gradually to the shore.

The fresh mountain breezes made the air very salubrious, a perfect location for the players to prepare for the game ahead. The training was not hard as it was considered that the men were already in good condition owing to the great amount of work they had done prior to leaving Nottingham so their time at the hotel consisted mainly of gentle walks – only one session during the week included work with a football!

Positive reports came out of West Kirkby of the good health and spirits of the team but the committee still had contingency plans in case any of the players were unavailable at the last moment. A number of players were fit and standing by for the call should they be needed. Frank Wilkinson (half-back), George Shepperson (inside-forward), George Kerr (forward) and Arthur Henfrey (half-back/inside-forward) were all fit and available if needed.

Bolton's form as they approached the final was not good with only one win from their last six League games including a 2-2 draw with wooden spoonists Newton Heath. In vivid contrast, Notts had suffered only one defeat in their last ten Division Two games. While the players were tanning in West Kirby, Bolton had decided to remain in their own town to put in the work necessary to bring them to the peak of fitness.

On the eve of the final, two reporters from the *Nottingham Daily Express* called on the Notts players at their hotel. Because it was the day of the Grand National it was busy when they arrived at the Central Station to transfer to their train for the short trip to West Kirby. Part of their report follows:

In front of the West Kirby Hotel is a lawn where we found some of the Notts men engaged in bowls. Just across a field or two was the beach with a serpentine island in the offing - whatever that is. But the island is there and it adds a picturesque charm to the view. The estuary is about seven miles across and the Welsh hills look delicious in the spring sunshine. Nottingham holiday-makers must 'discover' West Kirby. Mr Hart, the manager of the hotel will be glad to welcome them, I have no doubt.

The environment of the station at West Kirby suggests some little 'hydro' in Derbyshire, with its new villas and highly respectable shops where they charge four times the worth for the few trifles they sell. We were just about to ask some urchins who were kicking a small ball about which was the way to the West Kirby Hotel when who should march up boldly and beaming but David Calderhead the very able and amiable captain of the Notts team. Excellent Davie how glad we were to see him and looking the picture of health and contentment. "How are you old man?" - "Never better. Come down to see the boys have you?" "Going to stay all night?" They're as right as ninepence." Davie explained that he was just off to Liverpool to meet Mrs Calderhead but if we hurried up we should find the boys at dinner. "Just a question before you go Davie" said we. "They tell us you have been going in for boxing, cycling, fencing, indian clubs....." "Oh rubbish" said he "We are doin' nothin', and we like it" "Shall you win?" "Well" said he with true Scottish caution, "We've just as good a chance as they have - and may be better. But here's the train. You go just down there by the church and turn ....."

Davie was off while we wished him luck and we turned down by the church presently finding the hotel some distance down a sandy lane. "Where are the Notts footballers?" we asked a rosy cheeked girl. "I'll show you" she said and opened a French window, beyond which was pretty green lawn. The Notts team were there some lying about in the sunshine, some engaged in bowls, Mr T. Harris, resplendent in flannel shirt and knickerbockers, measuring his full 5 feet 10½inches in the grass. The boys gave us quite a lively welcome. How brown they all were and full of spirits.

It was late on Monday evening when they arrived - thirteen in all, including Mr Harris and Goode the trainer. "At our first meal" said the jovial hon. secretary, "We crossed knives and spilled the salt. If we win the cup we shall send word to the Thirteen Club." – "If we win?" said one. "Look here" said the same speaker, taking me aside – I won't tell you his name for his prophecy may not come off - but "Look here" he said and I went to look "We shall win that cup just as certain as ...."

"Why not will win, you'll see!" came as an interuption. Exactly so, thought I, why not?

"And what do you think to the place?" – "The jolliest, prettiest, best place we've ever been at" said Hendry, who, standing up, looked the picture of healthy, vigorous young manhood. "We're boys again. Go out paddling over yonder every day, sprint along the beach, practice with the ball in the field there and generally have a good time."

"All in good health?" – "Yes, every one. Never better." "Where are Shelton and Watson and Daft?" – "Gone out to make a call on somebody who has invited them."

Bruce was sunning himself in the grass and was too thoroughly engrossed in the pleasure of living to show much energy. But he joined in the universal praise of the establishment and of the pleasures of the life they were leading. Harper, tall and bronzed, was busy teaching Logan how to bowl fast over hand, using the wooden 'jack' as a ball, Logan putting in his best work to the great danger of the primroses in the beds on the far side of the lawn. Donnelly, shy and reserved, expressed his satisfaction with the club's quarters, but hinted a wish that the fateful struggle of tomorrow was over. Bramley, I espied, looking down on us from an upper window embowered in greenery. He cheerily greeted, "How do" and followed his phrase so quickly that he was on the lawn almost with his words. Toone in best of health and spirits was deeply engaged in a geographical discussion with Goode, the trainer, as to the extent of the Welsh coast in view and whether a fogbank somewhere about the mouth of the estuary was Snowdon.

Conversation drifted from one topic to another, Nottingham friends were inquired after, the news was imparted that the Bolton team were training at Eastham, and that Paton was not likely to play in consequence of an injured knee. Hendry rhapsodised over the Goodison Park Ground, exclaiming that if a team could not win on that ground they ought to be......

And we lounged and chatted and smoked in the glorious sunshine and watched the gulls wheel round and saw a steamer glide smoothly along in the distance. Then we looked at our watches. Heavens! Ten minutes to catch the train and the station a mile away, and no cabs nearer than Liverpool. "Come, I'll show you" said Mr Tom Harris, and in knickerbockers, running shoes and flannel he darted off. He had been training a week and had always something of the athlete about him. We had our overcoats and bags. "Up this hill here. We must jump the churchyard wall, but the gate is open on your side." Breathless we ran. Horror! The bell was clanging at the station which was yet a quarter of a mile away. We sped like the wind and the boys hurrahed. Into the carriage we tumbled, blown, heated, bedewed. "Has it bin a race sir?" inquired the civil porter. "Ca-catching the train?" "Oh, was it the bell as frightened you?" We always rings that five minutes afore time!!"

As we were steaming out of the little station Mr Harris's genial voice was heard, "Coach and four to the Central after the match. Return by 7.30pm Midland."

The Bolton team did not arrive in the Liverpool area until Friday, making their headquarters at Eastham, at the time a pleasant village located on the Wirral side of the River Mersey. They travelled across the Mersey on Saturday morning, pausing at Liverpool city centre to take lunch, ironically at The Star and Garter Hotel on St. John's Lane. Notts County, after a short train journey, arrived in Liverpool some time later. Both sides were then transported by horse drawn coach out to Goodison Park.

By 1892/93 it was necessary to relocate the FA Cup final in order to accommodate the ever-increasing number of fans who wished to see the game. For that reason, it had been moved to Manchester's Fallowfield Stadium.

The 1893 FA Cup Final Everton v Wolverhampton Wanderers at Fallowfield

However, the venue left a lot to be desired. During the excitement of the game barricades were swept away leaving fans encroaching on the touchline while thousands of other people were unable to see anything of the game due to the lack of appropriate banking or steps. So, when the decision was made for a venue for the 1894 final the FA, after inspecting the list of the possible grounds, chose Goodison Park. It was then the most advanced stadium in the country, boasting hot-water boilers, large double baths, a referee's changing room and a press stand capable of seating one hundred journalists.

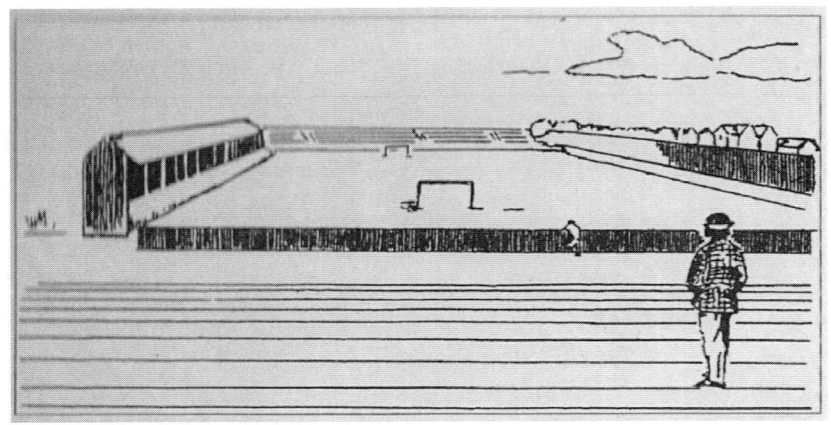

A sketch of Goodison Park that appeared in *The Liverpool Echo* in 1892

The ground was adapted to hold a 50,000 capacity crowd with the additional advantage that all spectators would be able to see the play, a boast that very few other grounds in this country at that time could make. It was estimated that should the weather turn out wet, 25,000 spectators would still be able to view the match under shelter. The Everton executive with the help of the local officials, further enhanced the setting by adding temporary seating along the Goodison Road side of the ground.

Goodison Park in 1905

Mr. R. Lythgoe, a member of the FA and a well known Liverpool referee, he had refereed Notts on a number of occasions during the season, was responsible for the arrangements for the accommodation of both the spectators and the press representatives, of whom there were over 100 present. In order to get updates of the match out to the waiting public Mr Lythgoe had arranged for a Hansom cab service to run every 15 minutes during the game to the nearby Victoria Street post office from where the messages were dispatched through a pneumatic tube to the central office at Paradise Street. From there they would be distributed accordingly.

The morning of the game got off to a sombre start when a message arrived informing the club of the sudden death of Alex 'Sandy' Ferguson, who had appeared at right-back for Notts in the FA Cup final just three years earlier, beaten then by Blackburn Rovers. He was only 27-years-old, had joined from Rangers and although he had been resident in and playing for Newark FC his death had occurred while on a visit back to Glasgow.

Alex 'Sandy' Ferguson

For the Notts fans, Midland Railway ran two excursions to Liverpool from Nottingham, the first left Nottingham at 9.50am and arrived at Liverpool at one o'clock. The Notts directors travelled by this train and would return by the same train accompanied by the team, leaving Liverpool at 7.30 pm and arriving in Nottingham by 10.30pm A second trip was run at 11.50am which arrived at Walton at 2.35pm, returning at 7.30pm for 10.55pm in Nottingham.

On the Manchester, Sheffield and Lincolnshire route a fast special was run, stopping to pick up passengers at Daybrook, Bulwell Forest and Hucknall Torkard. This train left the Great Northern Railway Station at Nottingham at 8.10am and was due at Liverpool Central at 11.20am. Messrs Swan and Leach also organised a trip which left Nottingham at 11.50am and arrived at Walton at three o'clock. Other excursions were also run from other parts of the country.

Bolton's route to the final had been against three Division Two sides (Small Heath, Newcastle and Liverpool) before meeting First Division Wednesday in the semi-final. At this stage of the season Liverpool were undefeated in Division Two with the title almost in their grasp, a club Notts had failed to beat in either of their league fixtures, yet they were brushed aside 3-0 by Bolton in the quarter-final - so Notts could not afford to underestimate the size of the task ahead of them.

The Wanderers made the journey from Eastham to Liverpool early in the day while Notts arrived at the Central Station from West Kirby at just before three o'clock where a coach and four was waiting to convey the party to the ground. Along the route the players were regularly recognised and cheered enthusiastically by their fans.

The sun was hiding behind the dense Liverpool smoke and the only gleams of colour were the brilliant white of the boards, which some three-feet high formed a frame around the playing surface and the red coats of a few soldiers. The ground was surrounded by houses and from every window and vantage point people peered trying to see the action. The windows were full of faces overlooking the enclosure. Men, women and children hung out eager to get a glimpse of the game.

Though the match was timed to commence at four o'clock the trams, buses and street vendors which plied their trade along the streets outside the ground were doing great business as early as one o'clock. A number of policemen were perched along the skyline of the grandstand's roofs.

An already large crowd was reinforced by a long procession of Notts supporters arriving at the ground and bringing up the rear were some noisy *Nottingham Football News* boys, eager to sell their mementos of the day. The Nottingham supporters were, however, immediately distributed in the crowd and effectively disappeared, although here and there black and white rosettes and club favours could still be seen and behind one of the goals a large black and white flag was continuously waved seeming to lead the cheers of the Notts contingent.

In the Press box there were a hundred or more eager football writers ready to set the scene and tell the exciting match details to distant towns and just before the kick-off the crowd witnessed the arrival of the Lord Mayor, Alderman W. B. Bowring, accompanied by Mrs Bowring.

The very excellent band of the Liverpool Police enlivened a wait of two hours by some inspiriting melodies, but the piece which elicited the loudest applause was the rendition of Arthur Sullivan's *Lost Chord* – and was it just coincidence that the band played *Get your hair cut* just as the Notts players came on to the field?

The two cup final teams as they appeared in *The Sporting Life* before the game:

Back row (players only): Osborne (Reserve), Calderhead, Hendry
Middle row: Bramley, Daft, Shelton, Toone and Harper
Front row: Watson, Kerr (Reserve), Logan, Donnelly, Bruce, Goode (Trainer)

Back row (players only): Somerville, Sutcliffe and Jones
Middle row: Tannahill, Paton, Hughes, Turner, Bentley and Dickenson
Front row: Willcocks, Cassidy and Weir (Reserve)

Five minutes before the stipulated kick-off time of four o'clock the Notts team were led into the arena by their captain David Calderhead and they were met with the most tremendous cheering as they went through a few preliminary kicks at goal. They were followed onto the turf by the Bolton team, led by their skipper David (Di) Jones, who also received an equally noisy reception. Both teams looked fit and well prepared with the slight sun tans gained at West Kirby adding to the Notts team's healthy appearance.

There was no wind worth mentioning and the sun was hidden behind dull heavy clouds which looked like thunder as the two captains came to the centre of the pitch where the referee, Mr Hughes, wasted no time with the preliminaries which saw Calderhead win the toss and just before the allocated time the two teams were in position and Mr Hughes gave the long awaited signal to start the game.

The first fifteen minutes were fast and hectic with little good football played with only rushing, heading and big kicking for some minutes while the players came to terms with their nerves and the important occasion. The speedy Notts wingers, Watson and Daft, put the Bolton defence under a lot of pressure in the early stages of the game. In particular the half-backs of Paton, Hughes and Gardiner described in the press as 'a sturdy strong-limbed trio' who were perhaps not the quickest of players but they certainly made up for any lack of pace with skill and a very determined attitude. Notts took the initiative and attacked the Bolton defence.

The ball was passed to Logan who quickly fed the ball to Bruce who sent a low fast shot just wide of the post. Harper stopped Cassidy in his tracks when he looked like carrying all before him. Play was hectic but Logan kept a cool head and twice sent out excellent passes to his wing men to start his forwards off on splendid runs but Notts could not get past the Bolton half-backs until Donnelly got hold and dribbling beautifully past Gardiner put the ball in the centre.

In rushed the Notts forwards as Sutcliffe ran out to meet the shot and successfully cleared the shot only for Bramley to hit a return shot which just missed the upright.

The quality of the football improved in technique as the players relaxed and began to play their usual games.

Logan was particularly prominent, his neat and splendidly effective passing, his pace and shooting earned him thunderous applause on a number of occasions.

Bolton were awarded a free-kick which was placed right into the Notts goalmouth but once again it was the inimitable Davie Calderhead who took control and quickly dealt with the danger and set his forwards off on another raid into Bolton territory.

Dangerous free kicks were given by either side now and Tannahill had a splendid clear opening but shot well over the bar. Next, Gardiner put a shot just a few inches wide. Notts were setting a fast paced game and Bolton were beginning to struggle to contain them. Following a rapid attack down the Notts right wing, a shot from Logan was blocked but immediately picked up by Donnelly who fired in a stinger of a shot which came back off Sutcliffe's left hand upright and this time it was Watson who picked up the loose ball and fired it into the net to signal an eruption of sound from the Notts fans after twenty-one minutes of play.

An appeal by the Bolton defence for the obstruction of Sutcliffe was disregarded by Mr Hughes and more extremely noisy cheering from the Notts fans as Mr Hughes pointed to the centre of the ground to confirm the goal. This was a tremendous boost to the Notts team, many of whom were present in the West Kirby Hotel the day before when Hendry said "If we score first we shall win" – they now had the chance to prove it.

At this stage Notts were playing fast attacking football with the Bolton defence struggling to contain them and more shots rained in at Sutcliffe but his goalkeeping was excellent and almost alone he was responsible for preventing Notts from adding to their lead. Bruce struck the post with a powerful shot. The Wanderers could not get the ball about as quickly as their opponents and when Bentley ought to have scored he shot feebly and it was not difficult for Toone to clear. Logan then made a solo run but when he got close his shot went into the side netting. Toone cleared from Bentley and the best bit of passing done so far by the Wanderers forwards ended in Wilson shooting only just wide.

Somerville twice stopped Daft and Bruce and then Jones running alongside Logan grassed him and cleared when a goal seemed likely to be scored. A splendid bit of combined play between Daft, Watson and Logan ended in the latter player taking the ball himself and after darting between Hughes and Somerville took aim and scored with a powerful shot that gave Sutcliffe no possible chance.

As the Notts fans burst into excited cheering there was once again a holding up of hands and vain appeals by the Bolton defenders but to no avail and Notts were two to the good.

Bolton worked hard to get back into the game but the Notts defence were able to dispossess them every time they came close to the Notts goal. The Wanderers appeared to lose a little heart at this stage while Notts on the other hand played with the confidence gained by having a two-goal lead and the way they were dictating the game.

Sutcliffe was playing outstandingly well and at times stood alone between Notts and a higher scoreline. In making a second save he fell and the ball ran loose, with four Notts men closing in on the ball but he was up in an instant to reclaim it and amid a burst of applause threw the ball well up the field. Next, Watson for Notts sent in a shot which skimmed just over the bar. Charge after charge was made by Notts, Logan forcing a corner which produced a second which came to nothing but how Bolton escaped without conceding another goal was down largely to the outstanding performance of their keeper Sutcliffe.

Just before half time Logan turned Somerville, his old team-mate at Ayr FC, one way, then the other with the Bolton defender eventually conceding a corner to bring the attack to a temporary halt. The corner came to nothing and play progressed during the closing stages of the first forty-five minutes in the Wanderers' goalmouth but Bolton's defence ensured there was no further score and the interval was sounded with Notts still two goals ahead.

The teams were allowed an interval of seven minutes after which Notts appeared first followed a couple of minutes later by the Bolton team and on re-appearing both teams were given a very enthusiastic welcome. Mr Hughes restarted the game, Logan kicked off but it was Bolton who went straight onto the attack. They went off like greyhounds determined to get back into the game. Wilson and Cassidy attacked the Notts goal togther, but Toone rushed out of his goal and dived full length to collect the ball and gained control of a dangerous situation.

A long punt into the centre by Tannahill was missed by Hendry and Toone had to leave his goal quickly to clear the ball. It didn't go far though and Cassidy was quickly on to the loose ball and sent in a fast low drive. Toone sprang back to his post in time to meet the shot which struck the upright and then Toone scrambled it over the goal line giving away a corner. Bruce cleared the danger from the corner with a powerful kick down the field and the next moment Logan was heading towards the Bolton goal at high speed with the ball at his feet, but on this occasion the attack came to nothing as the Bolton defenders successfully saw off the danger.

The football was now end-to-end, first Shelton stopped Cassidy and then at the other end Bruce and Daft, raced away but Somerville and Paton successfully halted the breakaway. Off went Cassidy at top speed, he beat Harper who was lying up the field and Hendry went forward to meet him. The Wanderer, however, tricked Hendry by knocking the ball one side of him and running past him on the other side and was just in the act of collecting the ball again when Toone rushed out and flung himself down and in doing so sent the ball back to Hendry who had time to clear the ball.

It was a good effort by Cassidy and had he been supported by his team mates, a goal may well have been the result. The Wanderers attacked again and after an initial clearance by Toone, Wilson picked up the loose ball and struck a shot that was heading for the top corner of the goal until Toone, at full stretch, touched the ball around the post and gave away a corner which came to nothing.

Logan, Donnelly and Watson raced up field with some slick interpassing resulting in a shot from Logan which was saved and cleared by Sutcliffe. It was then Cassidy's turn to race away at great speed but Hendry was in the way and in the collision the Wanderer was sent head-over-heels while Hendry calmly sent the ball sailing back up the field. All the play was now in the Bolton half with Notts' speed and swift passing getting the better of their opponents and hard luck alone prevented further scoring from Notts. Bramley missed by a few inches with a shot despatched by his favoured right foot. Notts were again on the attack and Logan got clean away and passed the ball to Daft who brought another fine save out of Sutcliffe.

Daft made a superb run down the left before putting in a cross straight to Logan, who raced clear of the sturdy Bolton defence before sending in a hard shot straight at Sutcliffe, who found the shot too hot to handle and the ball fell to the floor. Logan, 'sharp as a cat' was onto it and guided the ball through Sutcliffe's legs and into the net for Notts' third goal – much to the unbridled delight of the Notts supporters.

Somerville kicks behind for Safety.

An artist's impression of Somerville kicking behind for safety in the final

The cheering was tremendous and a big Notts flag was waved hysterically at one end of the ground, rattles were sprung and every Notts supporter made themselves generally as prominent as possible. This was about 18 minutes from the restart and the Boltonians appeared to be a beaten side and surely only the most remarkable bad luck could now stop Notts winning the cup. The followers of Notts were actually wild with delight at this further success, and a frenzied roar of applause greeted Logan as he walked back to the centre, whilst his team mates crowded round him and warmly shook hands with him.

Notts were now attacking the Wanderers defence time after time and with Paton failing to hold Daft, who centred to Logan who was once again the 'thorn in the side' of the Bolton defence as he carried the ball at high speed leaving both Gardiner and Hughes in his wake before being halted just by the goalpost by a Bolton defender but he remained cool and still managed to find a way to send the ball through the players in front of him and into the goal past Sutcliffe to complete a superb hat-trick amid more ecstatic cheers from the Notts faithful.

Reporters on the game posed the question – 'Had there ever been such a complete performance by a centre-forward in an FA Cup final as they had witnessed that afternoon?

When the Aintree races were finished many of the locals returning tried to gain access to the game, some were successful but others were turned away. Many Bolton fans began to leave the ground at this point convinced the game was over in favour of the Lacemen. The Notts men were looking head and shoulders better than their opponents who were being made to look a poor side. Logan and Donnelly each came within an ace of scoring and Sutcliffe kicked out a good shot from Watson.

Tannahill on the Bolton right wing got well up but his centre was not taken and Daft was soon making tracks for the other end of the field. Again and again Notts swept into the attack and never was such a fine defence, as the one from Bolton, given such a torrid time. Donnelly sent in a grand shot, Sutcliffe only just managing to save as Bruce got at him. Wilson then made a good run but finished up with a wild shot. Sutcliffe fell on the ball to save from

Logan and after a few more spasmodic efforts on the part of the Trotters, Daft all but beat Sutcliffe.

Bentley and Cassidy were each checked when dangerous and then Daft and Shelton each sent the ball over the bar. The Boltonians, however, pulled themselves together for a final effort as the gates of the ground were, according to the Lancashire tradition of the time, thrown open for free entrance in the last few minutes. Tannahill changed places with Wilson and Bentley, Cassidy and Tannahill playing clever passes with each other made some headway. A shot came in which Toone saved and pushed the ball out, but not far enough and he was on the ground as Cassidy collected the loose ball for an easy chance and scored for Bolton in the last minute of the match. Before the kick-off had been properly taken the whistle sounded and the game ended. It was all over and Notts County had won the FA Cup 4-1 much to the delight of their noisy followers.

Immediately after the game Lord Kinnaird presented the trophy to David Calderhead, the proud captain of Notts County, wishing him hearty congratulations on the team's splendid display as he did so.

Lord Kinnaird[21]

After seventeen years of trying, Notts County would finally be taking the FA Cup back to Nottingham for the first time in the history of the prestigious trophy. According to the various reports the triumph of the Notts team was thoroughly deserved as they were the better side with Bolton out manoeuvred and out-fought in all areas of the pitch. In the early stages the Wanderers had attacked well and Notts had a fair share of good fortune in keeping their goal intact.

Both sides eventually settled down and played some good football but after twenty-one minutes when Watson scored their first goal Notts took control and from that point on Bolton never looked as if they would win the game. There is little doubt that a major factor in the win for Notts was their superior speed. They set a high tempo to the game and maintained it right to the end.

---

[21] *Lord Kinnaird, was initially a public school footballer. Playing in long white trousers and quartered cap, and sporting a superb, flowing red beard, he was a great crowd pleaser, who, at the 1882 cup final stood on his head in front of the stands. He became an FA committeeman at the age of 21, in 1868, became treasurer in 1877 and president in 1890. He remained president for the next 33 years until his death in 1923, just months before the opening of Wembley Stadium.*

The temperature, of course, was exceptionally hot on the day and may have affected the result in some measure, but it was decidedly significant the manner in which the fleet-footed Notts forwards successfully got round and about the heavier Bolton back division, while at the back, Calderhead, the centre-half, played a real captain's role as he marshalled his men and led by example calmly dispossessing the opposition and then feeding and prompting his forwards with skilful and precise passes.

While most of the Bolton team failed to produce their best form, one man, the hardest worked man in the Bolton team, certainly did. Sutcliffe, the Bolton keeper, played an outstanding game. His exhibition of goalkeeping was of the highest level and had it not been for his extraordinary display between the posts the score against Bolton might easily have been doubled.

From *The Lancashire Daily Post*: *"The best team won, for Notts were far ahead of their opponents in speed, attack, resource and shooting. They established themselves favourites quite early and retained the position to the finish. It was a brilliant victory and a popular one all round."*

It was a really good team performance so it seems hardly fair to single out any one player for special praise, but Logan's feat of scoring three goals out of the four was so outstanding that the sporting press did pick him out for individual treatment.

In *The Athletic News*, 'The Tramp' heaped praise on all the team but singled out Logan thus: *"Logan's work speaks for itself. Three goals out of four in a final tie is an enduring testimonial to his brilliance and confirms his reputation as one of the deadliest shots in the British Isles. He was a clipper in full sail all through."*

The Manchester Courier printed, *"The game will be recollected by the conspicuous part played by Logan, the Notts forward. He kicked no fewer than three of the four goals, besides which was a regular thorn in the side of the Wanderers' defence. He kept his wings going and was individually the smartest man on the ground."*

The Birmingham Post: *"If anyone deserved special mention it is Logan who led the team with rare skill and judgment."*

The Birmingham Gazette: *"...and the hero of the day was Logan, the late centre forward of the Villa. It was indeed "Logan's Final"*

If Notts could reproduce their FA Cup final form when they play their test match game in four weeks' time it was going to take a very good side to stop them regaining their coveted place in amongst the elite of English football.

In Nottingham there was plenty of evidence of the keen interest that had been taken in the events at Goodison Park. In the streets of the town the colours of the Notts club were freely worn and from four o'clock onwards news of the progress of the game was eagerly awaited by large crowds at the various news agencies where the match scores would be posted. When it became known that at half time Notts were leading by two goals to nil great excitement was displayed and hopes were high that the cup would come to Nottingham for the first time. When the result came through soon after half-past five giving the score as four goals to one in favour of Notts there were huge celebrations taking place in many parts of the borough and notably at the headquarters of the Notts club at the Lion Hotel.

The winning team and the rest of their party were invited to attend a Liverpool hotel where they could celebrate their victory until it was time to leave to catch their train home. Never were officials and players more justly proud and elated than were those of Notts County with the historic, but dearly prized, old trophy taking pride of place on the top table at Liverpool on Saturday night.

The FA Cup won by Notts County in 1894

The cup was conveyed to Liverpool Central and the assembled vast crowds cheered and cheered with almost frenzied delight as the cup was produced from its well-worn wooden case. The players were the recipients of the most gratifying compliments and Mr Deplidge's appearance was the signal for a prolonged outburst of cheering so loud and enthusiastic that the horses in the station yard took fright.

Up came the huge saloon train and instantly there was a rush for the two specially reserved saloons marked with large letters stating: "Notts Directors." It required quite a struggle to get through the boisterous jovial and enthusiastic crowd but once safely inside the carriage the door was closed and the cup brandished aloft from the window. More cheering, more delight, more enthusiasm, more endearing expressions for the players and then good-bye to the seaport.

With their usual thoroughness the Notts directors had borne in mind the wants of their players and luncheon baskets were produced for each player. After they had consumed their meals there was only one topic of conversation as the match was relived over and over. All the players were warm in their praise of Sutcliffe, whose display they described as magnificent. "But for him," said Calderhead, "we would have won by a lot more goals."

All however, were quite satisfied with the result and even if they had won by a dozen goals they could not have been more happy and contented. Cheery little Donnelly said, "It's the proudest day of my life" while Calderhead, Logan, Hendry and others declared that their cup of happiness was full. Bruce, usually the most bashful man in the team, was so delighted that he yielded to a unanimous request for a song and right merrily he sang a charming little Highland ballad to the rest of the party. Other songs followed and the enthusiasm was at its height when the train came to a sudden stop at Stockport. There were whispered conversations between the directors and then out of the train bounced director William Gunn, returning to the saloon a few minutes later with the first instalment of a dozen bottles of champagne with which the health of the directors, players and everybody else was drunk, the English cup being used as a most suitable goblet. Of course there were some speeches and Mr Deplidge very gracefully complimented the team on their grand performances. Nottingham was reached in good time at about 10:30 and a coach and four awaited the party outside the station.

William Gunn – Notts County FC director

By nine o'clock there was a very large crowd around the station – particularly around the entrance, which in 1894 was on Station Street. Special police arrangements had been made to ensure there was not a rush onto the platform but a large number of people had bought tickets to the next station along the line in order to gain official access to the platform. By half-past nine Carrington Street had a lining of sightseers and the ranks were several deep about the juncton with Station Street while thousands were congregated in front of the station.

By ten o'clock there was a continuous crowd from St Peter's Church to the station, while from Canal Street onwards there was only a narrow line left for the passage of cabs and Station Street was completely thronged. Station Street is a miserably gloomy thoroughfare that would smudge out any other spectacle but though it concealed the sights it could not smother the noise – the cheerful effervescence of a huge crowd in a state of intense delight.

The only trace of colour in the street was the Wellington Hotel by its display of night-lights in rows of claret glasses at the windows of each storey, made the 'goings on' in the darkness slightly more visible. A line of youths had climbed up to sit on one of the railway walls and banged their heels on the enamelled advertisement sheets as they joined in with the music and singing.

As half-past ten approached the crowd began to seethe with excitement. Thump, thump, thump, went a drum, and some people at a distance began to hum, *See the Conquering Hero Comes* while others poured forward to wedge themselves into the dense crowd in front of the station entrance, that would have the privilege of the first welcoming shout. A cheer rose into a crescendo and swept like a breaking wave all along the street and then hushed into a silence that allowed the brass band to be heard as it played *The Man Who Broke the Bank at Monte Carlo* for the last long minute or two before the train was due. The crowd immediately joined in, singing along with the band as the expectation continued to build.

Then, when feeling had reached boiling point a shrill yell came along the station wall from the line of youngsters who suddenly forgot their clattering heel-taps and instead there could be heard the dull rumble of the incoming train. A moment's lull during which the opening notes of *See the Conquering Hero Comes* were heard and then Station Street bellowed with all its voices, waved all its arms and hustled all its bones in the biggest rugby scrum of the season.

As the train conveying the team emerged from beneath the bridge to come alongside the platform a mighty cheer went up. Alighting onto the platform the players were warmly greeted by their supporters and the cheers were given yet another boost as the club secretary, Tom Harris, raised the cup aloft. Outside the station an open carriage drawn by four horses was drawn up to await the winners and their leading supporters. The vast crowd were quickly aware of the arrival of the team and half-a-dozen sturdy fellows seized hold of Logan and carried him shoulder-high to the coach amidst the wildest excitement. Another minute and the team were in the coach while Tom Harris sat alongside the coachman and held the cup aloft in the gloom.

The coach and horses were following the brass band playing Handel's *See The Conquering Hero Comes* although the procession was moving extremely slowly because of the huge crowds. Happy were they who had taken up their station at the Canal Street crossing with Messrs Cullen's electric light at their service. The crowd had climbed walls and hung from lamp posts in an attempt to gain a good vantage point to see their heroes.

The extremely slow pace at which the triumphal procession advanced gave everybody a chance to see the team with the cup. Up Station Street, through Carrington Street and Lister Gate to the club's headquarters, namely the Lion Hotel in Clumber Street and each time Secretary Tom Harris held the cup aloft, the crowd went wild. There were thousands of spectators along both sides of the route taken which itself was gaily decorated with Chinese lamps, flags, bunting and the colours of the club as people literally shouted themselves hoarse.

It was a splendid reception, worthy of the team that had brought the FA Cup to Nottingham for the very first time in its history. As the procession turned into Carrington Street there was more light thanks to the electric lamps at a number of the business premises so the scene was even more strikingly impressive. As the crowd moved with the team it became necessary to temporarily suspend the movement of the tramway traffic. Some of the more enthusiastic of the Notts supporters attempted to clamber aboard the coach as it crawled along the road.

The team finally reached the Lion Hotel after 45 minutes, a very picturesque setting with flags flying from every window, decorations in the clubs colours, lights burning on the balcony and other bunting. Huge crowds of people outside the hotel were cheering and singing their heroes' praises which created quite a reception for the team and club officials.

A row of policemen kept the fans at bay until all the players and the rest of the party were inside then only as the door closed with all safely inside did the police relax their control of the crowd. Mr Edward Booth, the licensed victualler of the Lion Hotel, had made preparations for the reception of his guests and the hotel was crowded with enthusiasts waiting to tender their congratulations.

Upstairs in the large dining hall the team was received and it didn't take long before Tom Harris, still carrying the cup, went out onto the balcony to display the cup and ask for 'Three cheers for Notts' which the crowd below immediately delivered. Joe Goode the trainer, was given a word of praise for the great care and attention he had given the players during the time he had held the role.

That night the cup was filled, emptied and refilled again and again with Mr Booth's best champagne. Amongst the many speeches made that night was a very gracious one from Mr George Seldon, one of a number of people in attendance representing the Nottingham Forest committee. He congratulated Notts on their success and proposed a toast that both Nottingham clubs should go on and prosper in the future.

As soon as the immediate celebrations that evening were at an end Jimmy was given permission to make a visit home to Ayr for a few days where his wife was very close to giving birth to their second child.

Four days after the final on Wednesday, April 4, the cup-winning celebrations continued as the team and directors were entertained, once again at the Lion Hotel, this time at a banquet by Lord Henry Cavendish-Bentinck the Conservative candidate for Nottingham South.

The place was full of local celebrities, JPs, councillors, renowned sportsmen etc. Members of the Notts FC board who attended were: R. Deplidge (chairman), T. E. Harris (secretary), R. Coppack (treasurer), W. Gunn, H. J. Vann, A. Sibert, J. G. Thomas, H. Heath, W. T. Bramley, J.W. Shepperson and T. R. Featherstone (directors). Cup winning players present were: George Toone, John Hendry, Charles Bramley, David Calderhead, Alf Shelton, Arthur Watson, Sam Donnelly, Dan Bruce and Harry Daft – only Theo Harper and Jimmy Logan (who was at home in Scotland) did not put in an appearance.

Congratulatory speeches were made praising the club, the board, the players and Joe Goode received plenty of praise for the condition in which he kept the players, not just for the cup final but all season long. After the speeches Mr Harris read out a couple of messages. The first, a telegram from Mr J. J. Bentley of Notts' cup final opponents Bolton Wanderers, said; *"Allow me to congratulate your team on their big but thoroughly deserved victory yesterday."* The second was a letter from H. S. Radford, secretary of Nottingham Forest FC which said *"Dear Sir, Will you convey to your players and executive the congratulations of the Forest Club on your splendid victory today. Your men, by their devotion to the club's interests and the manner in which they have played in the Cup ties, are a credit to the town and they richly deserved their success. I am sure you will accept the congratulations of your old opponents in the spirit in which they are offered."* After these messages of congratulations many volunteers were up and singing their favourite songs. It was reported as being an excellent evening by all concerned.

The Notts County FC 1894 FA Cup Winning team
Back: Charles Bramley, Theophilus Harper, David Calderhead, George Toone,
John Hendry, Alfred Shelton, Joe Goode (trainer)
Front: Arthur Watson, Sam Donnelly, Jimmy Logan, Daniel Bruce, Harry Daft

The following appeared in the *Coventry Evening Telegraph* on Monday, April 2, 1894: *By winning the English Cup final Notts County team and their trainer (Goode) come in for a sum of £300, which Mr. Deplidge (chairman of the Notts directors) had promised them in the event of success crowning their game and the cup going to Nottingham.*

As FA Cup holders Notts County FC were in demand and received plenty of invitations from clubs wishing to play them in friendly games. For a club never far away from the next financial crisis it must have been difficult to turn down some of the guaranteed amounts of money they were being offered. Against that they also had to balance the fact that they still had work to do with an important final league game to play before the end of season test match which would decide in which division they played their football the following season.

So the final month of the season was more about Notts, as a club, making the most of their new celebrity status and 'cashing in' as best they could, while they could. Friendly matches were played with Crouch End (won 6-1) for £30, Everton (lost 0-3) for £20 and a long trek to Scotland to meet Rangers (lost 1-3) for a guarantee of £50.

FOOTBALL MATCHES.

GRAND EVENING MATCH — TO-NIGHT (MONDAY).
RANGERS
Scottish Cup-Holders, versus
NOTTS COUNTY
English Cup-Holders.
Ibrox Park. Kick-off at 6.30 prompt. Admission 6d.
Ladies Free. Covered Stand 6d., North Stand 3d. each person.

Advert for the Rangers v Notts game from the *Scottish Sport* newspaper

On Friday, April 6, Jimmy Logan's second son, William, brother to Jimmy junior was born at the family home at Union Avenue in Ayr.

The next day, the Notts team travelled to Birmingham to play Small Heath in their final League fixture of the season in the hope that it would be the last game they played in the Second Division. Both clubs had already qualified for the test matches but this game would determine which of them finished second behind Liverpool and it would therefore decide which opponents each would face in those games.

The winner would probably play Darwen while the loser would be against traditionally the stronger Preston North End. Unfortunately, Logan was unable to take part in the match, having 'not yet recovered from his indisposition', although he had returned from Scotland and did travel with the team to Birmingham. Notts were simply 'not at the races', played poorly and were convincingly beaten 3-0.

The foot of the First Division at the close of the 1893/94 season

	Pl	W	D	L	F	A	Pts
The Wednesday	30	9	8	13	48	57	26
Bolton Wanderers	30	10	4	16	38	52	24
Preston North End	30	10	3	17	44	56	23
Darwen	30	7	5	18	37	83	19
Newton Heath	30	6	2	22	36	72	14

The top of the Second Division at the close of the 1893/94 season.

	Pl	W	D	L	F	A	Pts
Liverpool	28	22	6	0	77	18	50
Small Heath	28	21	0	7	103	44	42
Notts County	**28**	**18**	**3**	**7**	**70**	**31**	**39**
Newcastle	28	15	2	11	71	58	32
Grimsby	28	15	2	11	71	58	32

The result meant Notts would meet Preston in a test match to determine which of them would be appearing in the First Division during the 1894/95 season. Liverpool would meet Newton Heath while Small Heath would meet Darwen. Bolton, Notts' FA Cup final opponents won their last game of the season 2-0 against Sunderland to avoid meeting Notts again, this time in the test matches, by a single point.

At a meeting of the Football League Management Committee at Manchester on April 10 the test matches were confirmed to be played on Saturday, April 28, and in the event of a drawn game, matches must be played to a finish on the following Monday on the same grounds.

Small Heath	v	Darwen (at Stoke)
Newton Heath	v	Liverpool (at Blackburn)
Preston North End	**v**	**Notts County (at Sheffield)**

The FA Cup celebrations continued with a smoking concert at the Albert Hall, Nottingham on Friday, April 13. There was a large attendance and the gallery was occupied almost exclusively by ladies. The platform was decorated with ferns and other plants while the front of the organ was partially covered with national flags. The much coveted FA Cup, decorated in the club's colours was on display on the top table. Amongst those present were county councillors, the Notts County directors, local celebrities and most of the Notts County players.

Those present were entertained musically by solos, duets, violin solos and humorous songs, including a ballad singer, dressed in black and white and sang his own version of *The man who broke the bank at Monte Carlo* entitled 'The Team that Broke the Hearts of Bolton Wanderers'. The entertainment was very well received by all present and was met with tumultuous applause. Speeches then praised the directors for guiding the club to the winning of the cup and for guiding the club through financially difficult times during the last few years.

The players were then presented with their medals in the following order; David Calderhead, George Toone, John Hendry, Theo Harper, Charles Bramley, Arthur Watson, Sam Donnelly, Jimmy Logan and Dan Bruce. Harry Daft and Alf Shelton were absent. Each player was loudly cheered as they received their medal. At midnight the concert was terminated with the singing of Robert Burns' *Auld Lang Syne*.

**The winner's medal each Notts player received.
This one belonged to Theo Harper, the right-back.
I am forever grateful to the late Haydn Green who allowed me to borrow the
medal for a few days**

Immediately after the Midland League game between Newark and Loughborough on Saturday, April 21, a Newark team played Notts County for the benefit of Margaret, the widow of Alex 'Sandy' Ferguson, a member of Notts County's 1891 FA Cup Final team and later the captain of Newark FC who had died on March 28 while back visiting in Glasgow at the age of only 27 with news reaching the Notts squad on the morning of their second FA Cup Final appearance.

Notts had their full cup-winning team - but with a difference. Toone the England international goalkeeper was playing at centre-half with full-back Hendry lining up 'between the sticks' and Calderhead replacing him at full-back. The Newark team was a mixture of old Newark FC players and the more senior Notts players who had been team-mates of Sandy. The Newark team included Stuart Macrae, Frank Wilkinson, Bobby Jardine, Albert Williamson, Archie Osborne and George Kerr. Notts ran out 2-1 winners but more importantly the attendance was much better than at the earlier Midland League match and a fair sum would have been handed over to the widow of the late Newark captain and Notts FA Cup finalist.

So despite lifting the FA Cup and enjoying victories over seven First Division clubs in various competitions and friendly games during the season, it all counted for nothing and Notts had just 90 minutes in the test match against Preston North End to show that they were worthy of a return to the First Division. Preston were one of the most successful clubs in the Football League. This was the sixth season of the League and in the previous five Preston had finished no lower than second – this was the first time they had slipped below their own very high standards.

An injury to Hendry received in the game against Everton meant that he was unfit to play so Calderhead switched to full-back and Frank Wilkinson came in at centre-half. Both sides showed great anxiety and passes were going astray because of the added pressure of the occasion. Notts were having their share of the play but, once again, were playing below their cup tie form.

From a throw-in, Cowan centred beautifully and Henderson headed on and Drummond scored to put Preston ahead half an hour after the start of the game. Preston were now playing with confidence, while Notts appeared to have lost theirs. After some fine passing Ross found himself in front of goal and he scored a second goal to put Preston further ahead.

Preston took control of the game and Cowan followed a good run by thumping the ball against the cross-bar with a terrific shot. Notts were so far below their best form as they dithered and hesitated in all areas of the pitch - so different from their cup form. A rush uphill by Drummond drew Toone from his goal to clear but before he could recover his position Cunningham had sent the ball into the Notts net for the third time. Half time was signalled.

Play was resumed just before five o'clock. The Notts halves, by strong play, worked the ball into the Preston quarters but the forwards lacked the dash, fire and energy, which had characterised them all season. Preston were piling on the pressure and Notts could not clear the ball away. After seven minutes of the second half Cowan centred splendidly and Henderson met the ball and shot into the net for a 4-0 lead. Soon afterwards a heavy charge by Bramley hurt Cunningham and he had to leave the field. The next minute Notts finally got close to the Preston goal and Daft let fly with a beauty which struck the bar with a resounding thud. A very disappointing performance from Notts came to an end.

Notts were the only second-tier side taking part in the test matches that failed to gain promotion to the First Division. In the other matches Small Heath made few mistakes against Darwen as they secured a 3-1 victory and Liverpool, who had remained unbeaten in the League throughout the season, continued their excellent run of results with a 2-0 victory against Newton Heath.

So Notts failed to recapture the form of their incredible cup run.

Whether it was due to the extended celebrations or pure exhaustion on the part of the players from the busy programme of the 11 matches played in only 26 days after the final, we will never know. What we do know is that Notts failed completely to do themselves justice with probably their most disappointing performance of the season and were thrashed 4-0 in the all important test match. It was immediately suggested that the cup holders should be elected to the First Division, but the League would not hear of such a thing and Notts would have to try again the following season for that elusive promotion.[22]

The season ended on another low for the club when Blackburn Rovers reported Notts County for approaching their full-back John Murray through their player William Campbell.

John Murray

[22] *Notts County had to wait until 1896/97 to achieve the elusive promotion back to the top flight when only George Toone, Charles Bramley and David Calderhead, of the cup winning team still remained.*

A letter written by Notts' Campbell to John Murray was opened by a Blackburn club director – also named Murray - which exposed the approach. The letter was produced for the management committee of the English League where the letter suggested Notts were prepared to offer Murray terms. Notts were found guilty of this offence by the Football Association and the club was suspended for taking part in the first fourteen days of the 1894/95 season. Campbell was suspended until October 1, though moved on to Newark FC without playing a single first team game for the Magpies.

SUSPENSION OF NOTTS. COUNTY.

At 61, Chancery-lane, London, yesterday afternoon, Mr. J. C. Clegg, of Sheffield, presided over a council meeting of the above association, when some important business was transacted.

The report of the commission on (1) Mr. Lewis's complaint re Aston Villa spectators; (2) Notts. County approaching Murray, of Blackburn Rovers; and (3) Mr. Morris's report of misconduct of players in the match between Burnley and Accrington on March 24th, resulted in Notts. County being suspended until September 14th next, whilst Campbell was suspended until October 1st.

News of Notts County's suspension in the *Nottingham Evening Post* on May 29, 1894

The news for Jimmy Logan was more personal. And deeply tragic. Only a few months after the cup win, Jimmy and his family, after a summer break in Scotland, were in Nottingham, possibly to attend team mate Jack Hendry's marriage to local girl Alice Smith on July 23 at St George's parish church.

Tragedy struck, however, just two days before the wedding when Jimmy's son William, aged only three months, died from bronchitis. *Scottish Referee* carried the following paragraph; *"The many friends of Jimmy Logan, both in England and Scotland, will regret to hear that the popular Notts centre-forward has had the misfortune to lose his little infant boy during the past week. The child caught a chill when Logan was returning to Nottingham after his summer holidays in Scotland."* A few days later William was buried at the General Cemetery in Nottingham.

CHAPTER SIXTEEN

August 1894 – March 1895

Hero to Zero

IT CAME as no surprise when Notts re-engaged most of the FA Cup winning team for the following season. The players retained included George Toone, Jack Hendry, Theo Harper, Davie Calderhead, Alf Shelton, Charles Bramley, Frank Wilkinson, Harry Daft, Sam Donnelly, Jimmy Logan and Dan Bruce who all signed on the dotted line for 1894/95.

Once again, the priority was to restore their top flight status. With that in mind, the Magpies added to their ranks Brown a goalkeeper from Forest, Murray a full-back from local team Bulwell, Chadburn from Lincoln and Elijah Allsopp from Bury.

The club also announced it intended to run a reserve team in the Notts League composed mainly of amateurs against the likes of Forest Reserves, Sutton Town, Bulwell United, Bestwood Institute, Kimberley and two Hucknall teams St. Johns and Portland.

Arthur Watson   **Archie Osborne**   **George Kerr**

The departing players were Arthur Watson, who had expressed a desire to return to his previous club Mansfield Town, Archie Osborne, who joined Clyde and George Kerr, who also returned to Scotland and his favoured centre-forward position for his home town club Annbank.

On the August 6 Bank Holiday, Notts staged their third annual Athletics Sports Day at Trent Bridge.

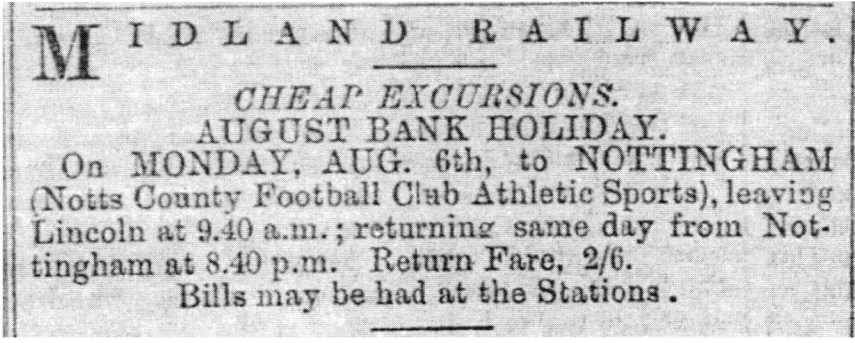

An advert in the *Lincolnshire Chronicle* offers transport to the club's Sports Day

After a wet start to the day the sun came out and the crowd climbed to around 6,000. The wicket in the centre of the field was staked off to avoid any damage, strings were laid down along the Gamston Lane side for the sprint races and the cycle track was marked out with four laps to the mile. Over 200 athletes had applied to compete and the organisation and day were a great success.

As previously mentioned, Notts began the season suspended for the first two weeks of the season, September 1-14, so their pre-season games consisted of games against the reserve team to get themselves into condition. It was reported that the suspension cost the club in the region of £200 – a huge amount for a club already experiencing financial difficulties. Without the funds brought in by the club's annual summer sports it is not improbable that Notts would have been dissolved.

Monday, August 20, was the first day of training for the new season and only two players, Harry Daft and Elijah Allsopp, were absent from the initial session at the Castle Ground. Of the players reported back some, including Logan, looked fit and ready to start a League match immediately. Others did not, among them the habitual worst offender Dan Bruce, having gained possibly seven pounds during the summer break. Still, no-one was in any doubt that Dan would be ready to go come Saturday, September 15.

Some 3,000 spectators warmly applauded and cheered the cup holders as they stepped onto the field. More practice sessions took place on Monday, August 27, then Thursday that week, Tuesday, September 4, and the following Saturday when new faces in the reserve team were tried out.

The players were in good spirits during these practice sessions, usually first team against the reserves with one or two players changing sides to add to the competition. In the second practice game the first team put four goals past Toone who was in goal for the reserves. At least one of the goals was completely illegal as Logan playfully bundled Toone into the back of his net whilst a team-mate scored a goal with Toone sprawled inside the goal helpless to save the shot.

Division Two table on September 14:

	Pl	W	D	L	GF	GA	Pts
Burton Wanderers	3	2	1	0	5	2	5
Bury	2	2	0	0	8	3	4
Grimsby Town	3	2	0	1	10	8	4
Darwen	2	2	0	0	11	0	4
Manchester City	3	1	1	1	7	6	3
Burton Swifts	2	1	0	1	7	6	2
Leicester Fosse	2	1	0	1	7	6	2
Walsall Town Swifts	2	1	0	1	4	4	4
Newcastle United	2	1	0	1	6	8	2
Lincoln City	2	1	0	1	5	8	2
Burslem Port Vale	2	1	0	1	2	4	2
Notts County	**0**	**0**	**0**	**0**	**0**	**0**	**0**
Rotherham Town	2	0	0	2	3	7	0
Woolwich Arsenal	2	0	0	2	3	8	0
Crewe Alexandra	2	0	0	2	1	8	0
Newton Heath	1	0	0	1	0	1	0

Notts' season finally got underway with a home game against Darwen on the Castle Ground on September 15. Darwen had won both their previous two games, scoring eleven goals while conceding none – so a tough starter.

Nine of the FA Cup-winning team turned out with only Arthur Watson (now Mansfield) and Sam Donnelly, whose mother had died the day before the game, missing. John Chadburn and Elijah Allsopp replaced them.

Around 10,000 were present and the Notts team were met with a tremendous reception as they entered the playing surface. Calderhead raced onto a fine pass from Daft to score past Briggs the Darwen custodian, to give Notts the lead after only twelve minutes. Darwen equalised but a fine shot by Bruce smacked against the crossbar and the ball rebounded straight to Chadburn who made no mistake in knocking it into the net to win the game 2-1. It wasn't Jimmy Logan's day, with his first shot going just the wrong side of the post and a later shot striking the post and being cleared.

Even so, the season started well, Notts winning five and drawing one of their first six games and Jimmy was once again amongst the goals, scoring five. However, after a game away at Woolwich Arsenal a twisted knee put him out for the next three League games. Jimmy's cup final team-mate Dan Bruce stepped into the breach, helping Notts win all three games in Jimmy's absence with Bruce netting three times.

On November 17, Notts played a friendly game away against Corinthian FC at the Kennington Oval, the famous amateur team, Notts shading an exciting tussle 4-3 (Bruce 3, Fletcher). A team photograph, below, was snapped before that encounter.

Notts County 1894/95
Back row: Tom Harris (Secretary), John Chadburn, Sam Donnelly, William Gunn (Director), Fred Fletcher, Elijah Allsopp, Joe Goode (Trainer)
Front row: John Hendry, Alf Shelton, Charles Bramley, David Calderhead, Dan Bruce, Alf Harrison, James Stothert.
The photograph was taken away at the Kennington Oval before the friendly with Corinthian FC at a time when Harry Daft, George Toone and Jimmy Logan were all missing with injury or illness so the team had an unusual look to it.
Keeper George Toone's replacement on the day was Alf Harrison who made only one League appearance for the club, in the next game at home to Bury. Yet here he is on the team photo for 1894/95

Notts had clawed their way up to third in the table and December 1 faced a trip to lowly Leicester Fosse. Jimmy returned from injury but he was chosen to play at inside-right allowing Bruce to retain the centre-forward role he had been performing so well. However Notts played badly and were crushed 5-1.

In fear of losing their coveted top three position, which ensured an end of season test match not unlike today's play-offs and thus chance to return to the top division, changes were made and the three members of the 'old guard' were the target.

Full-back Theo Harper and left-half Alf Shelton were dropped, but before Harry Daft joined them, he got wind of the club's intentions and submitted his resignation. The trio were all approaching thirty years of age. Daft joined his ex team-mate William Campbell who was by then the skipper at Newark.

Without them Notts lost 1-0 at Burton Wanderers with Jimmy taking Shelton's place at left-half, a position he had not played since his time at Ayr FC.

After that, Bruce was moved out to the left-wing with Jimmy re-installed at centre-forward with Harper and Shelton re-instated to their usual positions. Unfortunately Jimmy's best form deserted him and in the next nine games, apart from goals against two relegation/re-election threatened teams in Walsall and Crewe Alexandra, he fired seven blanks and comments were appearing in the sporting newspapers about his poor form.

As cup-winning right-back Theo Harper wound down his Notts career, a replacement was eagerly sought and in the second half of the season with no less than half-a-dozen different men (Walter Arnott, Dan Bruce, Walter Bull, Frank Guttridge, William Hall and James Stothart) were all tried in that position.

The New Year saw both Notts and Logan become very inconsistent. On Saturday, February 2, the FA Cup holders crashed out of the competition in the very first round 5-1 at The Wednesday with the *Nottinghamshire Guardian* writing; *"Logan was disappointing in the centre, as he has been in many recent matches."*

A week later Notts played Wednesday again, this time in the United Counties League and once again tasted defeat, this time 2-0 with the *Athletic News* summing up Jimmy's performance with, *"Logan was again weak in the centre."*

Notts' next game, on February 16, was a friendly at Trent Bridge against Small Heath (who later became Birmingham City). The management committee rested Allsopp, Donnelly and Bramley and also decided to try out a few positional changes. One of those changes was an amazing decision to put the 'out-of-form' centre-forward Jimmy Logan in their problem position at right-back!

The *Birmingham Daily Post* explaining; *"... placing Logan full-back instead of centre-forward, his efforts in the latter position having been not altogether successful this season."* Although Notts took the lead, it was not a surprise that Jimmy had a terrible time at right-back a local reporter writing: *'A run was made by the visitors with Walton easily getting the better of Logan and had no difficulty in equalising.'* and *'Walton, who had crossed over on the left side easily passed Logan who was quite helpless, and shot a second goal.'* So, after being in the lead, Jimmy was badly exposed, because he wasn't a right-back, making the half-time score 2-1 to Small Heath.

The second half saw Notts line up with only ten men as Jimmy failed to re-appear. As there was no sign of an injury, and substitutes not allowed, Jimmy was letting down the rest of his team-mates. Ironically, the 10-men performed better without him and salvaged a 3-3 draw.

The local press pulled no punches with: *'Logan at back was a failure, as may be understood when it is stated that Notts did quite as well, if not better, in the second half without him as they did in the first. The only cause assigned for his retirement was that he did not care for the remarks some of the spectators were making with regard to him.'*

That was to be Jimmy's final appearance for the Notts County first team.

Jimmy was dropped and the team rubbed salt into his wounds in the next game by beating Burslem Port Vale 10-0 with centre-forward Dan Bruce netting five of the goals.

'Retlaw' in the *Scottish Referee* summarised the situation as follows: *"Jimmy Logan the old Ayr, Sunderland and Aston Villa centre-forward, is doing badly for Notts County this season. Last year he earned a great name for himself by his brilliant, dashing play, and the three goals he scored against Bolton Wanderers in the final of the English Cup will long be remembered. But he seems to have lost all his old skill. He has been tried at left half-back, but without success and on Saturday last, against Small Heath, he partnered Hendry at full-back. This position suited Logan least of all and so annoyed did he become at the remarks of the crowd, who have forgotten his brilliant play of last season, that he left the field long before the finish of the game."*

Jimmy made one final appearance for Notts County – in the reserves – at Trent Bridge on Saturday, March 2, against Bestwood Institute in front of about 2,500 fans. The second team won 6-0 with Jimmy scoring a hat-trick. They were to be Jimmy's last goals for the club because in early March he left Nottingham and returned home to Scotland, treading a now familiar path from an English club back to his roots.

Notts responded by suspending Jimmy but it was a futile act as Jimmy had no intention of returning and when Dundee contacted Notts about a transfer to their club, it was reported that *'Notts placed no difficulty in the way of Logan's transfer, not even asking a fee.'*

The rise and fall was indeed dramatic. Rightly hailed as an FA Cup final hero, fêted by fans and the press alike for his historic hat-trick that proved to be a glorious match-winning contribution at Goodison Park, just a few short months later he was leaving, tail between his legs, a virtual outcast neither wanted by Notts County nor appreciated by their supporters.

From hero to zero was putting it mildly.

CHAPTER SEVENTEEN

March 1895 – June 1895

Dundee – a brief visit

AN AMALGAMATION of Our Boys and Dundee East End formed Dundee Football Club in May 1893 and the new club's application for membership of the Scottish League was accepted at that organisation's AGM the following month. For such a new team they were a good side competing in the Scottish First Division and had just reached the semi-final of the Scottish Cup.

Dundee FC 1895/96
Back row: Mr J. McIntosh, Mr T. Shaw, Mr W.T. Kennedy, Johnny Darroch, Fred Barrett, Charlie Burgess, Mr W. Saunders, Mr J. Black (referee), Adam Marshall (trainer)
Front row: Mr J. McMahon, Willie Thompson, Sandy Gilligan, Jimmy Dundas, Bill Hendry, Bill Longair, George Phillip, Alex Black, Sandy Keillor

Sandy Keillor, who had played in the same Scotland team as Jimmy back in 1891, was a member of the Dundee squad of players that Jimmy had joined. By March 1895 they were battling to avoid having to apply for re-election - finish in the bottom three and that was your fate. Dundee, with four games to play, all away from home at Hearts, Third Lanark, Celtic and Clyde sat fourth from bottom of the table.

The bottom six teams in the Scottish League First Division as at March 18, 1895:

	Pl	W	D	L	F	A	Pts
St Bernards	14	7	1	6	35	31	15
3rd L.R.V.	14	7	1	6	40	33	15
Dundee	**14**	**5**	**2**	**7**	**24**	**24**	**12**
Clyde	13	6	0	7	31	37	12
Leith Athletic	16	3	0	13	26	57	6
Dumbarton	16	2	0	14	23	56	4

Jimmy had joined Dundee just a couple of weeks after the club had lost in the semi-final of the Scottish Cup to Renton in an epic tussle. The first game, at home, ended in a 1-1 draw with both goals being own goals! A late penalty miss by Dundee's Bill Sawyers meant the teams had to meet again in a replay. The replay, played at Hampden Park in front of 20,000 was another draw – this time 3-3.

The third and decisive tie was played at Parkhead in front of 29,000 and Renton finally prevailed 3-0. The Cup was eventually won by St Bernard's who beat Renton 2-1 in the final.

After registration clearance, Jimmy was available for the game at Heart of Midlothian on Saturday, March 30. It was a good day to play Hearts because three of their Scottish internationals David Russell (who had hidden in disguise in the Ayr FC stand back in 1890/91), Isaac Begbie and John Walker had been called away to play for Scotland against Ireland in the Home International Championships at Celtic Park in Glasgow.

Not for the first time in his football career Jimmy had been ill all week leading up to his debut. Even without their three internationals Hearts were too strong, winning easily 4-0. With Jimmy probably feeling weak and listless from his illness he was still reported in the *Glasgow Herald* as follows: "*...the Hearts back division were having a warm time warding off hot shots from Logan...*" so under the circumstances a promising debut against a team which a couple of weeks later would be crowned champions.

Jimmy would make his home debut at Carolina Port a week after the Hearts game. The Carolina Port ground was located between Eastern Wharf and Camperdown Street, east of the Dundee city centre. It had a capacity of 12,500 including a 1,500-seater stand. It was opened at the end of the 1891/92 season when it was host to the Forfarshire Cup Final with Montrose beating Dundee East End 5-3 (East End's fourth consecutive cup final defeat). Dundee took over the ground midway through the 1893/94 season when they moved from their West Craigie Park.[23]

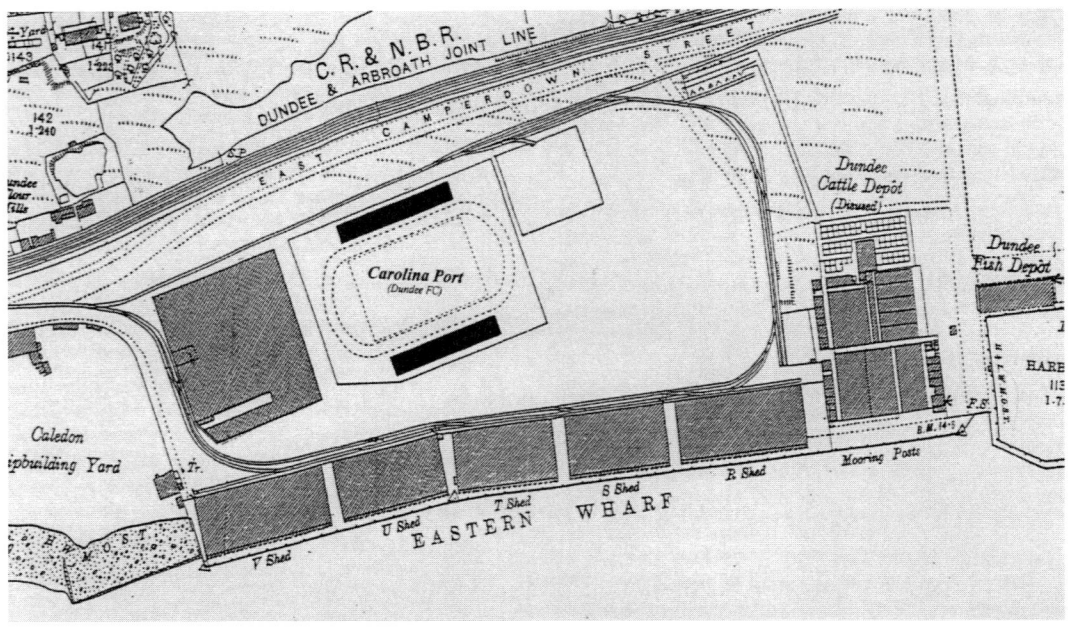

A map showing approximately where Carolina Port pitch would have been situated

---

[23] *When Dundee moved out of Carolina Park to move to Dens Park in 1899 the site was very quickly absorbed into the expanding docklands.*

An illustration showing Carolina Port – where a handy rubbish dump made a free 'grandstand'

Dundee FC in action against unknown opposition at Carolina Port in the 1890s

Jimmy's home debut was a friendly against Kilmarnock arranged because Dundee had no League game on April 6 and it was important to keep the team in good condition as they continued their fight against re-election. A close encounter ended 1-1 with the *Dundee Evening Telegraph* reporting: "*Logan was anything but a success. That he is – or was – a player one could easily see, but he either would not, or was not able to do himself justice.*"

Dundee's next game on the Spring Holiday, Monday, April 8, was another friendly at home against Jimmy's old team Sunderland (who had finished runners-up to Aston Villa in the previous 1893/94 season) but he was absent from the game and it is unclear if he was injured, rested or just unavailable for some reason as Dundee lost 2-0.

A week later it was the turn of Queen's Park to visit Carolina Park for a friendly. Once again there was no sign of Jimmy Logan and once again Dundee lost 2-0 then on Saturday, April 20, it was the turn of Blackburn Rovers to visit Carolina Park and claim a 3-1 win, once again the name of Logan was missing from the home team sheet.

In the middle of his time at Dundee, on Monday, April 22, he was back in action on a football field but it was for his old club Ayr rather than his current one. Jimmy was invited by his first senior club to make a guest appearance for them in a prestigious friendly at Somerset Park against Preston North End who were in the process of a tour around a number of Scottish clubs.

Also guesting for Ayr were Queen's Park and Scotland internationals William Gulliland and Tom Waddell – Gulliland and Logan being Scottish international team mates in the 4-3 win over Wales. A gusty wind made good football difficult but the 3,000 crowd still enjoyed the entertainment which finished in a 1-1 draw with Drummond scoring for Preston and Gulliland equalising for Ayr.

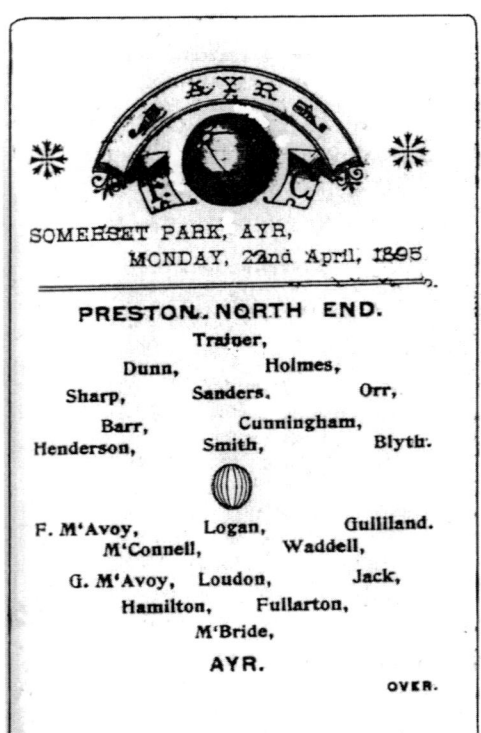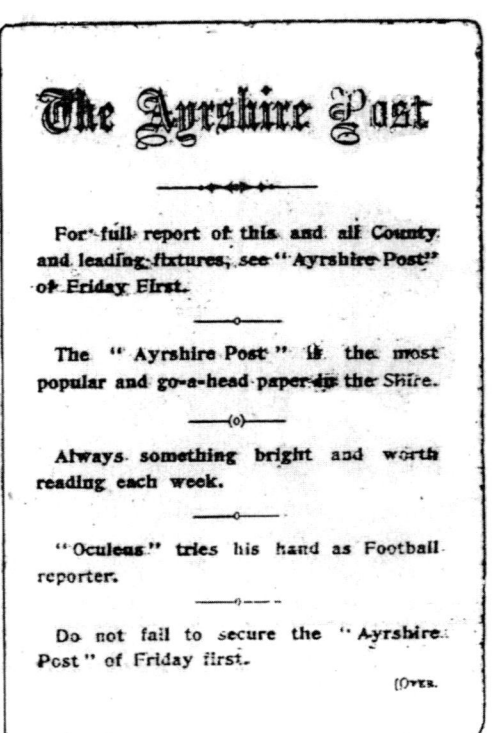

A copy of the match card from the Ayr FC v Preston North End match

It was back to the league struggle for Dundee and the next two Saturdays saw a 3-1 win at Third Lanark followed by a 2-1 defeat against Celtic at Celtic Park. Jimmy Logan was in neither team but after his appearance for Ayr against Preston it was clear he was not ill or injured.

The defeat to Celtic meant that Dundee's fate would hang on the final game of the season against fellow-strugglers Clyde – both teams had played 17 games and both teams had 14 points. The loser's future would be out of their hands as they faced a vote by the Scottish Football League as to who should keep their First Division status and who should be relegated to the Second Division.

A final friendly against East Stirlingshire on May 11 in preparation saw Jimmy Logan restored to centre-forward. Dundee played well and ran out 3-0 winners. *The Dundee Courier* reported that Jimmy Logan was *'slightly better than he was the last time he appeared'* – hardly a glowing tribute.

The Dundee FC 1895/96 team in their 'civvies'.
Standing: Adam Marshall (trainer), Johnny Darroch, Francis Barrett, Joe Fleming.
Middle row: Jimmy Dundas, Bill Longair, Sandy Keillor
Front row: Bill Thompson, Davie McInroy, Willie Maxwell, Bill Sawyers, Sandy Gilligan

Scottish First Division May 13, 1895:

	Pl	W	D	L	F	A	Pts
Heart of Midlothian	18	15	1	2	50	18	31
Celtic	18	11	4	3	50	29	26
Rangers	18	10	2	6	41	26	22
Third Lanark	18	10	1	7	51	39	21
St Mirren	18	9	1	8	34	34	19
St Bernards	18	8	1	9	37	40	17
Dundee	**17**	**6**	**2**	**9**	**28**	**31**	**14**
Clyde	17	7	0	10	36	47	14
Dumbarton	18	3	1	14	27	58	7
Leith Athletic	18	3	1	14	32	64	7

The Dundee team set off for Clyde on Saturday, May 18, leaving Tay Bridge Station at ten o'clock in the morning knowing that a draw would maintain their safe fourth-from-bottom berth – while Clyde HAD to win to guarantee safety. Jimmy Logan started at centre-forward knowing that he had not scored a single goal for Dundee but there would be no better time than this crucial game to open his account.

Dundee began well and had the best of it in the first half but the forwards could not find the goal their play deserved. Early in the second half Dundee lost Bill Thompson through injury and so played most of the second half with only ten men. It was a classic 'game of two halves'. Dundee dominated the first half without managing to score and then Clyde took advantage of their superior numbers and scored twice to win the game and achieve safety, while Dundee FC had to await their fate in the League meeting.

Scottish First Division 1894/95 – final table

	Pl	W	D	L	F	A	Pts
Heart of Midlothian	18	15	1	2	50	18	31
Celtic	18	11	4	3	50	29	26
Rangers	18	10	2	6	41	26	22
Third Lanark	18	10	1	7	51	39	21
St Mirren	18	9	1	8	34	34	19
St Bernards	18	8	1	9	37	40	17
Clyde	18	8	0	10	38	47	16
Dundee	**18**	**6**	**2**	**10**	**28**	**33**	**14**
Leith Athletic	18	3	1	14	32	64	7
Dumbarton	18	3	1	14	27	58	7

The SFL met at Glasgow on Monday, June 3. The bottom three clubs, Dundee, Leith Athletic and Dumbarton, applied for re-election with Hibernians (Champions of the Second Division) and Motherwell (runners-up of the Second Division) applying for election to the First Division.

The outcome was that both Dundee and Dumbarton were re-elected while Leith Athletic were relegated to be replaced by Second Division champions Hibernians.

How much of the nail-biting wait for news of Dundee's fate affected Jimmy Logan is impossible to know, but what is known is that within only a few days it was announced in the sporting newspapers that, approaching his 25th birthday, he had signed for Newcastle United.

In early June that summer, Dundee FC advertised for a club secretary:

The advertisement that appeared in the local Dundee press and also some of the sporting newspapers

There were around 50 applicants for the role and the successful candidate was Mr Frank Watt, who at the time was a referee at the highest level in Scotland and also Secretary of the East of Scotland Football Association.

Mr Watt was popular in football circles and had excellent testimonials from several of the most prominent men in Scottish football. Mr Watt began his new duties on July 1.

Frank Watt at the time of his appointment as secretary of Dundee

On face value, this appointment would not affect Jimmy Logan as he had played his final game for Dundee on May 18, six weeks before Frank Watt began his work at Dundee FC. Did Frank talk to Jimmy about staying on at Dundee for the coming 1895/96 season? Did Jimmy turn him down? We will never know the answer to those questions but the paths of Frank and Jimmy would cross again sooner than either man realised at this time.

CHAPTER EIGHTEEN

July 1895 – January 1896

Jimmy joins Newcastle United

JIMMY arrived at a Newcastle United FC going through a complete overall of their playing squad as they prepared for the forthcoming season. A year earlier the club had changed from their red shirts to the now familiar and famous black and white stripes.

Local rivals Sunderland had just ended the 1894/95 season as champions while the Tyneside club were tenth in the Second Division, their final result of the campaign being a humiliating 9-0 defeat to Burton Wanderers. Everyone at the club was determined to improve and close the gap on their Wearside rivals.

Only three players from the previous season, William Graham, Robert McDermidd and William Thompson had been offered and signed contracts. What followed was the influx of a new squad of players, with a strong emphasis on recruits from north of the border, namely: William McKay (Rangers), William Miller (Kilmarnock), John Henderson (Clyde), Jimmy Logan (Notts County/Dundee), William Wardrope (Motherwell), John Clements (Rotherham Town), Andrew Aitken (Ayr Parkhouse), James Stott (Grimsby), James Collins (Nottingham Forest), Robert Foyes (St Bernards), Malcolm Lennox (Glasgow Perthshire), George Donald (Glasgow Ashfield) and Charlie Quinn (Manchester City).

Newcastle United FC 1895/96
(Photo courtesy of P. Joannou, Newcastle United Archive)
The newly assembled Newcastle United players line up early in the 1895/96 season
Back row: J.S. Ferguson (Secretary), James Collins, John Clements, Jimmy Logan,
John Peers (trainer)
Middle row: Robert McDermidd, William McKay, John Henderson, William
Graham, James Stott
Front row: William Thompson, Andrew Aitken, William Wardrope, William Miller

In late July the *Newcastle Daily Chronicle* carried news of yet another bout of illness that laid Jimmy low: *"J Logan, the centre-forward of the team, has now thoroughly recovered from his severe attacks of influenza and says he was never in better health. He played magnificently for Notts County the season before last, when they won the Cup. His goal-getting was something extraordinary and he scored over 60 goals himself.[24] Last season he was thrice stricken down with influenza, from the effects of which he never thoroughly recovered, until too late in the season to be of much assistance. As a scientific centre-forward he is hard to beat."*

It came as a shock to some that Jimmy Logan had signed for Newcastle as, according to *The Walsall Advertiser*, he was expected to join Walsall FC that summer! Walsall had failed to gain re-election to the Football League at the end of the 1894/95 season so they spent the 1895/96 season in the Midland League.

Most likely, Jimmy chose Newcastle over Walsall for two reasons. Geography and money. Newcastle is closer to his Ayr home and one would hope that the wages in the Football League were higher than those in the Midland League.

While there were plenty of positives said about Logan during his move to Newcastle, there were also the occasional dissenting voices, like the following from *The Lancashire Evening Post*: *"Newcastle United report that they have secured Logan (late Notts), Mackay (Glasgow Rangers) and Ailken (Kilmarnock). All are good men. Logan is a splendid player, but one of the most awkward and unreliable men a team could have. He led Notts a rare dance last season, sometimes standing on the field for a quarter of an hour without attempting to get the ball."*

Home for Newcastle United was St James' Park. The field was first used by Newcastle Rangers FC in 1880 and subsequently by West End FC, who having merged with East End FC, changed their name to Newcastle United in 1892.

In those early days facilities were very basic with some shallow banking at each end of the ground and duckboards for standing spectators. St James' Park didn't have a changing room so the Newcastle players changed at the Lord Hill Inn on Barrack Road which runs close to the ground, while the away team would usually be found changing in a different nearby pub.

The fifth annual meeting of the shareholders of the Newcastle United was held on Friday, August 9, and showed that the club was in a relatively healthy financial situation. The expenditure for last season included: Players signing on fees £140, Players travelling and hotel expenses £364, Gate expenses £212 and Players and trainers' wages £1100 leaving the club with a profit for the season of £100. Reference was also made to the share subscription which had raised £220, which was used to pull together the 'first class team' in readiness for the coming season.

The players had been instructed to be in Newcastle the weekend before the commencement of training on Monday, August 12, a week earlier than most teams. However, the club felt there were so many new players that needed to blend together that the extra week would be needed.

With that in mind, a large crowd of supporters assembled at Newcastle Central Station on Friday evening, August 9, as it was expected that all the new Scottish signings would be arriving on the 7:20pm train. As it happened, only two players, John Henderson the goalkeeper from Clyde and William McKay a centre-forward from Rangers were on the train – but both received a very hearty welcome as they stepped onto the platform.

---

[24] *I could not substantiate this claim – I could 'only' find 38 goals he scored with Aston Villa and Notts County in the 1893/94 season.*

Newcastle United FC also announced that a new trainer, Mr John Peers, had been appointed to ensure the players were as fit as they could possibly be. Peers replaced Harry Kirk who had also been trainer at Notts County for about five years ending in October 1893.

St James' Park as it looked in 1904

Although training commenced on August 12 no full-scale practice games were able to be staged until 12 days later due to improvements to both the pitch and the surrounding ground facilities. The main improvements were to the stand where the press box had been raised five feet and an area for officials had been completed.

The pitch too had been well cared for and was covered by at least an inch or two of very thick turf. Once the ground was available, the preparations for the season began with the usual training and practice games amongst themselves. A game between the League team (first team) and the Alliance team (reserves) kicked off the schedule on August 24, followed by two more warm up games, at home, against opposition from north of the border, Hibernian on Monday, September 2, and then Celtic two days later.

The daily training was watched with interest by the Newcastle supporters and for the first practice game over 5,000 people assembled around the ground to watch. Heavy rain made the ground slippery and good passing football very difficult, but Foyers, Aitken, Miller, Stott and Logan were all said to have 'maintained their reputations' in a 2-2 draw.

About 6,000 spectators turned up at St James' Park to see Newcastle take on Hibernian with a 6 o'clock kick-off. After only ten minutes, Kennedy receiving a pass from the left hit a fine shot to put the visitors ahead. The home team had plenty of attacks but Groves and McCall at the back dealt with all that was thrown at them. At the interval, the visitors still led 1-0.

Early in the second half McKay and Logan broke away only for the visiting goalkeeper to scramble the ball away from in front of goal. Moments later a cracking shot from Logan grazed the wrong side of the cross-bar. Eventually Newcastle equalised after smart work between McCall and Logan resulted in a good ball to McKay who shot into the net. Hibernian took the result 2-1 though with a late goal from Kennedy which the Newcastle goalkeeper Henderson could not reach.

Two days later it was Celtic's turn at St James' Park. Anyone in the Sunderland area wanting to make a day of it could see the game and move on to the theatre before returning home later that evening.

FOOTBALL MATCH AT NEWCASTLE.
NEWCASTLE UNITED v. CELTIC.
GEORGE ALEXANDER'S COMPANY AT TYNE THEATRE.
On WEDNESDAY, the 4th of September, an Excursion Train will leave SUNDERLAND at 2 p.m. (with bookings from Monkwearmouth), for NEWCASTLE, returning at 11 p.m. the same day.

Another similar-sized crowd turned up to see an unchanged Newcastle take on Celtic. Newcastle were quickly into their stride and after good work from Wardrope and McKay the ball was passed to Logan who in turn put Milne through on goal who made no mistake beating the Celtic keeper very smartly.

No further scoring in the first half and it wasn't long into the second half when Newcastle went further ahead. After a spell of heavy pressure from the home team a quality centre by Milne was met by Logan who gave the visiting goalie no chance of a save.

Morrison of Celtic and Foyers of Newcastle collided and Morrison had to be carried off the field with an injured ankle. United were well on top and Logan fired in a powerful shot which bounced off the visiting custodian and had to be scrambled away. The third goal for Newcastle also came from the foot of Logan, who had been a thorn in Celtic's side all evening, just before the referee called time on the game.

The first competitive game of the season on September 7 was at home against a Loughborough side taking their Football League bow. The previous season the Leicestershire club had finished champions of the Midland League and applied for League status.

They were accepted but it was an inauspicious debut, turning out as it did to be a comfortable 3-0 win for Newcastle with Jimmy Logan scoring the third goal after a good team move. The local press described Jimmy's performance as: *"Logan was a good centre, playing judiciously to the wings and keeping them well together."*

On Wednesday, September 11, the Channel Fleet[25] dropped anchor at Sunderland and everything possible was done to make their visit to Wearside a memorable one. Banquets, balls, football and cricket matches were arranged for the sailors' entertainment. The football match in question was the League champions, Sunderland, at home to Newcastle United. In the first half McCreadie and Cowan scored for the home team, McKay and Logan replying for United but in the second half the champions re-asserted themselves to win 5-3.

---

25 *The Channel Fleet was the Royal Navy formation of warships that defended the waters of the English Channel from 1859 to 1909 and 1914 to 1915.*

Newcastle's second League game was away at Liverpool with the team catching the 4.05 train on Friday afternoon and staying overnight at the Star and Garter in Liverpool.

Inside the Star and Garter in Liverpool in 1894

The game was a very different one to the romp against Loughborough, a heavy 5-1 defeat away at Anfield in front of 8,000 people, Jimmy getting the solitary Newcastle goal. Liverpool began the game in sensational fashion setting a ferocious pace and were 2-0 up after only five minutes, a position that Newcastle were unable to come back from.

Jimmy's team-mate on the right wing that day was Charlie Quinn making his only appearance of the season. A few weeks later 22-year-old Quinn was arrested for attacking and wounding a young lady named Mary Taylor whose nose was broken in several places and was 'distorted'.

Quinn was sentenced to three months imprisonment with hard labour and never played for Newcastle United again. After his release from prison he stayed in the area and played for Blyth FC and Gateshead NER FC but was continually fined and in prison for short spells, usually for drunkenness.

Charlie Quinn

Before the next game, the club announced that further improvements had been made to the ground including new turnstiles at the Strawberry Lane entrance. After the heavy defeat by Liverpool, Newcastle needed a boost both for themselves and for their fans. Next up were Jimmy's old club, Notts County, a team that still contained five players who shared Jimmy's greatest moment in winning the 1894 FA Cup: George Toone, John Hendry, Davie Calderhead, Alf Shelton and Dan Bruce would surely all be determined to stop Jimmy showing his FA Cup final form in this game. The 7,000 spectators saw Newcastle go straight onto the front foot attacking Notts at every opportunity.

The press sang the teams praises; *'The forwards, led by Logan, who was in rare form, whenever they swarmed around the Notts goal, they rained shots upon it with a precision that made Toone feel very uneasy.'*

It was Jimmy Logan who drew first blood when a mistake from his old team-mate John Hendry let him in on goal and Jimmy incisively beat George Toone. Newcastle never slackened the pace and at half-time, with a hat-trick from Andy Aitken had the home team ahead with a convincing 4-0 scoreline.

Newcastle were not so outstanding in the second half allowing Bruce to notch a goal for the Lambs and a fourth for Aitken completed a 5-1 win for United. *The Athletic News* gave praise to the forwards with; *"The forwards proved themselves a reliable quintette, full of resource in attack. Undoubtedly the most conspicuous trio were Logan, Aitken and Wardrope."* This performance also had the Newcastle executive talking about this Newcastle team being *'the best that has ever represented Newcastle in first class football.'*

On Friday, September 27, the Newcastle team travelled to play Rotherham Town the following day. After their outstanding display against Notts County, everyone connected with Newcastle were optimistic that the team could bring back both points. The game took place at Clifton Lane, Rotherham in front of about 1,500 people on an exceedingly warm day.

Both teams toiled hard in the sun but the first half was an even affair with chances at both ends of the pitch but neither side could convert one so it ended 0-0. In the second period Rotherham took the lead through Hargreaves. Newcastle fought hard to find an equaliser when Logan was put through on goal and he made no mistake hitting it past the Rotherham goalkeeper. It finished a stalemate at 1-1.

The League season had started well for Jimmy with a goal in each of his first four games – including scoring in a 5-1 win over his previous English club – Notts County. Jimmy missed the next League fixture on October 5 at home to Liverpool with a foot injury sustained at Rotherham.

He had recovered in time for the FA Cup game against West Hartlepool NER. Initially, the draw gave West Hartlepool the choice of venue but Newcastle's directors were able to persuade the railway men, with the help of a financial offer, to move the game to St James' Park.

It was a good decision and Newcastle were too smart and too fit for the non-League side who played in the Teeside League. The home team ran riot with goals from Stott, Collins, Graham and Baxter was pressurised into an own goal so the 4-0 half-time scoreline had a very healthy look to it. Newcastle kept up the pressure in the second half with further goals from Thompson, Collins and Logan twice giving a final scoreline of 8-0.

The first of two League games against Newton Heath[26] followed, the first on Saturday, October 19, away at Bank Lane, Clayton before 7,000 spectators. Newton Heath attacked for most of the first 45 minutes but without success as Newcastle defended with enthusiasm and half-time was reached scoreless.

---

[26] *Newton Heath became Manchester United on 28th April 1902*

The second half was more even and a shot from Logan was just the wrong side of the post. At the opposite end Peters brought the ball down and put in a shot which deflected off Kennedy and into the net past the stranded goalkeeper to break the stalemate. A few minutes later the Heathens went further ahead when Peters again got possession out on the left and crossed for Clarkin to head in the second goal. In the final minutes some loose play in the Heathens defence lost possession to Logan who advanced before firing past the home custodian for a consolation goal.

That meant that in his last eight outings Jimmy had scored ten goals with very positive comments being said about him. At this point in his Newcastle career he was in a very good place, regular appearances in the side and regular goalscorer. Jimmy's life, though, never seemed to run that smoothly for very long.

A dapper looking Jimmy Logan as he appeared in the local press during his time at Newcastle

On Saturday, October 26, during the return game against Newton Heath Jimmy was injured seriously enough for him to retire midway through the game – not a thing you did lightly before the days of substitutes – leaving his ten teammates to hang on for a 2-1 win. The injury caused him to miss the next three league games at home against Middlesbrough, plus home and away against Darwen, which the team won two and drew the other.

Jimmy returned on Saturday, November 23, against Rendel in the FA Cup at St James' Park in front of 3,000 spectators. With the slope in their favour, United attacked strongly and took the lead early in the game through an Aitken penalty. Thompson scored a second and Logan a third and Wardope scored a fourth, making the half-time score 4-0. United had most of the play in the second half but could only add one more goal from Aitken. Final score, an emphatic 5-0 victory.

In December there was also another very significant new arrival at the club - and he wasn't a player. Newcastle had decided to appoint a secretary to oversee the running of the club in all aspects. Eventually their No.1 target accepted the offer and who should it be but Frank Watt, the current secretary of Dundee FC who had only been in place since the first of July. Frank was a respected football figure in Scotland, where he'd worked as a referee, administrator and secretary and was known for his keen eye for a player.

Frank Watt – Newcastle United secretary/manager

It is unclear whether or not Jimmy Logan's time at Dundee ended before the arrival of Frank Watt or if Frank even managed to see him play for the club. Were Jimmy's relatively below-par performances at Dundee passed on by word of mouth to Frank? It is unclear but Frank Watt's appointment coincided with Jimmy Logan being axed from the first team for the next TEN games.

His only football action appears to have been an appearance for the reserve team (referred to as Newcastle A) against local rivals Sunderland at St James' Park at the end of December. There was a heavy fall of snow throughout the afternoon but the two teams still managed an exciting game, Sunderland taking the honours with a 3-2 win. The only mention of Logan in *The Athletic News* match report was to say; *"Logan did not play anything like up to his true form."*

It was Saturday, January 11, before Jimmy was recalled to the first team at home to Grimsby but according to *The Athletic News* it was not a decision received well by everyone: *"There were, however, grave misgivings at the outset whether the re-arrangement of the home team by the introduction of Logan would conduce to the harmony of the combination. Not a few of the general public wondered at the change, as there could be no possible ground for displacing McKay from centre, a position in which he had played with much distinction for the last month."*

The match went very badly, Grimsby recording a resounding 5-1 win in front of some very disgruntled Newcastle fans. *The Sheffield Independent* saw the reaction after the game as follows: *"Occasionally one hears of referees and visiting players being hooted and mobbed, but it is rarely indeed that the crowd goes for its own players. This latter, however, happened at Newcastle on Saturday, where the home team were defeated by Grimsby Town by five goals to one. After the match the Newcastle players were hounded by the people and several ugly rushes were made for them, which were with difficulty repelled by the few who protected them. Logan, the ex-Notts County man, seemed to be the special object of this display and an effort, happily unsuccessful, was made by the infuriated mob to storm the hotel where the players dressed. It was with considerable difficulty that the landlord of the hotel and several others protected Logan from violence. Such shameful and cowardly conduct cannot be too severely condemned. The crowd were themselves to blame for Logan's failure to play in his best form, for, simply because he happened to make a rather bad mistake in the first few minutes, they never left off jeering him."*

The next game, at home to Woolwich Arsenal, McKay was back in the team and Logan was out, with McKay scoring in a 3-1 win as the fans and club returned to being on an 'even keel'. The Grimsby game would be Jimmy Logan's last for Newcastle United and within days rumours were plentiful that Jimmy was on his way out of the club and on Saturday, January 25, *The Newcastle Daily Journal* confirmed those rumours to be true with the following paragraph:

> Logan of Newcastle United has been transferred to Loughborough, and the player named left for his new quarters yesterday afternoon.

CHAPTER NINETEEN

January 1896 – May 1896

Can Jimmy help to save Loughborough?

LOUGHBOROUGH FC finished the 1894/95 season as champions of the Midland League, seven points clear of their nearest rival Stoke Swifts. On the strength of that success, on May 20, 1895, the club received 18 votes and a place in the Second Division of the Football League replacing Walsall Town Swifts. After the successful season in the Midland League the trainer, Jackson, left to join Liverpool so in July 1895 an advert was placed in the local press to find a replacement.

> LOUGHBOROUGH ATHLETIC AND FOOTBALL CLUB Wants experienced Trainer for the coming season.—Apply Ll. Watkins, Secretary, Loughborough.

The advert for a new trainer that appeared in the *Nottingham Evening Post*

From over 200 applicants, three were chosen to attend a meeting at the club headquarters at the Greyhound Hotel for the purpose of appointing the new trainer. The man chosen was Richard Prince, a 43 year old born near Crewe in Cheshire but moved while young to Bolton. He was an experienced trainer having previously been with both Bolton Wanderers and Preston North End. More recently he had trained a number of successful sprinters.

Richard Prince – the Loughborough FC trainer in 1895/96 - photographed in 1902

It was a tough step-up in standard for the club and they were struggling near the bottom of the Second Division table. The defence was regarded as acceptable, in fact, of the six defensive players (goalkeeper, two backs and three half-backs) five of them would go on to play in all 30 League games that season, including Jimmy's landlord John Berry. The forwards and goalscoring was the team's main problem.

In the eight League games from the end of November 1895 to the end of January 1896 the team had scored only three goals. In a very tight financial situation, the committee decided to release some of their professional players. The reduction in the wage bill allowed the committee one last throw of the dice in an attempt to pull themselves away from the foot of the table.

Out went a number of players who had helped the club win the Midland League title the season before, Ben Bull was transferred to Liverpool after the Merseyside club came in with a £40 bid the club couldn't refuse. Out also went inside-left Arthur Ward (who's brother Walter continued on the left wing), centre-forward Tom Cotterill who had only scored twice and inside-forward Joe Clark returned home to Dundee.

In came inside-forward Billy Andrews in December 1895 from Bolton Wanderers, Arthur Roulston a goal-scoring winger from Castle Donington and Billy Jones an inside-forward from Willington Athletic. The Luffs also paid out a large sum of £40 as they went for a proven goalscorer, a man who had scored against Loughborough in the opening game of the season for Newcastle United at St James' Park and had also scored a hat-trick for Notts County during the Trent Bridge club's 4-1 triumph over Bolton Wanderers in the 1894 FA Cup Final – Jimmy Logan.

With Jimmy's arrival it meant the Luffs now had two FA Cup winners in their starting XI – Jimmy, class of 1894 and left-back George Swift who had won it the year before with Wolverhampton Wanderers.

George Swift – FA Cup winner with Wolverhampton Wanderers in 1893

Jimmy arrived in Loughborough in January 1896 and it would have been good that he recognised at least one familiar face in half-back John Hamilton – his old Ayr FC team-mate who had joined Wolverhampton Wanderers in 1894.

John Hamilton during his time at Fulham (1903-1908)

The club had arranged for Jimmy to lodge with full back John Berry and his family at 108 Leopold Street. At the time, John and his wife Alice had two children, John, who was two, and Amelia who was only six-months-old.

John Berry pictured during the 1891/92 season with Burton Swifts

John Berry was born in Blackburn, Lancashire but moved to Burton-on-Trent in the early 1890s where he met local girl Alice Gamble and they married in 1893. While in Burton he played for Burton Swifts from 1891 to the summer of 1895 when he was offered a contract by Loughborough. Some professional players, like Jimmy Logan, would live alone in 'digs' and travel home to see his family at every opportunity, while others, like John Berry would set up the family home wherever they were playing.

The house in Leopold Street where Jimmy lodged during his time in Loughborough

Although Jimmy arrived in Loughborough in January, he wasn't eligible to play until February 1 and so his debut came against Manchester City at the Athletic Grounds in Loughborough.

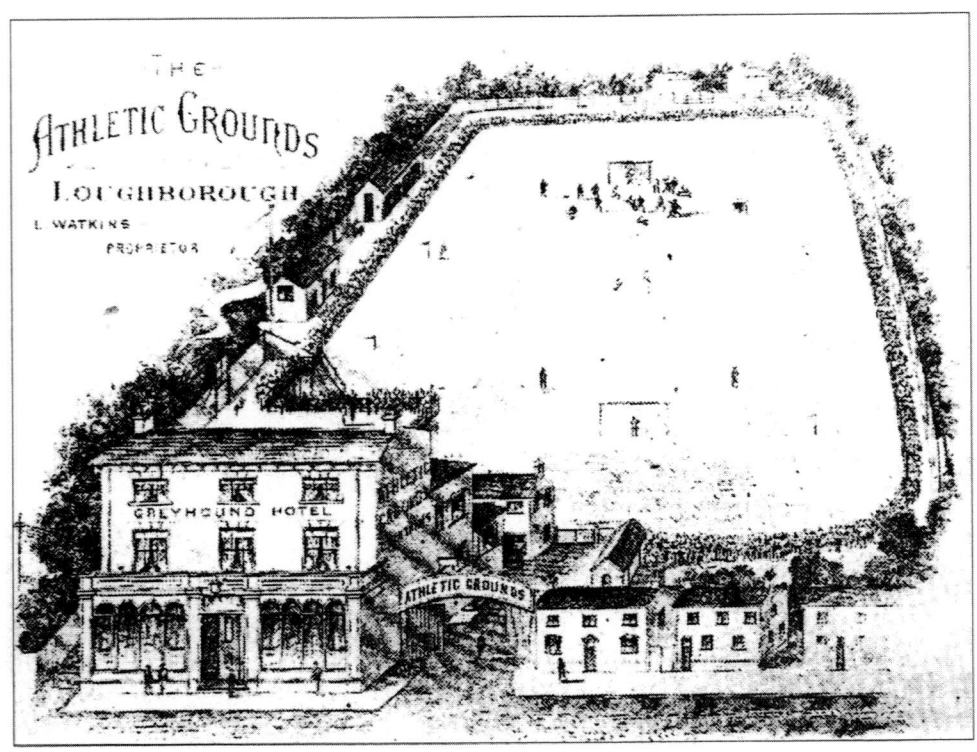

Athletic Grounds, behind the Greyhound Hotel on Nottingham Road, in the 1890s

Despite Jimmy scoring in both his first two League games, the 'new era' didn't get off to a great start with a 4-2 home defeat and a 5-1 away reverse against Manchester City and a draw away at Darwen. After that though there was an improvement in performances as the new players settled in with three victories in the next four games – a defeat against Rotherham Town but victories over Woolwich Arsenal, Newcastle United and Darwen would have given the club confidence and hope that they could still achieve their ambition. Despite the run of good results the Luffs were still in the bottom three and facing having to apply for re-election to Division Two of the Football League.

Easter would be the crucial time of the season which would probably decide their fate, facing four games, three away from home, in only five days:

April 3 (Good Friday)	Away at Crewe Alexandra
April 4 (Saturday)	Away at Newton Heath
April 6 (Easter Monday)	Home to Rotherham Town
April 7 (Tuesday)	Away at Burslem Port Vale

The following paragraph appeared in a number of the sporting newspapers:

"A report was received from Mr A. Kingscott, the referee, as to the misconduct of spectators at the match Crewe Alexandra v Grimsby, at Crewe, on March 7th. He stated that he was subjected to a very hostile demonstration, being kicked and hustled by the crowd, and having mud thrown at him. The Crewe committee came to his assistance, and the club officials had written admitting the charges, and expressing their deep regret at what had happened. It was eventually decided that the Alexandra ground be closed from Monday 30th March, to the end of the season, and the club were ordered to make better ground arrangements."

This meant that instead of Loughborough FC playing at Crewe's usual home ground at that time of the Alexandra Recreation Ground, the game would now be played at The Vicarage ground at nearby Sandbach, the home ground of Sandbach St Mary's FC.

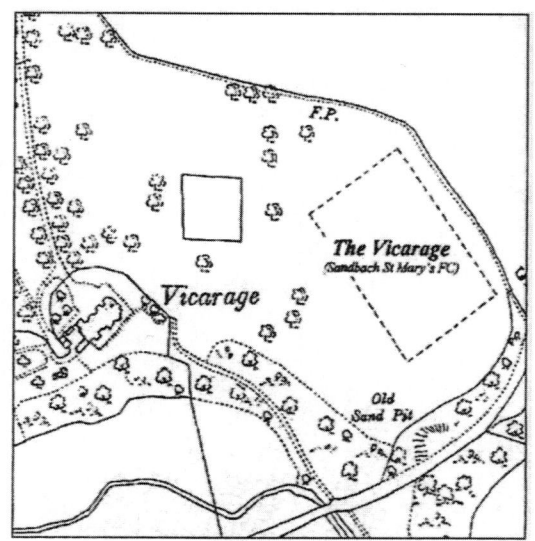

The Vicarage – located about one mile south-east of Sandbach. The pitch was sited in a field behind and on the east side of the vicarage. There were no facilities with spectators stood on the east side of the pitch alongside a footpath and hedge while one of the outbuildings at the vicarage would have been used for changing rooms

The Vicarage still exists but now is privately owned, called Tall Chimneys and rented out as separate flats, while the pitch behind the building was returned to normal agricultural use. This game was the only time the ground was used to stage a Football League match, so Jimmy was in a select group of only 22 people ever to participate in such a game there

The first of these crucial Easter games was played at Sandbach, on a pitch that was very wet and slippery. The team for this game was; Hugh Monteith in goal, John Berry and George Swift backs, Walter Rose, John Hamilton and Henry Middleton halfbacks and a forward line of John Smith, William Andrews, Jimmy Logan, William Jones and Walter Ward.

In the first half the visitors had considerably the best of the game and Ward put the Luffs ahead as the home goalkeeper lost his footing on the slippery surface and presented him with the opportunity. A second goal from Jones came from a free-kick. Crewe fought back with Peake reducing the arrears so at half-time Loughborough were leading 2-1.

In the second half Crewe made strenuous efforts to score but while the defence stood firm, Monteith was outstanding in goal for Loughborough. Monteith, another Ayrshire product, was a tall powerfully built coal miner who had joined Loughborough from Celtic.

In desperation, one of the Crewe players jumped at the Luffs custodian feet-first but Monteith 'met fire with fire' and the resulting clash saw the Crewe man 'standing on his head'. The Crewe players were less keen to get too close to Monteith after that and the Luffs held on for the win and the two precious points.

Hugh Monteith

Loughborough's trainer Richard Prince had two brothers, William and John, who both lived in the Crewe area so while the rest of the team returned home he stayed on in Crewe to meet one or both of his brothers – but he was under instructions to bring the kit hamper which contained the jerseys, knickers, socks, boots, etc. and to meet up with the team the following day at Clayton.

The team returned by train but would need to be up fairly early the following morning to travel back to the north west to play Newton Heath[27] at Bank Street, Clayton, Manchester – only around 35 miles from Sandbach. If money had been more plentiful surely the team would have stayed overnight in the Manchester area.

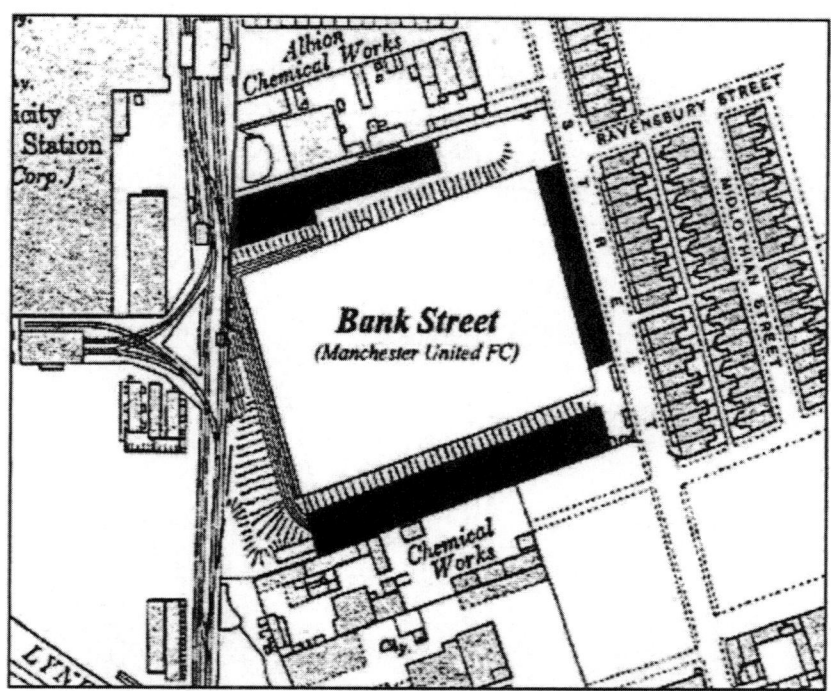

The positioning of the Bank Street ground from a 1908 map

The next day, Saturday, April 4, the same Loughborough team that had defeated Crewe the day before journeyed to Clayton in Manchester to play the return match with Newton Heath. The team and club official left Loughborough by the 9:40 train.

To the surprise of all the players and Mr Wells, the club official, who accompanied the team, trainer Richard Prince had not arrived on the scene when they put in their appearance at the ground. It was hoped he would, however, ultimately turn up.

They hoped against hope and at the hour fixed for the commencement a search was instituted for some spare "toggery." They were not very successful, several jerseys of various colours and a few knickers, suitable only for schoolboys, were scraped together.

Half an hour after the appointed time the teams entered the field, and a stranger would have thought a burlesque match was to be played - not a serious Football League fixture.

The 4,000 spectators laughed heartily at the Loughborough players' plight, with the latter also entering into the humour of the situation. Every one of the players wore their ordinary everyday boots. Monteith had his black trousers on and a black sweater with red stripes across the body and the arms. Smith turned his trousers up as far as his knees, and Jones continued throughout in his trousers, which were slit right up. Ward's knickers collapsed, and he was off the field for about half-an-hour for emergency repairs. Swift's knickers did not

---

[27] *Newton Heath became Manchester United on 28th April 1902*

reach anywhere near his knees, and the jerseys, which were of a nondescript character, were mostly composed of black and gold.

It was a dull day; Swift won the toss and as soon as the Heathens kicked off the game Loughborough were on the attack. Attempts by Ward and then Logan were saved comfortably by Ridgeway, the Heathens goalkeeper.

Succeeding this, Swift shot over the line, following good work by Middleton, after which McNaught got the ball away cleverly, and Clarkin reached the Loughborough end, where he centred and Donaldson beat Monteith, only for the goal to be disallowed. A legitimate goal, however, soon afterwards accrued, as after Monteith had saved nicely from Smith, that player scored from a scrimmage in goal, after Cartright had shot in.

The visitors played gamely, Hamilton at centre-half at this point putting in good work, and from a free kick, taken by Berry, Erentz only got the ball away in the nick of time. Principally by fine back play, to which McNaught contributed a good share, the Loughborough territory was often invaded, but the forwards performed with very little combination, Donaldson, however, being worthy of praise for hard work in the centre.

Against Vance and Smith, Rose was ever prominent. Indeed, as a whole there was very little to choose between the teams, with each end of the ground being alternately visited, whilst neither goalkeeper was tested for some time.

Presently Monteith, by rushing out of goal, forestalled Donaldson, who was almost certain to have scored from a splendid centre by Clarkin, and a little later he repulsed a fine effort by Vance. The Heathens pressed heavily towards half-time, but failed to score, and the home team therefore commenced the second half with a lead of one goal to none.

Manchester United 2-3 Arsenal, an FA Cup fourth-round tie taking place at Bank Street, Clayton, in Manchester[28] March 10 1906

In the second half play was very one-sided, and the home players had matters pretty much their own way. Both wings sent in good centres and Donaldson turned one into a goal, his shot striking the post and going into the net, Monteith having no chance to stop it. Logan, Smith and Andrews were prominent with a good run towards the home half, but Stafford intervened, and transferred play with a huge kick, and then much pressure was brought to bear upon the Loughborough goal, all the forwards having shots, but they found Monteith,

[28] *Manchester United moved to its current stadium, Old Trafford, in 1910. The car park for the Manchester Velodrome is now located on the site where the Bank Street ground used to be with a plaque on a wall marking the place.*

Swift, and his partner in their best mood, and try as they would they could not break through. Even the home halves had shots, and McNaught went forward, but no amount of pressure could induce the ball to again go into the net, and the home side had to rest content with a win by a couple of goals. Result: Newton Heath 2-0 Loughborough

But for the unfortunate incident above referred to Loughborough may possibly have beaten the Heathens. The fact that only two goals were scored against them speaks well for the application of the team, and their readiness to adapt themselves to any situation. The players' everyday boots were in a sad state at the finish of the game.

As an aside, modern day stories of this game tell of the players getting drenched in a heavy downpour and having to travel home in their sodden everyday clothes. As I have said before newspapers copy other newspapers. I have read numerous match reports (many clearly copied from other newspapers) of the game but could not find a single one that mentioned the word 'rain' at all. A couple of reports mentioned the day as being 'dull', while others said the ground was 'soft' but the majority described the weather as being 'fine' or the weather was not mentioned at all, where a heavy downpour of rain would surely have warranted a mention in at least one newspaper. Certainly the players would have been sweaty, muddy and weary – but not drenched by rain.

The players now had the chance for a day off (Easter Sunday) from their busy schedule before facing Rotherham Town at the Athletics Ground on Easter Monday – as long as the trainer Richard Prince had returned with the kit by then!

While the rest of the team suffered no ill effects except a few bruises and aching limbs, Jimmy Logan was ill in bed at home and unable to help the team in their next three games in their fight to get away from the foot of the table. Had two games in two days been too much for Jimmy's suspect body to cope with? He would normally have a few days to recover after each game, often even a week, but the tough Easter schedule may have been too much for him.

The Loughborough team were a different proposition now though and two victories in two home games against Rotherham Town (3-0) and Burslem Port Vale (3-0) followed by a draw away at Burslem Port Vale (1-1) greatly eased the club's problems.

The final game of the season for Loughborough took place at the Athletic Grounds against Crewe Alexandra a game that saw the return from illness of Jimmy Logan. Although not fully recovered he felt strong enough to re-join the team. At the kick-off the Luffs were immediately on the attack and it was Roulston who got in the first shot on goal, which crashed against the board behind the goal.

The Luffs were soon well on top with all members of the 'front five' registering at least one attempt on goal but Robinson in the Crewe goal led a charmed life as he kicked and fisted the shots away. Jones and Ward were outstanding in the Luffs attacks *and Logan threw himself into the conflict with much more vim*[29] *than usual.* Even the half-backs and full-backs were joining in the attacks with shots on goal.

The first goal finally arrived when Ward who picked up the ball, moved to the goal line before crossing the ball over goalkeeper Robinson where Andrews met the cross with a shot that gave Robinson no chance of saving it. Andrews scored again before the interval. Despite being completely on top it was just the two goals from Andrews that separated the teams at the break.

The second half saw Crewe improve and when Monteith did well to save a good shot from Barnett but the ball bounced away and Peake was on hand to score and pull a goal back for Crewe. After this Crewe tried hard to equalise but the next goal came at the opposite end when a scrimmage ensued in front of the Crewe goal and Jimmy Logan scored with a loose

---

[29] *Lively and energetic enthusiasm*

ball for the Luffs third and then, just before the final whistle Jones headed in from Roulston's corner kick making the final score 4-1.

The turnaround in Loughborough's fortunes was quite dramatic thanks to Jimmy and the other signings brought in. After the away game at Manchester City on February 24, the foot of the Second Division table looked like this:

Pos	Team	PL	W	D	L	F	A	Pts
10	Burton Swifts	23	9	3	11	34	45	21
11	Notts County	22	8	2	12	42	43	18
12	Rotherham Town	23	6	2	15	25	71	14
13	Lincoln City	21	5	3	13	38	54	13
14	Burslem Port Vale	19	5	2	12	28	53	12
15	Crewe Alexandra	22	4	3	15	25	64	11
16	**Loughborough**	**20**	**2**	**4**	**14**	**20**	**55**	**8**

With only ten games remaining, the picture at the foot of the table was a bleak one and prospects of evading re-election looked grim at best, especially as Loughborough had won only two of their first 20 League games.

Pos	Team	PL	W	D	L	F	A	Pts
10	Notts County	30	12	2	16	57	54	26
11	Burton Swifts	30	10	4	16	39	69	24
12	**Loughborough**	**30**	**9**	**5**	**16**	**40**	**66**	**23**
13	Lincoln City	30	9	4	17	53	75	22
14	Burslem Port Vale	30	7	4	19	43	78	18
15	Rotherham Town	30	7	3	20	34	97	17
16	Crewe Alexandra	30	5	3	22	30	95	13

Ten games later and the picture at the foot of the Division Two Table showed the Luffs unbelievable climb to safety. Their record over the last ten games being:

Played 10 Won 7 Drew 1 Lost 2 Goals For 20 Goals Against 11 Points 15 (out of 20)

The game against Crewe was the Luffs last game of the season at the Athletic Grounds so the club were left with a free Saturday (presumably the club hired the ground through the winter until the end of April before the summer games took over the ground) so the club decided to have a fancy dress football match.

Both the first and second teams were involved and the teams were mixed up. Prior to the game the players paraded through the town in their 'outlandish costumes'. About a thousand people had paid to enter the enclosure shortly before the game commenced, with £15 being raised, which all helped the club's precarious financial situation.

Some of the players were 'disguised' as follows:
'Captain' George Swift made a very convincing Inspector of Police.
Walter Ward, John Hamilton and Jack Berry were police constables.
Jimmy Logan, who had recovered sufficiently from his illness, was made up as a 'black faced minstrel entertainer'.
A. Cutler looked as if he had 'sprung from a cotton plantation'.
Hugh Montieth was a school urchin.
Walter Rose and Arthur Roulstone were members of the Awkward Squad

William Andrews was an eccentric

Harry Middleton had a strange 'get up' of top coat and petticoats.

Fred Foulds was a cowboy

John Mounteney, Joseph Clark, Charles Dickson and West were all clowns thanks to the efforts of Messrs. Jennings from the Alexandra Theatre.

Others were dressed as actors, soldiers and sailors etc.

Referee Walter Adcock was dressed as an Admiral and issued with a bell rather than a whistle.

The kick-off was made at 3:15 by councillor W.H. Wootton. The game that followed was absolute mayhem. The players initially played to the Association rules but at times the game turned into rugby with the 'policemen' adding to the ridiculous scene by occasionally escorting players from the field and into the dressing room which wound up the referee who was frantically ringing his bell!

The game finished in a draw with three Association goals and and fifteen Rugby points to each side. Afterwards the teams did justice to a good tea provided in the pavilion and in the evening the Borough Band, which had been on duty during the afternoon, played music for dancing and an enjoyable evening brought the season to a close.

At the beginning of May Jimmy appeared to be making a gradual recovery and was planning a trip back home to Scotland with two of his Loughborough team-mates William Andrews and Hugh Monteith. The journey was planned for Friday, May 22.

On Saturday, May 16, Jimmy's health had taken a turn for the worst and he took to his bed at 108 Leopold Street. No serious consequences had been anticipated until that Saturday when the internal complaint from which he suffered led to complications and in the end brought on pneumonia. He was still not well enough to travel with his team-mates to Scotland on the Friday.

Despite the attentions of the club doctor Mr. A Eddowes, Jimmy died on Monday afternoon on May 25.

The informant on the death certificate was Jimmy's father James. This was the last opportunity for James to recognise that his son Jimmy was a professional footballer. Jimmy was in Loughborough because of his football career and no other reason. When asked his son's occupation James replied 'Confectioner (journeyman)'.

Jimmy's last serious actions on the football field had been to help and inspire Loughborough FC to climb from a desperate league position over the last ten games of the season. The football club arranged for the funeral to take place on the following Thursday afternoon and as a mark of respect arranged for the Midland League championship flag to fly at half-mast during the club sports on the Athletic Grounds on Tuesday afternoon.

Jimmy Logan was to be buried in a pauper's grave. This meant that the deceased, or the football club who were paying for the burial, had no funds with which to buy a grave space and therefore the only cost would be the digging fee. One man present at the funeral had only three years earlier purchased a street of ten buildings and also the family burial plot back in Troon had a very tall elaborate gravestone on it. Jimmy's father James Logan could have ensured that Jimmy had a decent burial, but, for whatever reasons, he chose not to.

The funeral of Jimmy Logan took place at Loughborough Cemetery on the afternoon of Thursday, May 28. The cortege left 108 Leopold Street shortly after three o'clock and all the way to the burial ground it was the object of the attention of many sympathisers.

A short service was held in the little church at the cemetery and also at the graveside where a considerable number of people assembled, with the Rev. W. Fowler curater of the All Saints Parish Church officiating. Amongst the large number of people present were Mary, Jimmy's widow, Jimmy's father James, Mrs Calderhead wife of Jimmy's captain David

Calderhead at Notts County and members of the Loughborough Football Club committee H Dormer, G Mee, W Adcock, W Tebbutt and E Cooke.

Most of the Loughborough professional players had left the town to return home after reaching the end of the season but H T Dunn (secretary) and A D'Arcy (reserve team trainer) were present and six players, Jack Berry, Arthur Roulstone, John Plackett, C Coltman, Walter Rose and George Spibey did duty as coffin bearers. Among the wreaths were ones from; 'A loving wife', Mr and Mrs Berry, Mrs Hyde and the Loughborough Football Club committee. The coffin was of polished elm with brass fittings.

The unmarked ground to the right of the picture is where Jimmy Logan was buried in 1896 at Loughborough Cemetery

CHAPTER TWENTY

1897 - 2019

Epilogue

On March 5, 1897, nine months after Jimmy Logan's death, his widow Mary married William Sager, a German Master Mariner in Glasgow and for a short while they lived at 9 Twyfield Place in Ayr. The houses in Twyfield Place run very close and parallel to one of the touchlines at Somerset Park, the home of Ayr FC, Jimmy's first senior club. The Sager family had moved to England around 1870 and were proprietors of first The Pilot Boat Hotel and then later the Commercial Hotel, both in the quay area of Falmouth in Cornwall.

In time for the 1897/98 season Ayr FC joined Division Two of the Scottish Football League.

February 8 1898 saw the birth of John Logan's fourth child, a daughter, Mary Esther Logan, born at the family home at 13, Laburnum Terrace, in Derry, Northern Ireland, where John was still a confectioner.

In July 1900, at the end of the 1899/1900 season, Loughborough Football Club folded after serious financial problems. Crowds had dwindled from a few thousand to only one hundred by the end of that season; their last eighteen games were all without a win, with only one win all season.

The 1901 census found Jimmy's widow Mary (now Mrs Sager) and son James aged 8 on the night of the census they were visiting friends Henry and Mary Pritchard in Glamorgan, Wales.

The 1901 census also showed that John and his family of five children had left Northern Ireland and were by then living at 6 Greyhound Terrace, Greyhound Lane in Croydon with John now a yard foreman.

Between 1901 and 1911 Jimmy's widow Mary (now Mrs Sager) appeared to have left Britain and emigrated but information to confirm this could not be found. Once Mary had left Ayr, Jimmy's son James continued to live with his grandparents James and Elizabeth at 38 Union Avenue.

1903 saw the death of Jimmy's sister Janet Logan (married name Hawkins) aged only 35. She and her daughter Elizabeth Hawkins had been living at 38 Union Avenue for some time after she and her husband had separated. Elizabeth Hawkins continued to live with her grandmother. Of James and Elizabeth's six children only two survived to a 'mature' age.

1905 Jimmy's parents James and Elizabeth went to solicitors John W. & G. Lockhart in Ayr and drew up a Will – the money to be divided equally between their surviving children John and Elizabeth Giffen Logan (married surname Lawson). Provision was also made for the children of John and Elizabeth and also granddaughter Elizabeth Hawkins (the daughter of their deceased daughter Janet) who was also living at 38 Union Avenue with her grandparents. However, there was no mention at all in the Will of Jimmy's son, James, who was also living with them at Union Avenue – for such a young boy to be the only grandchild excluded from his grandparents' Will surely confirms that serious differences between Jimmy and his father must have existed during Jimmy's lifetime.

In 1906 Jimmy's father James passed away on June 18 and John came up from Croydon to deal with all the business. His father James was buried in the family plot in Troon cemetery. Widow Elizabeth continued to live at Union Avenue with grandaughter Elizabeth and grandson James.

In 1910 the name of Ayr Football Club disappeared forever when the club amalgamated with Ayr Parkhouse FC to become Ayr United FC who continue to play at Somerset Park.

This is the only instance of a merger between two League clubs from the same town in the history of Scottish football.

In the 1911 census Jimmy's son James, by then a mason, was aged 18 and living with his granny Elizabeth (Jimmy's mother) at what was still the family home at 38 Union Avenue. Also living there was granddaughter Elizabeth Hawkins aged 19.

The following year, 1912, Elizabeth died leaving young James and Elizabeth Hawkins potentially homeless and with little family to speak of. Once again, Jimmy's elder brother John travelled up from Croydon to Ayr for his mother's funeral and she was also buried in the family plot in Troon. After all the details had been taken care of, John took young James back down to Croydon to live with his family, which at that time was his wife Mary and their six children. Elizabeth Hawkins went initially to live with her father Henry Hawkins in Denny near Stirling but returned to Ayr soon after and fell ill and died in 1914 aged only 21.

The Logan plot (or lair) at Troon cemetery therefore contains:

Elizabeth Giffen Logan	died 1876 aged 1	(Jimmy's sister)
Thomas Logan	died 1876 aged 10	(Jimmy's brother)
Janet Connell	died 1897 aged 81	(Jimmy's grandmother)
Janet Hawkins	died 1903 aged 35	(Jimmy's sister)
Captain James Logan	died 1906 aged 70	(Jimmy's father)
Elizabeth Giffen Logan	died 1912 aged 72	(Jimmy's mother)
Elizabeth Hawkins	died 1914 aged 21	(Jimmy's niece)

1925 saw Jimmy's son James, now 33 and a Poultry Farm Manager, marry Kathleen Alice Bone 21, also of Croydon.

1926 saw the birth of James and Kathleen's first child, a son Douglas.

1933 saw the birth of James and Kathleen's second child, a daughter June.

1939 saw James, now a house painter, and Kathleen living at 66 Beddington Grove in Surrey.

John Logan's wife Mary died aged 71 at Worthing in West Sussex in 1942.

John Logan died aged 83 in Dumfries in Scotland in 1947.

In the mid 1990s David Kirkby, published a book entitled *The Luffs*, it was the story of Loughborough Athletic Football Club in their Football League years 1895-1900 this made David curious about the 'lost' Jimmy Logan grave and began, along with John Belton from Loughborough FC, talking about erecting a headstone on Jimmy's grave in Loughborough Cemetery.

There were two stumbling blocks to their plans. The first was the high cost of doing it and secondly Charnwood Borough Council at that time had a rigid policy that because Jimmy was buried in a pauper's grave with a 'non-family' member (i.e. a stranger) gravestones or monuments were not allowed to be erected in those circumstances.

A further attempt in late 2004 was also made and was minuted by the Notts County Supporters Trust[30] but once again it came up against a brick wall that was the local council's strict 'no headstones' policy. Instead, Loughborough FC's John Belton decided to name the pathway leading up to Loughborough FC's current ground James Logan Way, with a sign attached to a nearby fence.

---

[30] *Notts County Supporters Trust Meeting No. 36 dated January 18 2005*

The path named James Logan Way produced by John Belton of Loughborough FC

Eventually however both staff and attitudes changed at the council over a period of time so when Notts County FC fans Andy Black and Jimmy Willan approached the council some twelve years later in 2016, they received a far more welcoming reception from a council now far more ready to embrace their town's footballing history and a compromise was reached that if the other person buried in the grave (Charles Belton[31]) was also mentioned on the headstone they now had no objections to a headstone being put in place.

Not only did Andy and Jimmy erect a gravestone but they also organised the 'upgrading' of the James Logan Way pathway sign into a freestanding and more permanent sign.

The upgraded sign of James Logan Way created by Andy Black and Jimmy Willan

---

[31] *Charles Belton is a distant relative of the current Loughborough FC chairman John Belton*

So, on Tuesday, August 23, 2016 at 12 noon, in a ceremony at Loughborough Cemetery, Notts County's 1894 FA Cup hat-trick hero Jimmy Logan was finally honoured with the placing of a headstone on his grave, 120 years after his death.

Andy and Jimmy did an excellent job as the following two photographs show:

The various dignitaries at the Jimmy Logan graveside.
They were, from left to right, Andy Black (Notts County FC fan and co-organiser of the Jimmy Logan gravestone), John Belton (Chairman of Loughborough FC[32]), Les Bradd (All time Notts County record goalscorer and club ambassador), Richard McBrearty (representative of the Scottish FA and curator of the Scottish Football Museum), Councillor David Gaskell (Mayor of Charnwood), Mayoress Jan Gaskell and Jimmy Willan (Notts County FC fan and co-organiser of the Jimmy Logan gravestone)

---

[32] *The current Loughborough FC appeared when Loughborough Athletic dropped the "Athletic" suffix in 2001. The club were members of the Midland Football Combination, but resigned from the league in the summer of 2006 and now play in the Leicestershire Senior League.*

In
Memory of
JAMES LOGAN
24th June 1870 - 25th May 1896
Professional Footballer
and Scottish International
Notts County's hat trick hero
in the 1894 FA Cup final
Died after playing for
Loughborough F.C.

Here also lies CHARLES BELTON
27th May 1879

The superb headstone erected by Andy Black and Jimmy Willan – fit for a hero

APPENDIX

Out of interest, I put all the information I had regarding the numerous instances of Jimmy Logan's 'illnesses' and his 'inability to last the pace of a fast game' as well as Jimmy's death certificate in front of a Professor of Sports Science. Of course we can never be sure but these were his thoughts:

Dear Dave

Thanks for the opportunity to read the attached information about Jimmy Logan - what a tragedy and such a sad ending to a talented footballer. It would appear that the cause of death was severe pneumonia or as commonly called (wrongly) double pneumonia. Regarding his lack of stamina, it could have been poor lung function that may have been, as you suggest, asthma or 'exercise-induced asthma' which is quite common in today's athletes. If it was asthma then it is surprising that he played football, let alone to such a high standard. Furthermore, any sprints he performed would be followed, at the very least, by extreme efforts to breathe which would be obvious to all around him and, as a result, received some mention in match reports etc. Bearing in mind his background, he may not have had a healthy youth i.e. good nutrition and/or childhood illness such as rheumatic fever. It seems reasonable to suggest that he didn't have a healthy cardiovascular system which wouldn't allow him to recover following each sprint. As you know, even in a high tempo professional football match players rarely sprint for longer than 3-5 seconds. Fatigue sets in when the recovery between each sprint is less than about a minute or more. I suspect that Jimmy Logan probably had a less than average cardiovascular system (principally an underlying cardiac weakness) that was the result of his poor childhood nutrition (as well as genetics). The clue to why he succumbed to pneumonia when his team-mates did not is in the comment that he lodged with a team mate in Loughborough because of lack of money. I suspect that he wasn't able to have enough to eat and warmth to ensure that his immune system could successfully fight the bacteria infection that led to his death from pneumonia.

As an aside, I remember having to examine a professional cyclist who was released by his team because of underperformance. His GP thought that he had asthma, however when we ran him on the treadmill and did all the routine measurements we found that his performance was that of a recreational athlete. In fact he had to convince us that he was a professional cyclist by showing us photographs of his international race successes. What I think had happened is that he had continued training hard and competing when he had experienced a heavy cold, sore throat and a high temperature. This may have led to an infection of the mitral valve of the heart that reduces the heart's capacity to pump oxygen carrying blood to the working muscles and other tissues. As a result of this cardiac myopathy his aerobic capacity dropped significantly and so exercise intensities that were well within his range became intolerable. A well known runner who suffered from this condition was Steve Ovett in the latter part of his international middle-distance running career.

So when athletes have coughs and colds and ask can they continue training our advice is they can if the cold is 'from the neck up' but if they have a sore throat and feel achy then they shouldn't train for fear of the infection getting into the heart.

Sorry for the long winded reply. My best guess is that Jimmy Logan's lack of stamina was an underlying poor cardiovascular system, principally due to a less than normal heart condition and his susceptibility to pneumonia was brought on by an habitually poor nutrition that lead to deficiency in all the essential nutrients required to support adaptations to exercise and lack of nourishment of his defence mechanisms i.e. his immune system.

Best wishes and kind regards